The 2000 Presidential Election and the Foundations of Party Politics

The 2000 Presidential Election and the Foundations of Party Politics is an account of the closest presidential election in modern history. Although a study of just one election, it stakes claims applicable to all campaigns. This provocative work blends insights from the disciplines of communication and political science, explaining the accuracies and inaccuracies of each field. It draws on the largest continuous academic survey of the U.S. electorate and incorporates a detailed analysis of advertising buys with content analysis of network news. The authors argue that the 2000 outcome was close because the campaign made it so, thanks to well-conceived strategic initiatives first by the Bush campaign, then by the Gore campaign. The book shows how both ads and news coverage shaped the results of an election that according to forecasting models based on economic conditions should have been an easy victory for Gore.

Richard Johnston is Professor and Head of Political Science at the University of British Columbia and an Associate Member of Nuffield College, Oxford. He is author or coauthor of *Public Opinion and Public Policy in Canada: Questions of Confidence, Letting the People Decide: Dynamics of a Canadian Election*, and *The Challenge of Direct Democracy: The 1992 Canadian Referendum* and is co-winner of the Harold Adams Innis Prize for the best Canadian book in English in the social sciences. He was principal investigator of 1998 and 1992–3 Canadian Election Studies and codirector of the 2000 National Annenberg Election Survey.

Michael G. Hagen is Associate Research Professor and Director of the Center for Public Interest Polling at the Eagleton Institute of Politics, Rutgers University. He also has taught at the Annenberg School for Communication at the University of Pennsylvania, where he was codirector of the 2000 National Annenberg Election Survey. He is coauthor of *Race and Inequality: A Study in American Values* and a contributor to *Reasoning and Choice: Explorations in Political Psychology*, winner of the Woodrow Wilson Foundation Award for 1991, and has published in the *Annals of the American Academy of Political and Social Science*, the *British Journal of Political Science*, the *Journal of Politics*, *Political Behavior*, and *Public Opinion Quarterly*.

Kathleen Hall Jamieson is Professor of Communication and Director of the Annenberg Public Policy Center at the University of Pennsylvania. She is the author or coauthor of twelve books, including *Packaging the Presidency*, winner of the National Communication Association's Golden Anniversary Book Award, and *Eloquence in an Electronic Age*, winner of the NCA Winans Wichelns award.

The 2000 Presidential Election and the Foundations of Party Politics

RICHARD JOHNSTON
University of British Columbia

MICHAEL G. HAGEN
Rutgers University

KATHLEEN HALL JAMIESON
University of Pennsylvania

 **CAMBRIDGE**
UNIVERSITY PRESS

PUBLISHED BY THE PRESS SYNDICATE OF THE UNIVERSITY OF CAMBRIDGE
The Pitt Building, Trumpington Street, Cambridge, United Kingdom

CAMBRIDGE UNIVERSITY PRESS
The Edinburgh Building, Cambridge CB2 2RU, UK
40 West 20th Street, New York, NY 10011-4211, USA
477 Williamstown Road, Port Melbourne, VIC 3207, Australia
Ruiz de Alarcón 13, 28014 Madrid, Spain
Dock House, The Waterfront, Cape Town 8001, South Africa

http://www.cambridge.org

First published 2004

Printed in the United States of America

Typeface Sabon 10/13.5 pt. *System* LATEX 2$_\varepsilon$ [TB]

A catalog record for this book is available from the British Library.

Library of Congress Cataloging in Publication data available

ISBN 0 521 81389 1 hardback
ISBN 0 521 89078 0 paperback

To the memory of Ambassador Walter Annenberg, whose generosity made the National Annenberg Election Study possible, and to Leonore Annenberg, whose support of the Annenberg Policy Center has ensured that the Study will prosper in the decades to come.

Contents

Acknowledgments

This study would simply have been impossible without the generosity of Leonore and the late Walter Annenberg. The Annenbergs gave the policy center that bears their name resources on a scale sufficient to carry out the fieldwork and analyses and on a timeline that facilitated serious forward planning. Our dedication of this book to the Annenbergs only begins to express our gratitude.

Along the way we have accumulated many more intellectual and organizational debts. Translating the rough outline of a fieldwork strategy into the real thing was a pleasure in the company of Mary McIntosh and Chris Adasiewicz of Princeton Survey Research Associates (PSRA). At critical points, Chris and Mary defined grace under pressure. In part, the pressure reflected the sheer volume of time-sensitive demands we made on them, but it also reflected the very scale of the fieldwork. We all knew it was going to be big, but none of us could have thought through the implications of this scale for all the elements that go into clearing a sample, writing and debugging CATI code, and the like. Of course, the most direct impact of scale fell on the fieldwork house, Shulman Ronca Bucuvalas, Inc. (SRBI). We thank the entire SRBI staff for their consideration and hard work.

At various stages in design, fieldwork, and analysis, colleagues in a variety of institutions gave advice and support. Merrill Shanks and Henry Brady at Berkeley deserve pride of place. Merrill's CATI development work at the Berkeley Survey Research Center was critical to the early formulation of fieldwork principles that Johnston and Brady took to Canadian Election Studies in 1988 and that find their echo in the Annenberg study. Merrill had a more immediate impact on our study as well, as he essentially set the agenda for our treatment of issues and was a resonant sounding board for much of our thinking. Henry was, as usual, a remarkably fertile source of ideas about practically everything to do with the study. He also made room for us at his Center when we descended on the Bay Area.

Henry also was a critical player in organizing a June 1999 conference at the Annenberg Public Policy Center in Washington, DC, as were Larry Bartels and John Zaller. All along, Larry and John have been good-humored kibitzers, appropriately enough as much of this book reads like a dialogue with them. We also were fortunate to receive input at the conference from Gary Jacobson, Jeffrey Mondak, Diana Mutz, Vince Price, Russ Neuman, and Lynn Vavreck. Out of this conference came much of the study's ongoing instrumentation.

Two other colleagues need to be singled out. Chris Wlezien was a source of critical advice in the later stages of fieldwork and throughout the subsequent months and years. We believe he has saved us from blunders. We hope he agrees. Byron Shafer delivered audiences and trenchant comment to us, first in Oxford, later in Madison.

Graduate students at two institutions were critical to the production of data and, in some cases, analyses. At the Annenberg School these were David Dutwin, Erika Falk, Joyce Garczynski, Dannagal Goldthwaite, Kate Kenski, Kim Kirn, Kelli Lammie, Suzanne Morse, Brett Mueller, Dan Orr, Susan Sherr, Lesley Sillaman, Alex Slater, Svjetlana Tepavcevic, Paul Waldman, and Claire Wardle. At the University of British Columbia, these were Julia Lockhart, Scott Matthews, and Mark Pickup. We also thank Laura Lawrie for her expert copy editing.

Finally, we thank our families. They paid much of the price of our bicoastal collaboration, which required Johnston to spend a year in residence at the Annenberg School and required all of us to spend stretches holed up together in far-flung hotels. For our families' patience and support we are grateful.

It goes without saying, however, that all shortcomings in this book are our own responsibility.

I

Introduction

This book aims to unite two research traditions that are usually seen as competing. With some noteworthy exceptions on both sides of the disciplinary aisle, one tradition has been articulated mainly by communications scholars and the other mainly by political scientists. To perform the nuptials, we deploy unique bodies of evidence from one of the more compelling presidential elections in living memory, the virtual dead heat of 2000. In the campaign, all the factors that drive political science models were in play at least some of the time – abiding elements of social structure, geography, party identification, and ideology; the economy and other aspects of the record of the previous administration; the perceived fitness of each candidate for executive office; and issues reaching back to the New Deal. But these factors did not operate automatically. They were activated and in some cases critically altered by campaign communication – its overall volume, its partisan direction, the consistency of messages across communications channels, and the rhetorical sophistication of the messages themselves.

To make our case, we focus on three phases in the general campaign and on the critical transitions between them. The first phase was produced by the conventions and lasted for more than a month. In this phase, predictions from econometric forecasting models for a comfortable victory by Al Gore seemed bound for success, as, of course, was Gore himself. This phase came to an abrupt end and the second phase began in late September when perceptions of Al Gore's character – of his honesty in particular – crashed. Overnight he went from being the presumptive victor to fighting for his political life. In the third phase, he called up memories of the New Deal and succeeded in persuading a critical bloc of voters that George W. Bush was a threat to the Social Security system. In the byplay, however, Gore ignored the robust economy, which should have carried him to a comfortable victory. Still, his playing the New Deal card enabled him to win the popular vote.

But he lost the Electoral College and, with it, the election. The divergence between the popular vote and the Electoral vote is another theme of this book. In one sense, this takes us to the foundations of party politics and the origins of the republic. In another sense, it takes us to the frontier of political communication, in particular to the gap between parts of the television broadcast day. Al Gore won the popular vote by, at the end of the campaign, winning the battle for network news. George W. Bush won the Electoral College by, also at the end, winning the battle of the ads. These assertions are possible because by 2000, presidential elections had become a natural experiment on a continental scale. The New Deal-Social Security message that was critical to Gore's recovery was most effective where it did him the least good, in states he could not win and in states he could not lose. In closely fought states, states that were pivotal in the Electoral College, his message was blunted by the sheer weight of pro-Bush advertising.

In short, communication is critical in determining whether and if so how the economy, candidate traits, and issues function in a campaign. Sometimes the communication is directly by a candidate or a closely connected surrogate in intensely covered moments such as conventions or debates. Sometimes the channel is advertising or the news. It matters a lot if ads and news reinforce each other or work at odds. Failure to communicate can be as critical as active attempts at priming or moving opinion.

Saying such things aligns us with research in the tradition of communication studies that emphasizes contingency and the power of rhetoric. But much of that research is supposition, anecdote, or not strictly relevant to an aggregate phenomenon such as an election. The body of research on the other side, attuned more to "necessary" – as opposed to contingent – features of elections seems more robust, more thought through. But much of that research seems oddly antipolitical, ironically so, because most of it is by political scientists. Our view is that many of the propositions about recurring features of elections require communications factors for their proper operation. Explicating those communications factors reveals just where contingency lurks, where strategic choice by candidates is possible or even necessary, and where a candidate can go wrong.

Explicating communications factors also forces us to question the role of campaign communications in enlightening voters. At one level, the 2000 campaign clearly *did* enlighten the electorate. The incidence of basically correct perception of candidates' positions on issues was greater at the end than at the beginning. But not every effect of the campaign lay in the domain of interests and issues. The campaign also processed highly manipulated images of candidates' character. And within the domain of issues, much depended on what was said – and not said – and on the resources each side could command to get its message out.

Our claims rest on analyses of three bodies of data. Most important is a massive "rolling cross section" survey of the 2000 electorate, the National Annenberg Election Survey. Fieldwork began in November 1999 and finished in January 2001. This book focuses on the over thirty-seven thousand respondents interviewed between Independence Day and Election Day. Alongside the survey and sometimes joined to it are bodies of advertising data, organized by day and by media market. The spatiotemporal pattern in ad buys, when combined with the rolling cross-section survey data, enables us to estimate the impact of ads with considerable efficiency. Finally, we tie the rolling cross-section data to a detailed analysis of campaign coverage in major newspapers but, more importantly, on the national TV networks.

The next part of this chapter lays out the book's analytic stakes in some detail. Then we further describe the survey, advertising, and news data. Finally, we describe the order of argument and the plan of the book.

The Stakes

Forecasting Models and the Record of the Previous Administration
According to all forecasting models, Al Gore was supposed to win handily. Not only was the economy robust but also ratings of Bill Clinton's handling of his job were very high. Even discounting for the fact that Gore was not Clinton and that the Democrats were shooting

for a third consecutive term, Gore should not have lost. Zaller (1998) reinforced this expectation by claiming that Bill Clinton's popularity in the face of the Monica Lewinsky scandal confirmed the importance of "fundamentals," most importantly the economy. The predictions to this effect and the body of research from which they derive are ably captured by a symposium in *PS: Political Science and Politics* in 2001. The seeds of a difficulty already lurked in the research, however, especially in Gelman and King (1993) and Campbell (2000). Both argue that one function of a campaign is to prime the economy and so ensure that this most "fundamental" of considerations operates as forecasting models say it should. Both argue that the economy will always be primed in fact, as it would always be in one side's interest to do so, just by different sides in different contexts.

In the first transition of the 2000 campaign, exactly this happened when Bill Clinton told the Democrats in convention to be more optimistic about and to take credit for the economy over which he had presided. Democratic identifiers did as they were told. This did not increase partisan bias in economic perceptions, it just removed a partisan perversity in perception that reflects the ongoing class basis of U.S. politics. The convention thus fulfilled the preconditions for the presidential election forecasting models. But when Gore failed to champion the message of Democratic prosperity, the effect faded. Despite both robust economic indicators and general public satisfaction, the economy could not burnish Gore's prospects on its own. The rhetoric of the convention got the preconditions right; Gore's silence stilled its potential effect.

Gore's refusal to prime the economy may have reflected anxiety about associating himself too closely with his predecessor. This anxiety underscores a contingency taken for granted in the forecasting models. The standard claim is that popular approval of an administration mainly reflects its management of the economy. Other elements in popularity are similarly policy-driven or reflect ongoing partisan bias that carries no net predictive significance. Judgment on the incumbent's personal life is just not a factor. What forecasters did not forecast is that a president could be regarded as a competent chief executive but a bad human being, someone whose moral failings undercut his successor's ability to embrace prosperity. We surmise that Gore calculated that a tie to Bill Clinton the man would diminish his prospects more than a tie to the Clinton economy would enhance them. We suspect he was wrong. Whatever we think, the link between Al Gore and Bill Clinton created a contingency, a strategic choice and a challenge to Gore's rhetorical skill. The unfolding of the story reversed the logic outlined in Zaller (1998).

The Persuasibility of the Electorate

A pivotal event was the collapse in Al Gore's reputation as a man of character. There are many things to say about this but the first is that the collapse was quintessentially a media phenomenon, involving ads and news working in concert. A claim that media effects matter to the electoral bottom line is still controversial, notwithstanding the emergence of serious research with data from the field. For decades, the standing position in political science scholarship was the "minimal effects" model. It is useful to think of this model in terms of two mediating factors in any attempt at persuasive communication:

- How likely is the message to be received by the target audience?
- How likely are receivers, once they get the message, to yield to its persuasive content?

Among political scientists, these questions are associated with Zaller (1992). This sequence was first identified by the Yale studies of attitude change and social influence, typified by Hovland and Janis (1959) and brilliantly synthesized by McGuire (1968, 1969). It was independently identified by Converse (1962), although he seems never to have connected his insight to the Yale school one. Converse's 1962 idea lay mainly dormant, however, until Zaller (1990, 1991, 1992) resurrected it and explicitly linked it to McGuire's synthesis.[1] Early communications studies in sociology and social psychology drew skeptical conclusions about each mediating factor. The standard view was that persuasive messages are unlikely to reach their target audience, at least not in an unmediated way. Audience members who do get the message resist it. Those susceptible to the message never get it. Katz and Lazarsfeld's (1955) classic study of the two-step flow of

---

[1] Zaller's recovery of the older perspective was not unaided, but was the culminating manifestation of a perspective also exemplified by Sniderman (1975) and whose unifying thread leads to DiPalma and McClosky (1970).

social communication argued that the audience never gets the message, not in its original form. Most hear it only second hand, after it has been reinterpreted by opinion leaders to blunt its dynamic intent. Besides, most persons are well armed to resist messages. Berelson, Lazarsfeld, and McPhee (1954) documented cognitive bias in perception of candidates' issue positions, bias motivated by voters' own prior partisan commitments. Partisan stereotyping is another mechanism by which a persuasive message can be frustrated (Conover and Feldman, 1989).[2] By 1960, the various mutually reinforcing elements in the pattern had come to be seen as the "minimal effects" model (Klapper, 1960). The continuing grip of the model is nicely captured by Finkel (1993).

By the 1970s, however, skepticism about the minimal effects model could already by heard. Steven Chaffee, for instance, pointedly claimed that "the limited effects model is simply not believed" by the contributors to his edited volume (Chaffee, 1975: p. 19). It is telling, however, that this *cri de coeur* came from the field of communications research – with its professional stake in finding effects from the very thing it studies – not from political science. But Chaffee was not merely whistling in the wind. McCombs and Shaw (1972) had already staked out an empirical case that the media could at least set the agenda for political discourse and by 1981 their perspective had become commonplace.[3] By the 1980s political scientists were willing to pick up the thread. Erbring, Goldenberg, and Miller (1980) were the first to acknowledge agenda setting, and Iyengar and Kinder (1987) documented the phenomenon on a national scale. Outright persuasion was still not on the screen, however.[4] This changed with Page, Shapiro, and Dempsey (1987), who showed how the news moved opinion, although not on the time line of campaigns. Jamieson (1992) raised the specter of persuasion inside campaigns, as did Johnston, Blais, Brady,

[2] Where the Berelson et al. (1954) claim is that voters assimilate or contrast candidates' issue positions to resolve tension with their own positions, Conover and Feldman (1989) show that voters assign a candidate to the position typical of the candidate's own party.

[3] As instances, see Funkhouser (1973), McLeod, Becker, and Byrnes (1974), and Weaver (1981).

[4] Mutz (1998) points out, however, that much of what Iyengar and Kinder (and other analysts in the same mode) interpret as agenda-setting was probably persuasion in fact.

and Crête (1992), who found that news and ads affected judgment on party leaders and vote intention.[5]

It is one thing for persuasion to occur, it is another for its effect to be permanent. The electorate, once moved, may typically return to its original position. In a time-series sense, the electorate may be basically "stationary." It *is* moveable by an external shock, but without continuing pressure from whatever administered the shock (a stock market collapse in mid-campaign, for example), quasi-autonomic forces undo the initial movement. If such a shock occurs right at the end as an accident of timing, it may turn the electoral tide. But provided shocks occur early enough in the campaign, their effects will be undone. Such an aggregate pattern should prevail if the dominant mode of political cognition among individuals is "memory-based" (Lodge, McGraw, and Stroh, 1989; Lodge, Steenbergen, and Brau, 1995).[6] But Lodge and his colleagues argue that the dominant mode of political cognition is not memory-based but "on-line." On the on-line view, when a shock causes voters to shift their evaluation of a political object, they quickly forget the reason for the reevaluation, they just update and move on. They may shift again but only under the pressure of another shock. If this is indeed the dominant mode of political cognition, then campaign persuasion starts to look very consequential. The Lodge et al. claim is not universally accepted, however, and evidence for it is mainly experimental.[7]

This book provides a direct test. The fact that we identify phases in the 2000 campaign testifies, we argue, to the power of on-line cognition. Particularly impressive is the shift that this section started with: the collapse of perceptions of Al Gore's character. We show that this is the pivotal event for the entire campaign and that it was induced by an intense, but very short burst of bad news whose effects were permanent. Gore was never able to undo the particular damage, and his recovery came about only because he was able to shift the agenda to another question. But other shocks – some of them remarkable in their initial impact – saw their effects dissipate and so were less consequential.

[5] The heart of the evidence in Johnston et al. (1992) lies in Table 8.6 and Figure 8.10. The effect of their claim may have been limited by being made in the context of a Canadian campaign, not a U.S. one.
[6] This implication is persuasively argued by Wlezien and Erikson (2002).
[7] Chief among the dissenters is Zaller (1992).

Evidently, alternative modes of political cognition coexist. Some voters may have better memories than others. Different modes may be triggered by different events or by different media channels, news versus ads, for instance.

News and Ads

Most of the evidence on the "minimal effects" record involves lack of impact from news. When audience research was in its infancy, so was political advertising as we now understand the term. As well, the minimal effects model could be said to turn on a communications stream that is geographically localized and mediated by personal influence. As such, its relevance may be more historical than current. Personal influence networks are less binding than they once were (Putnam, 2000) and so citizens may have no choice but to look to impersonal sources. Newspaper ownership and market share have consolidated (Mutz, 1998) even as the broadcast media have become the central news source. The media have become more intrusive and citizens may have become less resistant. Accordingly, as Mutz (1998) argues, we have witnessed increasingly pervasive *im*personal influence, reflecting growth in the collective consciousness of society.[8] Mutz's own work still concentrates on news, however, and for her the problematic thing is whether the news gets it right. But the changes she documents for mass media also apply to their role as carriers for ads.

The relatively slow rise in emphasis on ads reflects the historical record. The first presidential television ads were played only in 1952. The most controversial early ads – the Johnson campaign's "Daisy" ad, for instance – postdate most of the "minimal effects" classics in audience research. TV advertising has only recently acquired its current scale and scope, so it should be little surprise that academic research has only begun to catch up. Much of the work is devoted to characterizing the content of ads (Kern, 1989; Jamieson, 1996; West, 1997). As ads are

---

[8] Mutz sees this as mostly a good thing. She is not persuaded that the massification of influence processes threatens the quality of face-to-face processes, contrary to mass society theorists of the 1950s (Kornhauser, 1959) or their social capital heirs (notably Putnam, 2000). Indeed, she sees impersonal sources as a valuable means of encouraging deliberation, specifically by countering local pressures to conformity (Mutz and Martin, 2001). At the same time, she is sensitive to the fact that news media now carry a bigger burden than before.

even more ephemeral than broadcast news (at least we know when to look for news), merely gauging the volume of plays, much less assessing their impact, is difficult.[9]

The earliest ad impact study with dynamic evidence was of the 1988 Canadian election (Johnston et al., 1992), and that analysis required heroic assumptions. The earliest U.S.-based work was in the laboratory, most tellingly by Ansolabehere and Iyengar (1995).[10] Ansolabehere and Iyengar also managed to take their laboratory insights to the field. Their contribution has been partly obscured by controversy over their claim that negative ads depress turnout.[11] Ansolabehere and Iyengar also made claims about ads' directional impact, however, and their findings appear to leave the core claim of the older literature strangely intact. They show that although citizens' vote intentions can be shifted, ads are most effective when they work with, rather than against, predisposition.[12] But a major crack in the edifice appeared with Shaw (1999b), who argues with data organized by state and week of campaign that ad volumes make a net difference at the margin. Romer, Jamieson, and Cappella (2000) question Shaw's claim about the magnitude of ad effects but not the fact of their existence.

Perceptions of Candidate Traits

Shaw and Romer, Jamieson, and Cappella aside, most work on ad impact has worked with ad content and has generally focused on messages that clarify means-ends relationships in the domain of issues. The domain in question is inherently *positional*. But campaigns also process valence information. In most political science accounts the valence consideration in question is the economy. But another valence factor also commonly pervades ads: personality traits of the candidates. Honesty (unlike, say, abortion) is something everybody agrees is a good thing. Of course, perception will be biased, as Democratic identifiers typically

---

[9] Although capturing air time is difficult, political scientists have been studying the impact of ad volumes for some time, almost without realizing it, in studies of spending on Congressional elections.

[10] See also Johnson-Cartee and Copeland (1991) and Biocca (1991).

[11] The controversy is captured by Lau, Sigelman, Heldman, and Babbitt, Kahn and Kenney, Wattenberg and Brians, and Ansolabehere, Iyengar, and Simon in a 1999 exchange in the *American Political Science Review*.

[12] This argument also echoes an early observation by Patterson and McClure (1976) that voters learn more facts about candidates from ads than from news.

see the Democratic candidate in a good light, and so on. But this is just bias, not a position on an issue that actually divides the parties. Presumably, not all trait perception is projective in this sense. Many citizens have no partisan reason to project in the first place and even those who do project may yield to new evidence furnished by the campaign.

Exactly this happened in 2000. The transition between the first and the second phase of the campaign – the undoing of Al Gore – shows how perceptions of candidates' traits are shaped by communication. The most critical shift was in perceptions of Al Gore's honesty. The shift was induced by a rough coincidence of ad and news messages, where Republican ads basically handed a message to TV news. The news in turn undermined perceptions of Gore, a process that was only accelerated by the first debate, which was treated in TV news as a further example of the problems first identified in Republican ads. The fact that ads and news worked together at this point magnified the overall effect.[13] Gore's predicament was somewhat mitigated by the fact that the campaign also worsened perceptions of George W. Bush's basic competence. In the end, voters saw a tradeoff between Bush and Gore. Had the election taken place six weeks earlier, the choice before voters would have seemed simpler.

The factor that produced the shift, perception of Al Gore's personal character, is not commonly seen as a major electoral consideration. The literature on voting and elections takes due notice of candidate traits, to be sure. A multitrait battery is a regular feature of U.S. National Election Study (NES) instrumentation, going back to Kinder, Abelson, and Fiske (1979). (Indeed, a version of the Kinder battery in the Annenberg survey is the basis of our own claims about trait perceptions and effects.) Candidate assessment is a stage in the Miller-Shanks (1996) multistage model that is now the industry standard. But few would argue that personality perceptions are the key to distinguishing elections from each other. Bartels's (2002) recent review suggests that candidate perceptions were, if anything, a smaller factor in 2000 than in other years, although potentially important because

---

[13] This claim is not quite in the domain occupied by Ansolabehere and Iyengar (1994), who look at the impact of ads-news reinforcement on individuals. Our claims are about content links between the ad and news channels and about aggregate effects of ads and news on perception, opinion, and behavior.

of the closeness of the result. We confirm Bartels in detail – as far as he goes.

What his analysis misses, however, is that perceptions of Gore were the dynamic key to the campaign. What made them dynamically critical is that movement in trait perception tends to be unidirectional. Bias persists, indeed it increases, but no group in the electorate actually grew fonder of Gore as all others were growing less fond. Increase in bias came about only as some groups reevaluated Gore more quickly and more totally than others.

Personality and Issues

In the transition that initiated the third phase and in the third phase itself, the content of communication was about the intersection of issues and traits. Strong party predispositions were engaged and no persuasion occurred contrary to predisposition, exactly as Ansolabehere and Iyengar (1995) lead us to expect. But not every one was highly predisposed and, overall, opinion moved in one direction at the expense of the other, so the movement was potentially consequential for the bottom line. Gore's recovery occurred against the background of earlier attempts by the Bush campaign to position its candidate close to the center on key dimensions of an agenda traditionally "owned" by the Democrats. By adopting the rhetoric of "compassionate conservatism" and by articulation of Republican alternatives on Democratic issues, Bush may have neutralized some of Gore's natural advantage on education, prescription drugs, and Social Security. Gore certainly acted as if this was the case. And late in the campaign, he found the way to recapture Social Security as a Democratic issue. He spread his message through the debates, through a near-takeover of NBC news, and through ads. He used language that also called George W. Bush's personal trustworthiness into account. At this point, indeed, both sides showed how issue and personality claims can be mutually reinforcing. The Republican attempt to blunt Gore's comeback strategy was executed mainly through ads that challenged Gore's credibility as an interpreter of Bush's Social Security plan. The challenge called up images of personal untrustworthiness: If you can't trust the messenger, you can't trust his message. The attempt succeeded. Where no or few ads were placed, Gore's winning the news battle was the decisive fact.

In closely fought states, where the Bush campaign overwhelmed the airwaves, Gore's news-driven comeback stalled.

Ads, News, and Enlightenment

Was the campaign at bottom an *enlightening* event, in the sense intended by Gelman and King (1993)? That sense is the currently dominant position in the political science literature. It is clearly detectable in Ansolabehere and Iyengar (1995), for instance. This view freely concedes that campaigns induce real dynamics in vote intention. But these dynamics do not create the result so much as *reveal* it. The critical thing about the campaign is its very existence:

> ...without it election outcomes would be very different. Moreover, if one candidate were to slack off and not campaign as hard as usual, the campaigns would not be balanced and the election result would likely also change. Thus, under this explanation, presidential election campaigns play a central role in making it possible for voters to become informed so they can make decisions according to the equivalent of enlightened preferences when they get to the voting booth. This process then depends on the media to provide information, which they do throughout the campaign, and the voters to pay attention, which they do disproportionately just before election day. (p. 435)

Campaigns should sharpen the effect of fundamental considerations and move groups with preexisting, basically rational partisan commitments back where they belong. In this sense, then, a campaign reveals enlightened preferences.

The geography of the 2000 election enables us to test the claim for enlightenment with remarkable directness. By the late 1990s, the partisan camps had become evenly balanced and the geographic expression of that balance, quite stable. This stability, combined with the logic of the Electoral College, yielded strong indications of where the campaign actually must be fought. Fewer than half the states in 2000 merited any investment in advertising or in visits by candidates. The spot market in ads accommodated this fact, such that virtually no ads were placed on the networks; almost all were placed with local stations. Each campaign was thus able to place its ads for maximum strategic effect. As a result, a good half the electorate *never* saw an ad (other than as part of a TV news report, at least). Voters who lived in places where ads were aired could see them at the times of the campaign's choosing but not at others; mainly they could see ads only at the end. The states that attracted ads featured races that were expected to be close. But the 2000 race ended up being close in the country as a whole. So the hard-fought states were a microcosm of the whole electorate. There were a microcosm, that is, except for one particular: *only they got the full campaign "treatment."* This made the campaign potentially a natural experiment.

And at the end, critically, the ad signal became decisively unbalanced, as George W. Bush won the ad war. Movement of vote intention in the direction indicated by mere weight of ads, if the movement did not also occur where no ads played, would by itself call the enlightenment hypothesis in question. Fortuitously, from our point of view, the ad signal outright contradicted the news signal, as Al Gore won the battle of network news. If the dynamics of vote intention where the dominant signal favored Gore – network news by default where no ads could be seen – contradicted the dynamics where the ad signal favored Bush, the enlightenment hypothesis is really in trouble.

Electoral enlightenment can be argued from another perspective that has gained adherents in recent years, the "constructionist" model. This model, first exemplified by Graber (1988) and Gamson (1992), has achieved its fullest flowering in Just, Crigler, Alger, Cook, Kern, and West (1996). On this view, campaigns are important mainly as they give the election its *meaning*. The meaning of the event is determined not just by candidates or the mass media, but also through citizens' own active participation. In its emphasis on meaning, this perspective dovetails with earlier work on agenda-setting.

But agenda-setting acquires a critical edge only if it is linked to victory or defeat. Johnston et al. (1992), for instance, brought the agenda-setting perspective squarely back to the center of campaign strategy and showed how one construction of the 1988 Canadian choice served all the major parties better than another, alternative agenda. Johnston et al. showed further that that alternative was a plausible counterfactual. In the 2000 presidential campaign, the agenda moves available to each campaign were hardly straightforward. Should a campaign attempt, in general, to position its candidate relatively close to the center of opinion, or should it reinforce its base? The Republicans certainly seemed to position their candidate toward the center. The Democratic orientation seemed more confused, but then Al Gore faced a more serious challenge on his left flank than George W. Bush did on his right one.[14] Whatever each side said about itself, it painted the other as extremist, so voters could be forgiven if they felt confused. Were some attractive agenda moves blocked by the structure of preferences or perceptions? Al Gore may have believed this in relation to the economy, out of fear that priming the economy would also prime bad memories of Bill Clinton. Complexities such as these cast a shadow on the imagery in Gelman and King of the rival campaigns' knowing quite unproblematically what cards to play and having the resources to play them.

This is not to deny that campaigns enlighten voters. The 1988 Canadian event cited earlier was at one level a remarkable civic exercise. The parties engaged in intense debate on the core issue, as did many nonparty groups. Extraordinary numbers of private citizens took it upon themselves to read detailed commentaries on the trade agreement; many of them tried to read the agreement itself. *Citizens*, the very persons on whose existence Just et al. insist, populated the landscape. But the event was equally a field for manipulation, in the initial agenda moves and in the subsequent stylization of the stakes. We show that all this could be said of the 2000 presidential campaign as well. Advertising was dense in issue content. Both sides frequently focused on the same question. They did not, *pace* Simon (2002), merely talk past each other, each side emphasizing its own preferred agenda. As the campaign progressed voters saw the stakes more clearly, tightened the links between their issue positions and the vote, but also assimilated their positions on the key issue to their social position or to their general ideological orientation. But both campaigns also engaged in intensely strategic behavior, in resource allocation and in agenda moves. And otherwise identical voters responded differently according to the dominant mass media stimulus where they lived.

---

[14] Analytic models of elections are no help, as they are all over the map. The standard version of the rational-actor model, originating with Downs (1957), emphasizes centrist strategies. But theorists of that persuasion recognized early that centrist strategies were not all that dominant empirically. This led Aldrich (1983) to weigh party activists in the balance along with casual voters, with noncentrist results. Palfrey (1984) achieved similarly noncentrist results by invoking the specter of invasion from an ideological extreme. Rabinowitz and his colleagues (starting with Rabinowitz and Macdonald, 1989) argue that the Downs model, which they style as a "proximity" calculus, is flawed at its base as a description of voter psychology. Their alternative, "directional" model argues that centrist strategies almost never make sense.

Democratic/Republican Asymmetry

A minor but recurring theme is that Democrats and Republicans differ not just in their substantive policy preferences but also in how they respond to campaign stimuli. Where Bush supporters stood reliably behind the Republican, potential Gore supporters were less steadfast. Gore had to work harder than Bush to hold what, by registration and ideological disposition, "should" have been his base. This may have been an incidental feature of 2000, when Al Gore faced Ralph Nader on his left as well as George W. Bush on his right. But we suspect not. Instead, we show that the asymmetry runs through political cognition: Republicans and Democrats are qualitatively different in how they see candidates' ideological and issue positions. Cognitive asymmetry was first noticed by Brady and Sniderman (1985) and is a central element in Ansolabhere and Iyengar (1995). These insights, our book shows, have dynamic significance.

What We Do Not Do

There is much about the 2000 event that we touch only tangentially. Obviously, an account of the Electoral College and its implications for campaign strategy has lessons for the Florida debacle. No doubt the centrality of Social Security to both the Bush and the Gore campaigns reflects Florida's voting power (although not just Florida's). And the story we tell about the pro-Bush imbalance in ads also has special relevance for that state. But this book can do little more than set the Florida story up and show why the state was so pivotal. Besides, other states were also pivotal in 2000. One might ask about New Hampshire, for instance, whose four Electoral votes would have put Al Gore over the top, whatever happened in Florida.

Mention of both Florida and New Hampshire points to another facet of 2000 that we treat only in passing: the Nader campaign. Worry about Nader was visibly reflected in various aspects of the Gore campaign's strategy. In our multivariate estimations, we contrast Gore and Bush separately as alternatives to "neither of the above." Most respondents in our survey who rejected both Bush and Gore had no candidate preference at all, as far as we could tell. But a critical fraction whom we classified this way actively preferred Ralph Nader. Rarely do we single them out, however, as in a study focused on dynamics, the Nader candidacy must be a sideshow. Our own data did not reveal interesting

dynamics in third-party vote intention. We admit that our concentration on strategic choices by and on the balance of forces affecting the
two main candidates neglects key elements in a comprehensive account
of the 2000 result. But our goal was never to account for all the par-
ticulars, but rather to use the 2000 event to shed light on the dynamics
of election, whatever the year.

Data and Analyses

The most important data source for this book is the National Continuous Monitor component of the 2000 National Annenberg Election
Survey (NAES). The Monitor was in the field almost continuously from
November 1999 to January 2001, but we look at the period of highest sampling density, July to Election Day, when roughly three hundred completed interviews were completed each day. Apart from sheer
scale, the distinctive feature of the Monitor is its manner of release
to the field. The survey is a "rolling cross-section," managed so that
the day on which a respondent happens to be interviewed is as much
a product of random selection as that respondent's initial presence in
the sample. All that distinguishes one day's sample from another day's,
aside from sampling error, is something that has happened in the interval. Over-time comparison is possible with few or no controls, and the
sample can be partitioned pretty much at will. Details on the sample
and the design can be found in Romer, Kenski, Waldman, Adasiewicz,
and Jamieson (2004).

Supplementing the survey data and occasionally wedded to them are
data about advertising. The primary source of ad data is the Campaign
Media Analysis Group, or CMAG. CMAG data for 2000 cover the
seventy-five largest media markets, where 74.1 percent of the NAES
Monitor sample lives. This remarkable data source covers campaign
advertising by both official campaigns and by independent groups
aligned with the candidates. It also permits detailed content analysis,
a recurring feature of this book.[15] Supplementing CMAG for certain
purposes are the weekly advertising buys from each candidate's campaign. These give complete coverage of the nation and they represent

---

[15] The first published use of CMAG data is Freedman and Goldstein (1999).

the likelihood that ads will actually be seen. But they are limited to the official campaigns and do not permit analysis of content.

The Annenberg 2000 study also included detailed content analysis of news coverage. In this book, news coverage basically means the three national networks. Notwithstanding the proliferation of cable, networks remain the primary means of access to the campaign for ordinary television viewers. Approximately one household in four still does not have cable connections and cannot see any of the cable channels. Also cable news channels, unlike networks, do not concentrate their hard news coverage in a single part of the viewing day.

The Book

The first two chapters present the ultimate dependent variable – vote intention – and the ultimate independent variables – temporally constant factors in social structure, partisanship, and ideology.

Chapter 2 makes the case for division of the general campaign into three basic phases: Gore ahead, Bush ahead, Gore drawing even. The transition between the first and second phase was especially abrupt. The chapter also documents other shifts, none of which seemed to endure, and argues that these shifts are overlays on the two basic ones. The basic shifts endured, and the pattern that defined the first two phases was stronger at the end of each phase than at any earlier point in it. Until the very end, movement in Gore's share was mirrored by movement in Bush's share only incompletely. Gore-preference also traded off with no-preference. The major candidates' preference profiles were, in short, asymmetric: Bush forces were disciplined, neither gaining nor losing much; Gore forces were more fickle, potentially more numerous but difficult to hold in line. Finally, the overall amplitude of swings may have diminished over the course of the campaign, although the evidence for this is ambiguous.

This diminution in swing, such as it was, points to increasing polarization. Polarization with respect to what? *Chapter 3* considers the possibility that polarization was mainly toward fixed fundamentals: social structure, party identification, and ideology. If such polarization occurs, a critical question is the balance among considerations. Balance does seem to be the governing motif. The key social structural elements are offsetting in the sense that the one-sided groups tend also to be small. Party identification is arguably not as one-sidedly Democratic as it is commonly thought to be. Conservatives clearly outnumber liberals, so this dimension helps the Republicans. But moderates were far more likely to vote Democrat than Republican, so this dimension too nets out to a rough balance. The dynamic asymmetry flagged in Chapter 2 reflects a structural one described here: George W. Bush was more of a fixed object than Gore, more a focus of attraction or repulsion. Focus on fundamentals includes the geography of the system. Independently of state-by-state differences in social, partisan, and ideological composition there are enduring state partisan cultures. As a result, the 2000 state-by-state vote distribution was quite predictable from 1996 returns, and a core of highly competitive states can be identified. For all that fundamentals do a good job of assigning respondents to sides, the campaign did *not* increase polarization much with respect to fundamentals. The ebb and flow of preference largely cut through precommitted groups. Not all respondents could be assigned to such a group. The polarization identified in Chapter 2 was oriented to other considerations, and is a matter for further investigation in later chapters.

So Chapters 2 and 3 leave unanswered questions. Although abiding "fundamentals" account for much of the vote in a cross-sectional sense, they account for remarkably little of its dynamics. Instead, analysis of the ground for campaigning points toward a handful of states on which the rival campaigns were likely to concentrate. This geographic indication takes us into the realm of strategy, and the chapters that follow look at critical choices by the campaigns, as well as how the campaigns were received by the mass media and by voters.

Because of the interaction of geography and the electoral college, the campaign took the form of a natural experiment. If Chapter 3 identified the landscape over which the battle must take place, *Chapter 4* describes how strategic actors responded to the landscape and with what impact. Visits and ads were highly concentrated geographically. Ads in particular were focused on only a handful of states, and the identity of these states was highly predictable from analysis in Chapter 3. In general, within a state, if the campaigns advertised anywhere they advertised everywhere. The volume of ads ramped up dramatically at the very end of the campaign.

Over the full campaign, the Republicans bought somewhat more ads than the Democrats. Independent advertising offset this partially, and the overall Republican advantage was modest. But pro-Bush ads were markedly more concentrated than pro-Gore ones in the last days of the campaign. In the last week, the Bush advantage was nearly two-to-one. This advantage mattered to the outcome, as the advertising differential for any week affected candidate choice at the margin. Specifically, it affected choice of Al Gore, a further indication of the greater volatility of his proto-coalition. In closely fought states, Gore might have netted four percentage points more of the popular vote among persons with weak partisan commitments had he been able to match Republican ad spending. Partly offsetting this was that Al Gore won the news war at the end. The campaign thus was fought in two, divergent arenas. The three-phase chronology of Chapter 2 reflected the campaign in the free media and was mainly a story of low-volume, uncompetitive states. Where advertising was heavy – which at the end is to say, where pro-Bush advertising was especially heavy – the third phase was aborted, and Al Gore did not recover.

The next three chapters capture the content of the campaign, in its rhetorical focus and in the substance of voter response. Roughly speaking, each chapter accounts for a phase.

Chapter 5 suggests that the first phase exhibited characteristics predicted by econometric forecasting models. The nominating conventions sorted out citizens' perceptions in ways that were useful for Al Gore. In general, respondents saw the economy in a far more positive light than at practically any time in recent memory and they were willing to credit the Clinton-Gore administration with primary responsibility for this. In September, economic perceptions yielded the Gore campaign a net advantage. But after the convention Gore failed to take credit for the economy; his campaign ads mentioned it not once. As September yielded to October, the link of economic perception to the vote attenuated. By indirection, this confirms the intuition of earlier observers that campaigns prime the economy, indeed that they produce the very link that drives forecasting models. The 2000 campaign is the exception that proves the rule. Instead the ultimately dominant aspect of the Clinton-Gore stewardship was Bill Clinton's low personal reputation, which made him a drag on the Democratic ticket. Certainly, notwithstanding the economy and the president's high professional regard, Republican advertising did not hesitate to link Gore to Clinton. Tellingly, Gore himself never made the link.

Chapter 6 shows that the transition to the second phase was driven by judgments on the current candidates. Before mid-September respondents struggled to differentiate aspects of candidates' personalities; ostensible judgment on individual facets of character mainly reflected overall popularity. In late September, however, the candidates – Gore in particular – came into sharper focus, as did the personality tradeoff between Bush and Gore. If Al Gore seemed generally more competent, Bush seemed the more estimable character. At the end, the competing considerations were almost perfectly balanced. But *dynamically*, the critical fact was the permanent collapse in judgments on Gore's character, on his honesty in particular. This collapse defined the transition and permanently worsened the terms of the electoral equation for Gore. His recovery occurred in spite of this worsening. The collapse was induced by a firestorm of media controversy in late September, a peculiar concentration of stories that seemed to exemplify long-standing but as yet unprimed suspicions about Gore. If TV news was the conduit for these suspicions, the language in which they were voiced was handed to the media by the Republican campaign.

Chapter 7 shows that Al Gore closed the gap mainly by focusing on George W. Bush's proposal to divert some Social Security contributions into the stock market. On most questions that might have featured in the 2000 campaign – many actually did – Gore was aligned with popular majorities (Waldman and Jamieson, 2003). But two obvious exceptions, abolishing inheritance taxes and the Bush stock market plan, were central planks on the Republican platform. Gore attacked the Social Security proposal. As a result, in debates, ads, and news, the campaign was a site for learning on policy questions, notwithstanding the persistence of cognitive bias. Initially, however, Gore's attacks only clarified that he was further from the center of opinion than his opponent. Ultimately, these attacks began to move opinion, such that although a majority supported Bush's position right to the end, the balance clearly shifted toward Gore. And this shifting balance accounted for much of Gore's ultimate recovery. But the recovery was incomplete in states pivotal to the Electoral College for reasons first outlined in Chapter 4. As Gore increased his focus on Bush's Social Security proposals, the Republican advertising effort responded in kind. At the end, 80 percent of Republican ads mentioned Social Security, usually also impugning Gore's credibility as an opponent of the Bush plan. In places where Republican ads dominated, initial opinion shifts toward Gore's position were reversed. Once again, we see the divergence between arenas that operated to Gore's strategic disadvantage.

Chapter 8 accounts for the track record of claims about campaign effects. At some level, most propositions about campaigns, both claims that minimize the independent significance of campaigns and claims that take them seriously as forces in history, prove to be true. Some dynamics of the 2000 campaign seemed quite predictable. But others were not. Resources were not balanced at the end and the imbalance mattered to the result. Al Gore did not grasp an issue that predictive models said he would have. His failure to do so probably reflected a predicament that forecasting models have never acknowledged. The predicament took a particular form in 2000, but it suggests a more general pattern: At least one candidate, sometimes both, face strategic tradeoffs. Not all issues are positional, and movement in position or perception a "valence" domain like candidate personality can cut through predispositions efficiently. Not all citizens have strong predispositions on policy. If such voters cannot be anchored to, say, a clear view of appropriate reward or punishment for managing the economy, then it all may come down to which side buys the most ads in the last week.

2

The Evolution of Vote Intentions

In the general campaign – late August to Election Day – three phases stand out. Later chapters reveal that the first phase corresponded to predictions from forecasting models that emphasize the economy, that the second was induced by a shift in evaluations of candidates' personal characteristics, and that the third turned on a battle over issues. In this chapter, however, the focus is on what vote intentions tell us by themselves. In the first phase, Al Gore was clearly ahead, about as far ahead as forecasting models said he should be. In the second he was clearly behind, almost as far behind as earlier he was ahead. In the last phase, he drew even. The transition from the first phase to the second was abrupt and unmistakable. The transition from the second phase to the third is more debatable. Within each phase, less consequential shifts also occurred, but none lasted more than a few days and none fundamentally altered the course of the campaign.

Movement, whether enduring or temporary, in the candidates' vote shares was asymmetric. Shifts in Al Gore's share were not just the mirror image of shifts in George W. Bush's share. Until the very end, when the system appeared to undergo a qualitative transformation, Gore's share was more mobile than Bush's. Change in the relative standing of the two candidates stemmed heavily from the ebb and flow in Gore's own support. This also means that Gore intention was polarized more than Bush intention was against "none of the above." Bush's support was more disciplined, less likely to shrink but also harder to expand. Some of this Bush-Gore asymmetry reflected the fact that the threat was greater on Gore's left than on Bush's right. But Ralph Nader, the threat on the left, was a small part of this story. The asymmetry, we argue, is endemic to party competition in the United States. The asymmetric pattern in vote intention anticipates a broader set of findings later in the book. It also fits a pattern first identified in early voting studies and deepened by work in the 1980s, evidence of a qualitative divide at the core of party politics.

The amplitude of swings between candidates was smaller toward the end than at the beginning. Each drop in amplitude reflected a net mobilization of preference, depletion of the ranks of the uncommitted. But diminution was not gradual. Rather, the typical amplitude dropped abruptly after the conventions and then again, probably, at the end. This latter drop may be only an end-point illusion. All along, shifts that narrowed leads tended to be larger than shifts that widened them, such that the race became closer as the end approached. Such a pattern suggests that the electorate grew more polarized. This begs the obvious question, polarized with respect to what?

Phases in the Campaign

The division of the post-convention campaign into three major phases is based on a reading of Figure 2.1.[1] As the figure typifies this book's

---

[1] All analyses of vote intention in this book work with the following survey questions:

1. Now thinking about the general election in November, if you voted today in the general election for president and the candidates were George W. Bush, the Republican; Al Gore, the Democrat; Pat Buchanan of the Reform Party; and Ralph Nader of the Green Party, who would you vote for? *(Order of candidates' names was randomized.)*
2. Some states allow individuals to vote before Election Day, that is vote early at a polling station or by filling out an absentee ballot. How about you? Have you already voted in this year's presidential election or not?
3. For president, did you vote for George W. Bush, the Republican; Al Gore, the Democrat; Pat Buchanan of the Reform Party; Ralph Nader of the Green Party; or someone else? *(Order of candidates' names was randomized.)*

The four-candidate intention question was first asked on July 17. Before that we relied on pairwise items that offered different combinations of major-party nominees. This was a legacy of the primary election period, in which candidacies were still hypothetical. For methodological reasons, the pairwise question was also retained for the rest of the campaign, with the order between Gore and Bush determined by a random number. The order between the pairwise question and the four-candidate question was also randomized.

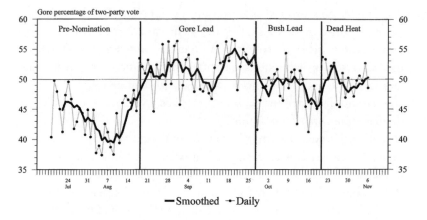

Note: Smoothed by five-day prior moving average.

FIGURE 2.1. The Critical Phases in Vote Intentions.

visual presentation of data, it merits extended description. The raw
material in the figure is the plot of daily values. Usually such a plot will
not be presented, but in this case the day-by-day plot is an important
supplement for analysis. It also conveys a sense of what the survey
data underlying this book really look like. Interpretation of daily plots
is difficult because of noise from sampling error. To distinguish signal from noise, some kind of smoothing is required. Any smoothing
function requires pooling of consecutive observations. But how many
observations and pooled in what way? In this book, pooling is almost
always by *prior moving average* (PMA), the simple mean value for the
day of interview and for some number of immediately preceding days.
In Figure 2.1, as in all figures in this book that use the entire survey
sample, smoothing is by five-day PMA, the day in question and the
four that precede it.[2]

The early voting sequence was first used on October 2. Over 10 percent of all persons
interviewed in the last week claimed to have voted already, and these constituted nearly
12 percent of all claiming some form of intention. In a two-party calculation, George
W. Bush's share of votes already cast was 57 percent.

All analyses in this book use unweighted data. Similarly, we invoked no screens for
supposed likely-voter status. We experimented with alternative screenings but none
produced as accurate a last-week forecast as the simple direction-of-vote question.
Some persons who claimed they would not vote nonetheless offered a candidate preference and many who said they would vote declined to choose a candidate.

[2] Our usage of the PMA differs slightly from more conventional usage, in which the
day in question is *not* included in the calculation and, instead all information is from

In the first postconvention phase, August 18 to September 27, Al
Gore enjoyed a clear lead. He was ahead of George W. Bush twenty-
eight days and behind twelve days, with the two candidates tied one
day. Gore's average share for the whole period was 52 percent. His
lead was bigger in late September than in late August. In the last fifteen
days of this phase, his average share was 53.7 percent. Interestingly, this
was just below the median predicted share from published forecasting
models.[3] At this point, there seemed no reason to doubt that vote
models predicated on information publicly available well in advance
of the event – information about the state of the national economy
and about the popularity of the President – would triumph, as would
Al Gore.

Between September 27 and 28, however, Gore's share plummeted.
The drop was fourteen points and, although Gore seemed to bounce
back, it was clear that the terms of the campaign had shifted against
him. He trailed Bush on the four days that initiated this phase. From
September 28 to October 20, Bush led on fifteen days, trailed on seven
days, and was tied with Gore one day. In those twenty-three days,
Bush's average share was 52 percent, just like Gore's in the preceding

preceding days. We adopt this particular setup to facilitate identification of turning
points. As much of our argument relies on temporal priority among potential causal
factors or between a putative cause and the vote intentions it might affect, we need
a smoothing function that allows precise localization of shifts. Including the day of
interest and preceding days permits just such localization. All other smoothing func-
tions that we are aware of include subsequent as well as preceding information and
so yield confusing indications about turning points.

Why a five-day PMA, and not some other number of days? We arrived at this conclu-
sion by comparing various PMA results with a tracking produced by Kalman filtering.
We began by putting the daily data of Figure 2.1 through "Samplemiser," an online filtering program (http://research.yale.edu/vote/samplemiser.html) developed by Donald
Green and Alan Gerber. A filtered and smoothed rendering of our data yields a plot
with almost exactly the same amount of daily "roughness" as our five-day PMA. It
would have been tempting just to use the Samplemiser plot, except that Samplemiser's
smoothing stage deploys information from following dates and so generates confusion
about turning points. By itself, filtering is strictly forward looking and makes turning
points clear. But it produces a much rougher plot than the simple PMA. So the five-day
PMA struck us as a very workable compromise. Besides, most of the other variables in
this book are not appropriate as Samplemiser input, so the PMA allows us to compare
variables that have been smoothed in exactly the same way. Where data are drawn
from subsamples, the number of days pooled is larger.

[3] The predictions are summarized in Wlezien (2001), Table 3. The median prediction
for the seven published forecasts was a Gore share of 55.2 percent; the mean was
56 percent. Two predictions were clear outliers at 60.3 percent each. Of the other five,
the median was 55 and the mean, 54.3.

phase. Also as in the previous phase, the frontrunner was further ahead at the end than at the beginning. In the last six days, Bush's share was 54.3 percent.

But Bush's advantage also slipped away. Of the last seventeen days (October 21–November 6), Bush was ahead eight days and Gore, nine. Gore's average share was 49.9 percent. The phase could be read as embodying a gradual trend toward Gore initiated by a massive but unsustainable pro-Gore pulse. Or it could be seen as ebb-and-flow around the 50-percent line. The boundary between this phase and the preceding one is not as obvious as the late September one, and alternative readings are possible. The October 20–21 boundary happens to mark Gore's first over-fifty reading in a week. The actual turning point appears to be earlier.

It could be that the whole period after September 28 is of a piece. The middle ten days to two weeks of this span saw an essentially even split between Bush and Gore. This was followed by a pro-Bush pulse that was then offset by a pro-Gore one, each in the aftermath of a debate. Alternatively, the last phase may have occupied only a handful of days. One can see Bush as clearly ahead mid-October until very near the end, except for a late-October pro-Gore pulse that mostly dissipated.

The most parsimonious reading, however, sets the effective boundary between the middle and last phases at the night of the 16th and 17th, following the last presidential debate. The second, foreign-policy debate clearly helped Bush. Some of that impact would probably have dissipated on its own (if impact from the third debate is any guide). But it probably would have strengthened Bush relative to the preceding weeks, deepening the pro-Bush tendencies that defined the campaign's middle phase. The third debate undid this impact, and then some. Impact from the third debate also dissipated, but the electoral center was nonetheless displaced toward Gore. And the trend of the last ten days clearly continued toward Gore, suggesting that the force originating in the last debate also benefited from further diffusion or reinforcement. Locating the boundary at the last debate also benefits from side information, which we analyze in detail later in the book. Suffice it to say here that Gore's recovery was assisted by the issue agenda of the last debate, which resonated in voters' own issue positions the very next day, even if impact from that issue shift on vote intentions was delayed a few days.

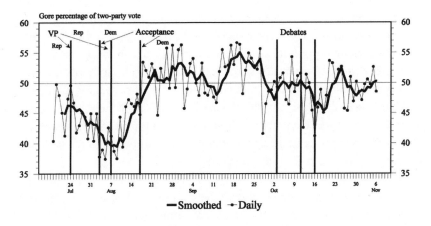

Note: Smoothed by five-day prior moving average.

FIGURE 2.2. Public Events and Vote Intentions.

Other Dynamics

Other shifts than those that mark phase transitions are clearly discernible. As most followed key public events, Figure 2.2 takes the same plot as in Figure 2.1 and superimposes a chronology of conventions and debates. This allows us to compare events for the existence and scale of impact. It also identifies shifts that cannot be attributed to any great public event.

The conventions clearly shifted the campaign's center of gravity. Each convention obviously favored its own party, thanks to heavily positive media coverage (as Chapter 4 shows). But the summary effect of the two conventions was to bring Al Gore into serious contention, indeed to give him the lead that defined the first phase of the general campaign. The pro-Republican shift was smaller than the pro-Democratic one, five or six points compared to ten or twelve. Each convention's overall impact came in two stages. The biggest shifts occurred *before* the conventions actually took place. Figure 2.2 marks the sequence of the most plausible moments connected to each event, the announcement of the vice-presidential choice and the presidential candidate's own acceptance speech. For each party, the turning point follows shortly on the vice-presidential announcement, although not immediately in each case. The biggest single jump in this period followed the presentation of Joe Lieberman as the Democratic nominee.

It followed the announcement by some days, however, and the shift in question was no larger a proportion of the overall pro-Democratic shift than the corresponding pro-Republican shift had been. Each convention's second shift stems from the acceptance speech. The daily tracking suggests that the effect is immediate, or nearly so. George W. Bush's share cleared 60 percent the very night of his speech and stayed there for at least three days. Al Gore's share surged the day after his speech, but the effect was no less abrupt and no less dramatic, a lift from the mid- to high-forties to the low-fifties.

Two of the three presidential debates also moved the center of gravity, in ways that we have already encountered. The first debate was *not* among these, however. The debate found Gore's share recovering from the cataclysm of September 27–28 and did nothing to disturb that recovery.[4] As mentioned, the second debate was a clear setback for Gore, while the third initiated his recovery. This interpretation requires imputing a shift that begins on a given day to an event that took place three days before. This hardly seems outrageous. It implies that debate impact is mediated, depending more on subsequent coverage of the event than on direct viewing. The interpretation is reinforced by the fact that the pattern is almost identical, apart from direction, between the second and third debates. No other incidents in the period offer themselves as explanatory possibilities.

If the third debate boosted Gore's share, the impetus did not last. From the 20th, he led five consecutive days, but on October 26 his share declined quickly. In the remaining days he was more often behind than ahead. Some counterforce may have driven his share back down. The simplest interpretation, however, is that the full impact of the last debate was unsustainable. These interpretations are not mutually exclusive. And its decay does not mean that this impulse was wholly ephemeral.

Two other shifts stand out, neither attributable to a public event. First was the ebbing of Gore's advantage in September. In the middle of the first phase, Gore clearly lost ground to Bush. Of the twelve days he

---

[4] The first debate did have an adverse impact on perceptions of Al Gore's honesty, as Chapter 6 shows, and so it reinforced a trend that was a defining element in the second phase. There is a hint of a pro-Republican shift in vote intentions after the vice presidential debate. Note in Figure 2.2 that the two observations following that event lie well below 50 percent. The impact, if impact it was, evaporated in three days.

was behind in the entire late August–September period, eight fell between September 1 and 12 and five were the consecutive days from the 8th to the 12th inclusive. On those five days, his average share was 48 percent. The second was his regaining of the ground. The 13th began an almost uninterrupted two-week Gore lead.

Asymmetric Mobilization

Before the last two weeks of the campaign, Al Gore seemed to be as much in a fight with indifference as with George W. Bush. Figure 2.3 makes this point by presenting Gore and Bush trackings separately. For one thing, Gore's share was generally more volatile than Bush's. On the smoothed series, Bush's share spans a range of eleven points, Gore's, of fourteen points. Between August 21 and September 13 all of Gore's gains and losses were the result of shifts in Gore's own share, unmatched by movement in Bush's share. Over that span, Bush's share scarcely moved. Of Gore's late-September recovery, no more than two-thirds was attributable to net exchange with his competitor:

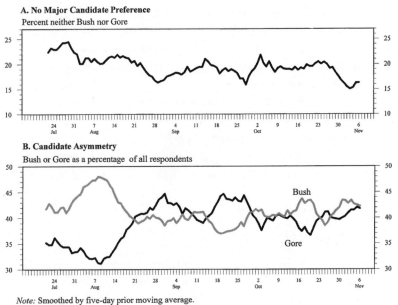

Note: Smoothed by five-day prior moving average.

FIGURE 2.3. Asymmetry between the Candidates.

as Gore went up six points, Bush went down only four. Gore's dramatic late September drop was mostly in his own share: where Gore's share dropped more than six points, Bush's share gained between two and three points. Bush's own share in Figure 2.1's early October phase, when he basically held the lead, was no higher than in mid-September when he was well behind. Gore, in contrast was five or six points behind his earlier standing. By implication, swings in Gore's share in Figure 2.3B (apart from his losses around the Republican convention) correspond mainly to ebbs and flows in no-preference. His decline from the first postconvention peak corresponds to a no-preference gain. His recovery corresponds to a no-preference drop. His abrupt late September drop is mirrored by the sharp rise in no-preference.

In mid-October, the asymmetry finally dissolved. Bush's gain after the second debate was exactly mirrored by Gore's loss; none of this is reflected in shifts in no-preference. Bush's loss after the last debate roughly mirrored Gore's gain. Thereafter *both* candidates gained at the expense of no-preference.

The pattern from mid-August to mid-October bespeaks a Republican base that is more disciplined than its Democratic counterpart. It may be intrinsically harder to mobilize potential Democrats than potential Republicans, but there may also be more potential Democrats out there to mobilize. The task for Republicans may not be so much to convert the indifferent as to reassure them that their indifference is warranted. This could be a peculiarity of 2000, when Ralph Nader lurked on Al Gore's left flank. Certainly, among those in the "no-candidate" group were persons who actively preferred Nader. But most persons with no major-candidate preference had no minor-candidate one either. The asymmetry in 2000 is also suggestive of a deeper, long-term qualitative difference between the parties, a matter to which we return below.

Diminishing Amplitude of Swings

Scope for movement shrank as the campaign approached its end. According to Figure 2.1, the widest swings occurred around the conventions. Even the modest pro-Republican shift of earlier August was as large as or larger than the critical late-September turn against Gore.

The swing toward Gore induced by the Democratic convention was twelve or thirteen points, easily the largest sustained shift of the whole campaign.

Between the conventions and the final two weeks, the amplitude of swings did not diminish further. Gore lost about four points in his early September recession, gained five or six points back in mid-September, lost five or six points in the critical late September swing, lost four more points because of the second debate, gained seven points temporarily because of the third debate, and lost five of these points right after October 25. The average across all these swings was about five points. Strikingly, the largest swing was the second last (Gore's big postdebate gain), and the very last (the partial dissipation of that big gain) was right at the average for the whole period.

The final swing, Gore's recovery at the end, spanned only two points. Yet it does look like the real thing – a real swing. The smoothed tracking does not misrepresent the underlying daily values and the recovery was steady and wavelike. Its minuscule span hints, however, that this shift is qualitatively distinct from all earlier shifts. Then again, its apparent distinctiveness may be an illusion, helped along by the fact that these are the last data points.

The stages by which swings diminished correspond – sort of – to stages in the decline of the no-preference share, as indicated by Figure 2.3A. From late July to Election Day, the percentage with no preference dropped eight to ten points over all. The Republican convention knocked three or four points off the no-preference total, and the Democratic convention had roughly the same effect. So by late August, eight to ten percent more of the electorate declared a major-candidate preference than did a month earlier. The other apparently transformative shift came with a week to ten days left, when the no-preference percentage abruptly dropped five points. The correspondence is loose, however, and should not be overstated. For one thing, the no-preference percentage drifted up and down after the conventions, but mostly it went back up. With two weeks to go, half the convention effect had been erased. And the drop at the end did not precisely coincide with the slowing down of shifts. In fact, the no-preference drop began with the abrupt reversal of Gore's postdebate advantage. Figure 2.3 indicates that this reversal was a compound of a small drop in Gore's own share combined with a rather larger gain in Bush's. Thereafter both candidates' shares increased, as we have already noted, and this fact is what made the final shift tortoiselike.[5]

This delay in the damping of swings may reflect another general pattern: shifts that made the race closer were larger than shifts that did the opposite. The best illustration of this is the convention sequence. Before the Republican event, the race was already quite one-sided, with Bush eight to ten points ahead. Against this background, it is remarkable that the Republican event was able to move the electorate still further away from competitive balance. The much bigger shift toward Al Gore induced by the Democratic convention seems less remarkable when we consider where it left his share: slightly larger than Bush's. The main exception to this generalization is the quite abrupt shift that put Gore well ahead in mid-September. But then, the next shift, which erased the lead, was even bigger and it yielded a more competitive balance. Of the impulses after each debate, the smaller one – after the second debate – made the race less competitive and bigger one – after the last debate – made the race more competitive. This asymmetric pattern seems typical of campaigns, according to Holbrook (1996) and Shaw (1999a).[6] To return to an earlier point, if a force makes the system less competitive, a subsequent force making the system more competitive will probably produce a bigger swing. Such sequences necessarily slow down any systematic tendency toward a general reduction in swing.[7]

---

[5] As far as we can tell, the 2000 pattern exemplifies a general pattern. Wlezien and Erickson (2002) deploy poll evidence cumulated from 1944 to 2000 to show that day-to-day variance in poll readings peaks right around the conventions. What they are unable to show is how the subsequent shrinkage, if any, in volatility plays out.

[6] Holbrook (1996) applied the generalization specifically to conventions. He posits that each election year has an "equilibrium" vote division, based on a forecasting model, and shows that the "bounce" from nominating conventions is greater if its direction is toward the implied equilibrium value than away from it. Shaw (1999a) finds asymmetry for a broad range of campaign events, although the directional difference is modest.

[7] Because of this asymmetry, campaigns also almost necessarily make the race closer as time passes. Certainly this is true for 2000, but then this could hardly have been otherwise given the ultimately razor-thin result. For the general pattern, see Campbell (2000), especially Table 7.4, which shows that although the typical frontrunner is far ahead on Labor Day (sixteen points ahead on average and often more than twenty points ahead), that lead is usually cut in half, still leaving a comfortable margin and affording few opportunities for the lead to change hands. Only in 1948 and 1960 did the Labor Day frontrunner lose. The 1980 election seems unique: the lead changed

Conclusions

The most important thing about the campaign is that it was divided into phases. The phases point us to an explanatory task: to account for what distinguished each phase from the others. No less important than the substance of the phases, however, was their mere existence. This points to the importance of "on-line" processing. And an electorate that processes on-line is an electorate to which campaigns matter in a very deep sense.

Accounting for Phases

The nominating conventions launched the first phase. The chronology of movement around the conventions is not surprising, as it exemplifies propositions convincingly established by Holbrook (1996). And the outcome, an increasingly comfortable lead for Al Gore, was exactly that predicted by econometric forecasting models. Chapter 5 adds flesh to this skeleton by showing how the conventions aligned economic perceptions in ways that were useful both for explanation and for Al Gore's prospects. The first general-campaign phase, then, represents a triumph for "fundamentals." Accounting for the evaporation of this pattern, for the sudden collapse of Al Gore's lead, is the task of Chapter 6. It takes us into the domain of candidate perception, in particular to judgments about Gore's honesty. This is also the place where Republican strategy and broadcast media choices intervened to disengage the electorate modestly but critically from the gravitational pull of fundamentals. Al Gore's comeback, the third phase, takes us into the realm of issues: voters' own positions and their perception of candidates' positions, and the processes of priming, learning, and persuasion. This is the subject of Chapter 7.

Phases and Political Cognition

What does it mean for a phase to be a phase? Two conditions seem necessary and together they are sufficient: First, the shift must be sudden, accomplished in no more than a few days; and second, the shift must endure. In the absolutely ideal case, all displacement should be

---

hands even though the eventual winner, Ronald Reagan, was ahead on both Labor Day and Election Day; and Reagan's margin was wider on Election Day than on Labor Day.

immediate and the initial displacement should be entirely preserved.[8] Certain discontinuities in 2000 were absolutely unmistakable. At least two of the four convention-related shifts – and arguably all four – occurred overnight; the shifts related to each acceptance speech certainly took this form and neither was obviously ephemeral. We shall never know what might have been the subsequent history of the pro-Bush shift that followed his acceptance speech had the Republican convention come after rather than before the Democratic one. What we do know is that the pro-Gore shifts induced by the Democratic convention lasted, so much so that they initiated the general campaign's first phase. It may be that some of the impulse from the Democratic convention dissipated on its own. Certainly Gore lost ground in early September. But the time path of his decline does not look like autonomic decay; before the downturn, his advantage had been sustained for a good two weeks. More likely, an active counterforce drove his share down. Later chapters suggest that this reflected a temporary Republican advantage in advertising. Regardless, there is no suggestion that the race would move back to the strongly pro-Bush values of early August. If the August-September pro-Gore phase started suddenly, so did it end suddenly. The five-day PMA makes it look as if the collapse required a few days, but the daily tracking makes a compelling case that the lead evaporated overnight, with some subsequent dissipation of the initial impulse.[9]

The transition from the middle phase to the last one was not so sudden. It is awkward that our insistence on discontinuity at the last debate rests on information yet to be presented. Certainly Al Gore was better off on Election Day than he was three weeks before. But his standing three weeks before, on the eve of the last debate, represented a low point not entirely typical even of the middle phase. That low point and the next high point were closely spaced and both might represent localized debate effects. Described this way, each event seems ephemeral. Each

---

[8] In the language of control theory, the shift would be a "step," indicating that the signal that produced the response is strong and relatively unmediated and that the electorate's response is "integrated," that is, that the signal's impact endures. See Shaw (1999a) and Wlezien and Erikson (2002).

[9] To continue themes from note 8, the late September shift combined elements of a "step" and a "spike," rapid in both onset and dissipation, but the dissipation was less than total.

emitted a strong enough signal to displace vote intention dramatically and suddenly, but the effect was swiftly cancelled. Closer scrutiny of the sequence makes a strategic interpretation equally plausible, however. Nullification of impact from the second debate may not have been autonomic, but instead the result of the counterforce applied by the third debate. Certainly, it seems reasonable to pose the counterfactual: what if the third debate had not taken place? As for the third debate itself, even if some of its impact dissipated, the electorate never again leaned decisively to Bush.

We propose that these shifts are essential to understanding the result. Other shifts were clearly visible and we return to them in a moment. But the phase transitions moved the very ground on which the campaign was fought, ground on which more ephemeral shifts were overlaid. The existence of phases indicates that at some level a campaign is, in the jargon of time-series analysis, a "random walk": If a shock displaces the system, it stays displaced; further movement requires another shock; the electorate does *not* automatically return to its prior state (Wlezien and Erikson, 2002). This time-series image further suggests that the political cognition is, again at some very basic level, "on-line," in the sense intended by Milton Lodge and his colleagues (Lodge et al., 1989; 1995). An electorate that behaves this way is an electorate for which the campaign is very important. If one side can succeed in moving it, the other side must take action to move it back. It cannot count on autonomic forces – memory expressing "fundamentals" – to do the job.

Coexistence of Patterns

But phase transitions are not the only visible movements, not even the most spectacular ones. All other shifts were erased seemingly by the mere passage of (not much) time, and this pattern corresponds to the other image in time-series analysis, of a "stationary" series. An electorate that is essentially stationary will experience shocks, forces that displace the partisan center of gravity. But as the shock itself wears off, the electorate should return, sooner or later, to its preshock position. An electorate that looks like this arguably employs "memory-based" cognition, as voters eventually reinterpret electoral shocks and assimilate novel information to preexisting stocks of knowledge. Voters may be distracted temporarily but eventually they or their proxies sort it out.

Some ephemeral shifts were gradual, certainly in onset, sometimes in dissipation. The early September dissipation of Gore's lead was like this. Other shifts were sudden but not entirely sustained. Impact from the second and third debates may also fit this description. And some of the shifts we interpret as marking phase transitions also exhibit stationary features. The late September transition is a case in point: daily readings indicate that Gore's collapse was massive initially but also that only some of the initial impact was preserved. What was preserved fundamentally redirected the campaign, however. Such a reading may also apply to the pro-Gore shift after the last debate. The coexistence of patterns warns us to be alert for heterogeneity in the electorate. This touches a theme signaled in Chapter 1: perhaps some voters have better memories than others.

And then there are the – possibly linked – facts that swings became less extreme with time and that movements that narrowed the race were larger than movements that widened it. Both facts bespeak an electorate undergoing polarization (Campbell 2000; Wlezien and Erikson, 2002). The key question is: polarization with respect to what? The standing interpretation would be: with respect to "fundamentals." By "fundamentals" is meant a set of relatively fixed factors – social structure, party identification, and ideology – and a moving factor – the record of the previous administration, especially in managing the economy. What all these factors have in common is that their distribution is known well in advance of the election. If this is all that polarization means, then the phases we identify are also ephemera, way stations toward a predetermined destination.

3

The Landscape

On one view, the main effect of a campaign is to enlighten voters about the means and ends dictated by "fundamentals" of competition in the current party system (Gelman and King, 1993; Zaller, 1998). The fundamentals assessed in this chapter are factors that endure across elections, indeed across decades.[1] Some reflect party differences originating in the New Deal but reinforced by the policies of Lyndon Johnson's Great Society. Others reflect the "culture wars" of more recent decades. Importantly, enduring differences are also expressed geographically, in variation across states. This variation created, in turn, the possibility that the 2000 campaign would be a natural experiment on a continental scale. Identifying differences is only the starting point, however. For this book, fundamental factors are most interesting as they constrain, or fail to constrain, the dynamics of preferences over the campaign.

Is the electorate indeed best characterized as a field of polarized interests, such that the campaign's primary effect is to increase preexisting gaps in vote intention, as citizens are reminded of the proper means to ends they hold dear? To the extent that this is so, shifts induced by the campaign should be mainly offsetting and the scope for the campaign to shape the result should, correspondingly, be small. The campaign would not be very interesting as a field for strategic play and

---

[1] The economy is another fundamental factor, but its implication varies from election. Consideration of the economy is postponed to Chapter 5.

counter play. Strategic initiatives may occur and, taken individually, may have their intended effect. But their cumulative impact should be to move blocs of voters to interests they hold, knowingly or not, all along. Gauging the rhetoric of such an event would be a waste of time, analytically speaking. The one really critical question is whether the underlying distribution of group interests is balanced, or whether it systematically favors one side over the other.

Or do the dynamics of the campaign appear in roughly the same way on both sides of most major gaps? If this is so, the scope for the campaign to shape the result is potentially great, for shifts among individuals are less likely to be offsetting, more likely to move the bottom line. The balance of resources between the campaigns becomes particularly important. So potentially does the rhetorical content of the campaign.

This chapter begins with the balance of underlying forces – in the social structure, in party identification, and in ideology. This includes an exploration of the system's geographic base, which is more than a simple state-by-state aggregation of individual differences in party orientation. Geography is particularly significant in its own right because of the Electoral College. The chapter also explores a qualitative difference between Democratic and Republican candidates in their links to the underlying group structure. Finally, the chapter goes to the central question, about the group basis of campaign dynamics.

The Balance of Forces

We look for balance or imbalance in three broad areas. First is social structure: differences among racial, religious, and economic groups, and between males and females. Then we consider party identification, the closest of these considerations to the vote. Party identification partly overlaps liberal-conservative ideology, the last factor we consider.

Social Structure

The claim that factors in the social structure are basically in balance rests on the evidence in Figure 3.1. Since many figures in the book resemble this one, another detour through pivotal analytical and presentational choices is required. Figure 3.1 embodies the first installment of the book's basic multivariate setup. The multinomial logistic

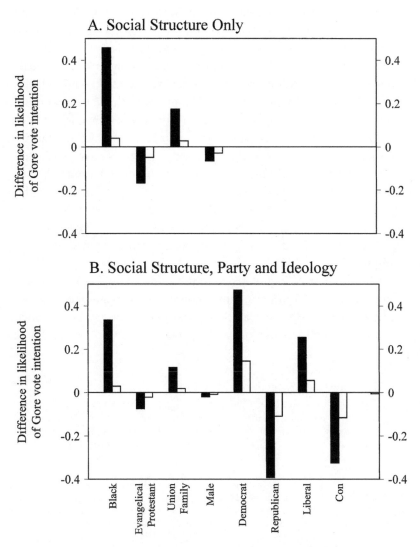

Note: Bars indicate difference in likelihood of Gore vote intention made by membership in group. Based on coefficients in Table A3.1.

FIGURE 3.1. Group Differences in Vote Intentions.

regression estimation on which it is based appears as Table A3.1 in Appendix A. The multinomial setup allows factors in the choice of one candidate to operate differently in choice of the other. Freeing the candidates in this way follows from the indication in Chapter 2 that

Gore preference exhibited more dynamics than Bush preference. But the substantive meaning of logit coefficients is not transparent, and so a recurring strategy in this book is to convert coefficients in appendix tables into plausible values for impact on the probability of candidate choice. In Figure 3.1, this means the difference made by membership in an indicated group as compared with nonmembership.[2] Because probability differences in Figure 3.1 refer to the *net* likelihood of choosing Gore rather than Bush, any asymmetry between Gore and Bush is washed over.[3] Other times, as in Figure 3.3, potential asymmetries are front and center. Probability differences are indicated by vertical black bars, above the zero line if membership helps Gore, below the line if it helps Bush. White bars represent the probability difference discounted for the size of the group. Discounting is accomplished by multiplying the probability difference by the group's proportion of the total sample.[4]

The first part of Figure 3.1 indicates that, taking both group distinctiveness and group size into account, the demographic bases of party competition were remarkably balanced. The four most powerful lines of differentiation among individuals were, in declining

---

[2] The steps in such a comparison are as follows:

1. The logit is calculated for the intercept, that is, for persons not in any of the groups denoted by a dummy variable and scored zero on any variable with a continuous distribution (in Table A3.1, the only such variable is the 1996 vote in the respondent's state cast as the difference from the national two-party division).
2. This logit is converted into a probability of choosing the indicated candidate by taking the antilog.
3. The logit for the indicated group is calculated by adding the coefficient for that group's dummy variable from Table A3.1 (implicitly, the coefficient is multiplied by one, in contrast to step 1, in which the coefficient is implicitly multiplied by zero).
4. This logit is converted into a probability, again by taking its antilog.
5. The difference between the two probabilities is then taken and converted into a vertical bar in Figure 3.1.

By construction in logit, impact of membership in any one group is contingent on membership in others, so the estimates in Figure 3.1 should be taken as illustrative more than authoritative.

[3] The net probability shift is simply the difference in the value yielded by step 5 in note 2 for Gore minus the corresponding value for Bush.

[4] Sample proportions are not always identical to census proportions, but there is little point in going outside the sample. The sample is no worse than the census in its portrayal of the potential electorate and certain groups – Evangelical Protestants and union families – have no census equivalent.

order: race, Evangelical religion, union membership, and gender.[5] African Americans were the most distinctive group by far, a true Democratic bastion. The difference between African Americans and all others, other things equal and averaged across the whole campaign, was over 40 percentage points. Gore's share among African Americans was close to 90 percent (over 90 percent at the end). White Evangelical Protestants were 17 percentage points less likely than other religious groups to support Gore.[6] The union/nonunion gap was about as wide – seventeen points – but favoring the Democrats. The gender gap was modest, with males seven points more favorable than females to Bush; of course, the "groups" on each side of the gender gap are enormous.

At first look, the Democrats have a more sharply defined base than the Republicans. The two pro-Democratic groups are more distinct than the two pro-Republican groups. And one of the Republican "groups" is males, more properly seen as one-half of an exhaustive contrast; we could easily have labeled the variable "female." This comports with a general view of the Democrats as a party of "special interests." But when each group's distinctiveness is weighted by its size, the demographic balance becomes quite even. The African

---

[5] Other groups might have been included in Figure 3.1 but they were either insufficiently distinct or too small. Hispanics were numerous enough potentially to be a key target group, and the Bush campaign certainly saw them this way. Hispanics constituted just under 10 percent of all persons with a major-candidate preference, so they were effectively only a slightly smaller group than African Americans. But they were not that distinct: about seven percentage points more likely than others to support Gore. Asian Americans *were* quite distinct – about 18 percentage points more likely than whites to support Gore – but they constituted only about 1.5 percent of the sample.

[6] The primary identifier for Evangelical group membership was response to the following question:

Do you consider yourself an evangelical or born-again Christian?

Persons who answered in the affirmative and who were neither African American nor Roman Catholic scored one on the Evangelical dummy variable. A majority of African Americans claimed to be born-again, but this made no difference to the vote. A modest percentage of Roman Catholics also made this claim and such persons were more likely than other Catholics to support Bush, but the difference was small, especially in comparison to the impact among white Protestants.

Although other religious contrasts were clearly visible, each involved uncomfortably small numbers. Mormons were sharply more pro-Bush and Jews, pro-Gore than all others. Traditionally important contrasts no longer carry the weight they used to. Catholics, for instance, are effectively indistinguishable from mainline Protestants. If all Protestants are lumped together, a Catholic/Protestant gap appears. But it is entirely the product of the distinctive behavior of Evangelicals and understates the gap at the real political boundary.

American/White Evangelical Protestant comparison is particularly instructive. The difference in probability induced by the race contrast is three times that induced by the religious one. But White Evangelical Protestants are over three times as numerous as African Americans. So when each group's coefficient is discounted for the group's size, as indicated by the white bars, the relative importance of the contrasts is roughly equalized. The same result holds when this calculation is applied to union membership and gender.

Party Identification

If the social bases of the system are balanced but rather weak, party and ideology, in contrast, produce huge gaps. Table 3.1A introduces these factors by describing their joint distribution. Democrats outnumber Republicans slightly.[7] The Democrats' numerical advantage is much smaller than typically found in the U.S. NES. This discrepancy is entirely the result of the interview mode, where Annenberg respondents were interviewed by telephone and most NES respondents were interviewed face-to-face.[8] It seems entirely reasonable to claim that the balanced picture of Table 3.1 is the politically relevant one, as even analyses that identify a considerable Democratic advantage in underlying identifications all concede that Democratic identifiers are less mobilized than Republican ones (Campbell, 2000). The mobilization differential evidently extends to availability for telephone interviews. The largest single group, in any case, was self-described Independents.[9]

---

[7] Party identification is captured by the root question in the standard NES sequence, the query about whether the respondent is a Democrat, a Republican, or an Independent. The Annenberg survey also asked partisans the strength of identification and Independents whether or not they lean to one or the other party, but we have chosen not to use these data for reasons we give below.

[8] Fortuitously, part of the 2000 NES sample was interviewed by telephone, and the party balance in this mode was essentially identical to that in Table 3.1.

[9] This last observation turns on taking at face value all persons who describe themselves as Independents in response to the root question. Not all agree that this is the correct classification, and the whole battery is a matter of controversy (at least among scholars at or associated with the University of California). Green and Palmquist (1990) and Keith et al. (1992), on one hand, argue that the intensity indicator is also useful and that Independent "leaners" ought to be treated as partisans. Miller and Shanks (1996), on the other hand, argue for the superiority of the root question. In the Annenberg rolling cross section data, the root question yields much more aggregate stability in the face of dynamic pressures in the campaign. As forces favored Gore, the intensity of identification strengthened among Democrats

TABLE 3.1. *Party and Ideology*

A. Joint Distribution

	Liberal	Moderate	Conservative	
Democrat	10.8	13.8	6.3	30.9
Independent	9.3	19.6	12.4	41.3
Republican	2.0	8.9	16.9	27.8
	22.1	42.3	35.6	(36876)

B. Joint Impact on Bush Intention

	Liberal	Moderate	Conservative	
Democrat	5.6	10.1	17.3	10.0
Independent	19.3	30.0	50.8	33.8
Republican	56.7	69.7	81.9	76.2
	16.0	31.8	59.8	38.3

C. Joint Impact on Gore Intention

	Liberal	Moderate	Conservative	
Democrat	75.3	69.8	60.3	69.8
Independent	39.5	34.8	17.1	30.5
Republican	18.1	10.8	3.8	7.1
	55.0	41.2	18.3	36.1

and weakened among Republicans, and the Democratic share among Independent "leaners" grew and the Republican share shrank. The opposite happened when forces favored Bush. At the end of the campaign, identification with each party intensified. For more detail on these patterns in the Annenberg data, see Hagen, Johnston, and Jamieson (2001). They echo patterns observed in NES and other data by Allsop and Weisberg (1988), Brody and Rothenberg (1988), Brody (1991) and Bartels (2000).

Our interest lies not in maximizing cross-sectional leverage but in minimizing longitudinal variance in what we wish to represent as an unmoved mover. So we have no choice but to use the simple but resilient response to the root question. Our findings about the relative resilience of the root and the enhanced indicators of party balance exactly parallel those in Weisberg and Kimball (1995), Table 3.4. Even by this measure, the party identification balance shifted modestly over the campaign, particularly in late September (again, see Hagen, Johnston, and Jamieson, 2001).

Ideological Self-Designation

If party identification was balanced, ideological self-designation was not. Conservatives outnumbered liberals massively, by a factor of about 5:3.[10] Although ideological moderates outnumber both extremes, the center is only slightly more populated than the right. At first glance, then, the ideological landscape favors the Republicans. Citizens that Republicans cannot mobilize by direct partisan appeals might be susceptible to ideological ones. When ideology is primed, more conservatives than liberals should respond, simply because there are more conservatives to begin with.[11]

Party and ideology are at one and the same time mutually reinforcing and a source of tension. The reinforcement is especially clear on the Republican side. Two-thirds of Republicans are conservative; fewer than one in ten is a liberal. So Republicans are an ideologically quite compact group. The tension is disproportionately on the side of

---

[10] Ideological self-designation is captured by this question:

Generally speaking, would you describe your political views as very conservative, conservative, moderate, liberal or very liberal?

Although each of the five steps in response captures a real difference in ideology and in likelihood of a Bush or Gore vote, we discard intensity differences on each side. This simplifies presentation and facilitates comparison with party identification.

[11] Although it is not a major theme in this book, it is worth noting that response to the liberal-conservative question is controlled by at least two dimensions. One is economic, a polarization on New Deal and Great Society issues. The other is cultural, a compound of disagreement over the place of women and homosexuals, secularism and Christian Biblical literalism, and guns and crime. As a broad generalization, the cultural dimension is more important than the economic one. These propositions are based on analyses reported in earlier drafts of this chapter. Further details are available from the authors on request.

Two-dimensional representations of U.S. political debate constitute a small but distinguished literature, for which the *locus classicus* is Shafer and Claggett (1995). The U.S. system is hardly unique in this two-dimensional structure. Most party systems have such an underpinning, in fact. Almost all party systems have had to cope with the "National" and the Industrial Revolutions (Lipset and Rokkan 1967). The challenges of the Industrial Revolution were common, more or less, to all polities and so produced cross-national convergence in the structure of political contestation. In contrast, each country had its own "National" Revolution, and the terms of the national settlement – including the prevailing conception of citizenship – produced each country's idiosyncrasies. In recent decades, the national and cultural dimensions may have changed shape in the face of "postindustrial" economic developments and rampant secularization (Inglehart 1997; Kitschelt 1994, 1995). Still, two separable policy dimensions stand out in country after country.

the Democrats, who are ideologically diverse. Liberals make up only about one-third of the Democratic base and conservatives constitute fully one-fifth. Almost half of Democratic identifiers are self-described moderates (in contrast to one-third moderate among Republican identifiers). The ideological contrast between parties helps account for the asymmetry observed in Chapter 2. Republicans' partisan impulses are much more likely than Democrats' to be reinforced by ideology. An extreme position in ideological tension – conservative Democrat and liberal Republican – is three times as prevalent on the Democratic as on the Republican side.

Independents are ideologically very diverse. They are more conservative, unsurprisingly, than Democrats, but they are no more dominated by the conservative pole than Democrats are by the liberal one. Almost one-quarter of Independents are liberals. Indeed almost as many liberals are Independent as Democrat, a significant fact in light of the Nader candidacy. And moderate Independents, who should be the most rootless group, are also the largest, one-fifth of the sample.

Panels B and C in the table present the joint impact of party identification and ideology on vote intention, averaged across the whole July–November span. Gore and Bush intention is presented separately, to allow asymmetry to appear. Party and ideology each made an independent contribution to the vote, but party also trumped ideology. Where gaps between liberals and conservatives were just over forty points, those between Democratic and Republican identifiers were over sixty points. Among Democratic and Republican identifiers, the conservative/liberal gaps were about fifteen points. Gaps between parties within ideological groups, in contrast, are over fifty points, and sometimes over sixty points. The parties are not that different in the pull they exert relative to ideology. There is slightly more defection among liberal Democrats than among conservative Republicans, but both groups were overwhelmingly loyal. Defection in less consistent groups is also very similar between the parties. So far, the decisive fact is not behavioral differences between groups, but the background distribution indicated by Panel A: A cross-pressured Republican is as likely to defect as a cross-pressured Democrat; there are just fewer cross-pressured Republicans.

What happens in the middle is complex but critical. First of all, moderates are not equidistant between conservatives and liberals. They are much more like liberals. Among persons with a major-candidate preference, Gore's shares in the liberal, moderate, and conservative groups respectively were 77, 56, and 23 percent. Moderates were thus seven percentage points more likely than all persons to choose Gore (Gore's two-party share in the whole sample over the whole period was 49 percent). More to the point, the gap between moderates and conservatives was thirty-three points. Between moderates and liberals, it was only twenty-one points. So the advantage that George W. Bush derived from conservatives' preponderance combined with their relatively high partisan consistency was offset by the fact that moderates were actually rather liberal.

But Al Gore was not able to derive as much advantage from this fact as he might have. The problem was not moderates, however; it was liberals. Ideology played its strongest directive role among Independents, as implied by our earlier observation about the dominance of party over ideology. Party can trump ideology, obviously, only where persons actually identify with a party. Among Independents, vote gaps between ideological extremes were very wide: thirty points between extremes in Bush preference; twenty points, in Gore preference. Now, Independents were less likely than either Democrats or Republicans to express a major-candidate intention. Where 80 percent of Democrats and Republicans supported a major-party candidate (usually their own, of course), only 64 percent of Independents made a choice. Similarly, moderates were less likely than conservatives to make a choice. But they were *not* less likely to do so than liberals. Where 78 percent of conservatives chose a major candidate, the percentages among moderates and liberals were, respectively, 73 and 71. This pattern is almost entirely the result of liberal Independents. Where conservative Independents leaned heavily toward Bush: (50.8 percent for Bush, 17.1 percent for Gore, a ratio favoring Bush of roughly 3:1), liberal ones were hesitant about Gore. Their support for him (39.5 percent) was only slightly greater than that of moderate Independents (34.8 percent) and their ratio favoring Gore over Bush was only 2:1. The problem, of course, was Ralph Nader. Although many liberal Independents, like Independents in general, had no preference for any candidate at all, this group was also the distinctive source of Nader support. So Gore was deprived of critical help from a natural constituency.

It is worth dwelling on the importance of ideology. Although moderates were the largest single group, they were still outnumbered by persons who accepted an ideological label. If ideology is dominated by party where party and ideology conflict, they usually do not conflict in fact, especially on the Republican side. And ideology is not absolutely suppressed when it does conflict with the party label. For the many who reject party labels, ideology is the most powerful guidepost, especially for Bush support. This sits uneasily with the observation that the U.S. system is deeply consensual, consisting mainly of variations on themes of liberalism (Hartz, 1955). Gerring (1998) makes a powerful case that students of parties fail to find ideology largely because they do not look for it. He argues that, even if Democrats and Republicans have reversed themselves in certain domains or have shifted their focus in others, remarkable continuities animate their respective appeals. And the fact that socialism, in particular, has been weak to nonexistent in the United States does not mean that the range of debate is narrower than elsewhere:

...the bounds of thinkable thought may be more conservative in the United States than in most countries; but they are not narrower. We must not confuse the rightward drift of American political culture with the rejection of ideology. The absence of socialism means that party conflict has taken place at one end of the ideological spectrum in the twentieth century; it does not mean that such conflict is any less intense. (Gerring, 1998, p. 54)

The survey data seem entirely consistent with this statement. At the same time, the data sit uneasily with claims that most voters are pragmatic and ignorant. Certainly, ignorance of political facts is widespread, and this ignorance makes a difference in voters' choices, in the sense that many uninformed voters, if they knew more, would make different choices from the ones they make in fact (Bartels, 1996). Response to individual policy questions tends to be only weakly related to response to other policy questions. Persons commonly hesitate to impute ideological orientations to themselves or to employ the language of ideology when asked open-ended questions about their likes and dislikes in politics (Converse, 1964; Smith, 1989). But the now-ubiquitous models that present liberal-conservative orientation as an operative master idea (Peffley and Hurwitz, 1985; Sniderman et al., 1991; Miller and Shanks, 1996) seem vindicated by Table 3.1.

Party and Ideology as Free-Standing Factors

If party identification and ideological self-designation are powerful forces, they also seem to be socially rather free-standing. The second panel of Figure 3.1 presents their effect along with impact from the four demographic factors discussed earlier. For party identification and liberal-conservative self-identification, Figure 3.1 adds little to the evidence in Table 3.1; indeed the figure is rather less subtle than the table. More interesting is what the party and ideology controls do to effects estimated for group membership. Each social structural effect shrinks, although all remain statistically significant. Some demographic impact is mediated through the long-term party and ideological predispositions those same group memberships help create. But not all of it. Controlling both party and ideology, African Americans are still thirty-five percentage points more likely to support Gore than others and union families are still over ten points more likely to support him.[12] Controls suppress more of the estimated impact from Evangelical religion and gender, however: coefficients on each term shrink dramatically when party identification and liberal-conservative self-placement are also controlled.[13]

Overall Balance

Taking all factors together, long-term forces seem remarkably balanced. Social groups that are one-sided also tend to be small. The small Democratic advantage in identification is more than offset by the marked Republican tilt in ideological locations, which is in turn offset by a Democratic tilt among self-described moderates. Of special relevance to 2000, however, is the irresoluteness of liberal Independents: they were not as consolidated around Gore as they might have been. This particular pattern is very much a product of Ralph Nader's candidacy: where liberal Democrats stayed with Gore, liberal Independents were especially vulnerable to Nader's appeal.

---

[12] These findings sit uneasily with Achen (1992), who claims that party identification should absorb impact from all background factors.

[13] The greater impact on the religious and the gender variables testifies indirectly to a point made in note 11. Liberal-conservative self-placement is driven more by cultural factors than by economic ones, and so is more closely associated with these cultural background variables. African Americans and union families, in contrast, are distinguished more for socioeconomic than for cultural liberalism.

Geographic Stability and the Battleground

The estimation on which Figure 3.1B is based also includes the 1996 two-party vote division in the individual's state. Table A3.1 in the Appendix indicates that the 1996 vote has a powerful effect in its own right. This implies that differences among states in vote propensity exceed those we might predict from states' differences in social structural, partisan, or ideological composition. Indeed, many aggregate differences among states work at odds with simple summing up of individual differences. For instance, the most one-sidedly Republican states are also racially homogeneous states, consistently with the individual-level differences. But Republican shares in these states are far higher than would be predicted from the states' racial homogeneity alone. And some of the strongest Republican states sit at the other end of the racial-composition continuum, in the South.

The critical fact for understanding the campaign is that, after decades of change, the geography of the party system seems to be stabilizing. The South has become more Republican, while the Northeast, the Pacific Coast states, and the Southwestern states immediately to their east – Nevada, Arizona, and New Mexico – have become more Democratic. These processes may have largely run their course, however, and the 2000 distribution of two-party shares across states was highly predictable from the 1996 distribution. Figure 3.2 illustrates this with state-level data. It presents a scatterplot of 1996 and 2000 results together with the line of relationship, calculated by Ordinary Least Squares regression (OLS).[14] The 1996–2000 relationship is very tight, a slope of 1.1:1. Republican places in 1996 were even more Republican in 2000, relatively speaking, and places that were Democratic in 1996 were even more Democratic in 2000, again relatively speaking. Between 1996 and 2000, the whole surface shifted downward, so states that gave Bill Clinton 54–55 percent of the vote are predicted by the estimation to give Al Gore about 50 percent of the vote.

Thanks to this, the 1996 data indicate the potential 2000 "Battleground." Eighteen states lay within ± four percentage points of the 1996 national two-party division and so would be predicted to

---

[14] The estimation focuses on the continental forty-eight states, the frame for our sample. It also excludes the District of Columbia, the most one-sidedly Democratic jurisdiction in the union.

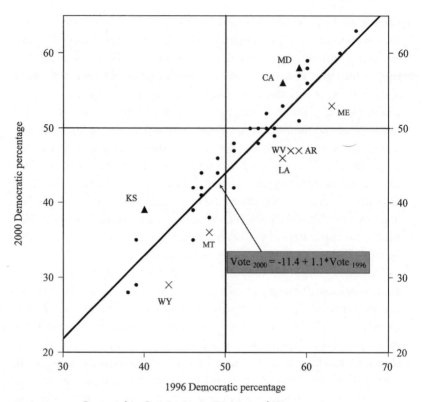

FIGURE 3.2. Geographic Continuity in Division of Vote.

lie within the same range of 50:50 in 2000. In descending order of 1996 Democratic share, these states were Maryland, Delaware, West Virginia, Michigan, California, Washington, Louisiana, Wisconsin, Iowa, New Hampshire, Pennsylvania, Oregon, New Mexico, Ohio, Missouri, Florida, Tennessee, and Arizona. Relaxing the criterion to ± 4.5 points adds two states, Nevada and Kentucky, both with a smaller Democratic share than in the first eighteen. Relaxing it to ± five points adds three more, Illinois, Minnesota, and Arkansas, all with Democratic shares larger than in the first twenty. So, by any reasonable criterion, a majority of states would fall *outside* the zone of contention. These states would be counters for the Electoral College but bystanders for the campaign.

The 1996–2000 relationship is not perfect, however. California and Maryland, which in 1996 had already tilted toward the Democratic end of a ± 4.0 band, stayed about as Democratic in 2000 as in 1996.

Kansas, in both 1996 and 2000 a solidly Republican state, was no more Republican in the latter year than the former. More critical, given the closeness of the result, are states that were less Democratic than they "should" have been. Three of these clearly were energy-producing states, perhaps reflecting the distinctive appeal of a Bush-Cheney ticket. Of these, Montana and Wyoming were already securely in the Bush camp. West Virginia, in contrast, "ought" to have given Al Gore a solid majority, a share of about 54 percent. Instead, 54 percent was the share won by George W. Bush. Three other states catch the eye. Maine remained in Gore's camp, but not by the margin he might have expected. Arkansas and Louisiana were outright losses that "should" have been wins. Some of the Arkansas displacement just reflected the removal of Bill Clinton from the top of the ticket. Rosenstone (1983) and Lewis-Beck and Rice (1983) converge in estimating that candidates derive a four-point net advantage in their home state, so Clinton's retirement alone made Arkansas competitive.[15] But Al Gore still "should" have carried the state. No story can be conjured up for Louisiana.

Nonetheless, Figure 3.2 says that prior information was readily available for party strategists to identify which states the Electoral College would make critical in 2000, which states would constitute the "battleground." Only some states would be worth visiting and spending advertising dollars in. These states would not be precisely a microcosm of the United States as a whole, but they would, almost by definition, have values close to the average on most politically-relevant characteristics.

The Relative Strength of Candidates' Links to Groups

Support for Bush was more rooted in demography and ideology than was support for Gore. This is indicated by Figure 3.3, which looks at probability differences separately by candidate; the probability is of choosing that candidate as opposed to remaining uncommitted. To

---

[15] Why then did Tennessee not move up the list? The answer may lie in the fact that Tennessee was already further up on the distribution than it would otherwise have been because of Al Gore's presence on the 1996 ticket. Rosenstone (1983) estimates that the vice presidential advantage is about 2.5 points, so Gore's expected marginal gain for moving to the top of the ticket would be at most 1.5 points. His outright loss of Tennessee seems mainly dictated by the fact that he ran over four points behind Clinton nationwide. His 1996–2000 swing in the state was less than four points, so he might still have derived some home state advantage.

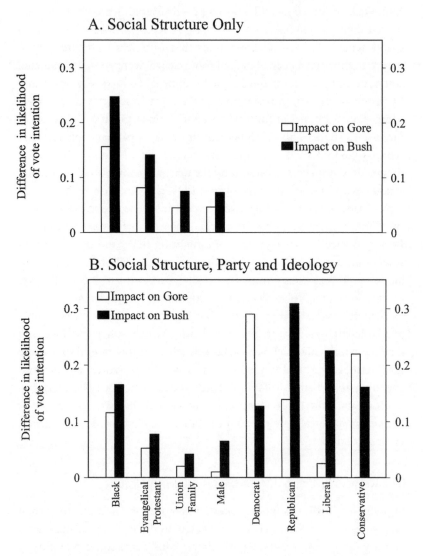

Note: Bars indicate difference in likelihood of vote intention made by membership in group. Based on coefficients in Table A3.1.

FIGURE 3.3. Group Differences in Vote Intentions by Candidate.

facilitate comparison between candidates, all vertical bars represent positive values, even though half the values are actually negative.

Social structural effects appear in the top part of the figure. Each group is more oriented to Bush than to Gore, sometimes in attraction, sometimes in repulsion. Relative to no-preference, African Americans were almost 60 percent more likely to avoid Bush than be drawn to Gore. Put another way, about 60 percent of the total race difference in Figure 3.1 is attributable to avoidance of Bush, only 40 percent to attraction to Gore. For Evangelical Protestants, Bush was the attraction. For union families, Bush was more repellant than Gore was attractive. Men were more attracted to Bush than repelled by Gore. Taking all the groups together, the Bush candidacy was more anchored in social structure.

Taking party into account, as shown by the bottom panel, only shrinks the overall effect estimated for social structure; it does not dissolve the asymmetry. The effects of party identification were not asymmetrical between Gore and Bush, just between an identifier's own candidate and other candidate. Partisans were more fixed on their own candidate than averse to the other. A Democrat had a thirty-point greater likelihood than an Independent of choosing Gore, but only a fifteen-point smaller likelihood than an Independent of choosing Bush. Roughly the same was true on the other side for Republicans.

Liberal-conservative self-placement worked the same way as group membership, that is, asymmetrically between candidates. Liberals were not much more likely than moderates to support Gore. But they were much less likely than moderates to support Bush. This essentially repeats the finding in Table 3.1, and testifies to the appeal of Ralph Nader. Conservatives were more repelled by Gore than drawn to Bush. To this point, ideological extremes mirror each other but reverse the pattern for party identification: if partisanship creates attraction more than aversion, ideology creates more repulsion than attraction. But conservatives were also distinctively drawn to Bush. So where Gore only repelled conservatives, Bush both repelled liberals and attracted conservatives.

All this dovetails with the dynamic asymmetry identified in Chapter 2. Party identification aside, Bush's candidacy was more deeply rooted than Gore's. Some of this was in its stronger appeal to its own support base. Some was in its repulsion of unsympathetic groups. The image for Bush, once again, is of support that is resilient but difficult to expand. The Bush/Gore contrast observed here seems completely consistent with the contrast in Chapter 2, in which Bush's candidacy was less susceptible than Gore's to short-term volatility.

Who Shifted?

The General Pattern

For the most part, differences between groups were not wider at the end than in late July. The outstanding group-based dynamic was that Gore's late September surge drew some normally unsympathetic groups toward him. At his peak, social differences in candidate support were relatively weak. His late September collapse was mainly flight by the same, normally unsympathetic groups that had temporarily moved toward him. Only African Americans exhibited countertendencies.

Figure 3.4 indicates that the two widest demographic cleavages – race and religion – also exhibited the most volatility. No trend is visible for the union/nonunion gap or the gender gap.[16] If anything, the union gap shrank. Black/Non-Black and Born-Again/Other differences did shift, and were smallest in the last week in September. They then crept back to their earlier width. The gap between blacks and whites did end up larger at the end than at the start. The widest gap of all was between Democrats and Republicans, but it did not

---

[16] The stability of the gender gap is especially striking in light of repeated attempts during the campaign to impute specific dynamics to women in particular. On NPR's *Talk of the Nation* on September 19, for instance, Richard Morin claimed that "women have moved 11 percentage points more for Gore. That movement is responsible for much of his improvement in the polls." Other commentators, notably Linda Hirshman and Eleanor Smeal, argued that women were either coy or indecisive. On either account, they were volatile in expressed preferences. More subtle was Anna Greenberg, cited in an October 21 2000 CNN story under Andria Hall's byline:

Well, what happened was prior to both the conventions, Gore was leading among women by about four points. And then after the Democratic convention he was leading among women by about 16 points. Since the debates, his support among women has been cut by about half. In the latest "Washington Post" poll, for instance, he's leading among women by about eight points.

The issue really is that women are more evenly divided between the parties than men are and so, as such, their support tends to be a little bit softer. It's not really that women are more undecided or swing voters per se, it's that they tend to be more evenly divided among the parties.

The first part of the statement is broadly consistent with the evidence in Figure 3.1, which implies that women were more evenly divided than men. So it is simple, uninteresting arithmetic that the lead changed hands more among women than men. More problematic is the hint in the second paragraph that a relatively close aggregate balance in a group signifies relatively great ambivalence in the individuals that constitute the group. Figure 3.4 is absolutely eloquent: *women cannot have been more volatile than men.* For a review of media commentary on the gender gap, see Lockhart (2002).

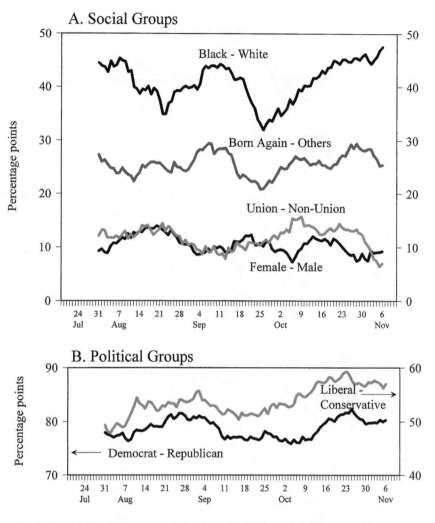

A. Social Groups

Black - White

Born Again - Others

Union - Non-Union

Female - Male

B. Political Groups

Liberal - Conservative

Democrat - Republican

Note: Entries are daily differences between indicated groups in Gore's percentage of two-party vote intentions. Smoothed by fourteen-day prior moving average.

FIGURE 3.4. Dynamics of Group Differences in Vote Intentions.

grow. The gap between liberals and conservatives, in contrast, grew: it was almost ten points wider at the end than at the beginning.

Figure 3.5 confirms that movement in cleavage widths was mostly generated by groups *un*sympathetic to Gore. It focuses on race, religion, and ideology, the three contrasts with dynamics worth discussing. As

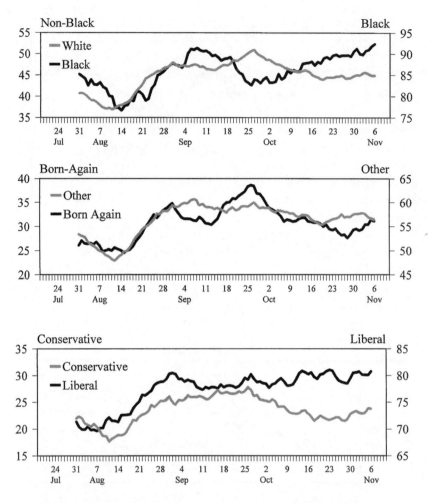

Note: Entries are Gore percentage of the two-party vote intentions, smoothed by fourteen-day prior moving average.

FIGURE 3.5. Dynamics of Vote Intentions in Key Groups.

emphasis is on dynamics, the figure does not portray the width of any of the gaps.[17] Had it done so, the width of the gaps would have overwhelmed the figure's vertical axis, and dynamics would have been all but invisible. Accordingly, the figure sets each vertical scale to the twenty-point range that best captures observations for the group. In

[17] Had the figure portrayed the gaps, their width would have overwhelmed the figure's vertical axis, and dynamics would have been all but invisible.

the top panel, for instance, the line for whites is oriented to the left axis with a range from 35 percent to 55 percent; the line for African Americans is oriented to the right axis, with a 75–95 percent scale.

Gore's support increased roughly in parallel among both sympathetic and unsympathetic groups through and after the Democratic convention. Among Whites and Born-Again Protestants, however, it continued to grow in late September, for a total gain in each case of about fifteen points. This is not to say that these groups gave majorities to Gore. Whites may have done so momentarily, but the Evangelical Protestants among them never did. No matter, the critical thing was that his standing in these groups improved; every vote was potentially useful. But Evangelical Protestants – and Whites more generally – fell away dramatically after the late-September moment, essentially never to return. Although conservatives did not rally to Gore as sharply as Born-Again Protestants did, they nonetheless participated in the general shift toward Gore. But they too fell away, on exactly the same timetable as the others: Their flight from Gore marked the end of what Chapter 2 identified as the first phase.

Dynamics on the other side were usually less interesting. Liberals and persons outside the Evangelical Protestant camp moved toward Gore after the conventions and then basically stayed put. His share among persons of "other" religion may have fallen back slightly. His share among liberals grew slightly. Among pro-Gore groups, only African Americans exhibited serious movement in both directions and at odds with the generalizations just ventured. They had moved almost as far toward Gore as they possibly could by early September. Then, when generally unsympathetic groups moved toward Gore, African Americans actually moved away from him. When other groups moved away or remained steady, African Americans moved back to him. His cumulative gain among African Americans from late September to Election Day was seven or eight points.

The Liberal-Conservative Gap

The cleanest pattern was for the gap between liberals and conservatives. This gap widened almost monotonically. It did narrow slightly in September, but that month's reversal was far smaller than for other contrasts. The overall widening of the liberal-conservative gap came in spite of the fact that ideology was sometimes at odds with party. Indeed, among partisans the gap did not widen at all. Not surprisingly, partisans at odds ideologically with their own party were more mobile than less cross-pressured persons. So conservative Democrats were quite drawn toward Bush by the Republican convention, although they then bounced back with the Democratic one. After the Democratic convention conservative Democrats responded further to the siren call of the Bush campaign, and finally drifted back toward Gore. On the Republican side, nothing can be said about liberals, as their numbers were too few. But moderates were drawn significantly toward Gore at mid-campaign and stayed there until the second debate, whereupon Gore lost ten points in this group. None of this yields a widening ideological gap. Indeed, it is a story of *narrowing* gaps, particularly as conservative Democrats chose party over ideology. Conservative Democrats ended up more supportive of Gore than *liberal* Independents were. Moderate Republicans approached a Gore share that rivaled that among conservative Independents at one point, but at the end they were nearly 10 points more likely to support Bush.

Ideological polarization was thus a story about Independents, persons for whom partisanship could not have been in tension with ideology. Figure 3.6 makes clear that it was here that most campaign dynamics occurred. Conservative Independents were the single group most responsive to the Republican convention but they were also very responsive to the Democratic one.[18] After the Democratic convention, however, this group drifted back in Bush's direction. Liberal Independents resisted the Republican convention and were highly responsive to the Democratic one. Moreover, once fixed in place by that event, they scarcely budged. The campaign took a preconvention gap of thirty points and by the eve of the election converted it into a gap of forty-five points.

The General Pattern

Did the campaign widen cleavages among traditionally partisan groups? For some groups and over certain intervals, the answer is Yes.

---

[18] In fact, conservative Independents moved as far back toward Gore as they had originally moved toward Bush. This is a bit deceptive, however, as the Democratic event exerted an even stronger pull on the other Independent groups and on conservative Democrats.

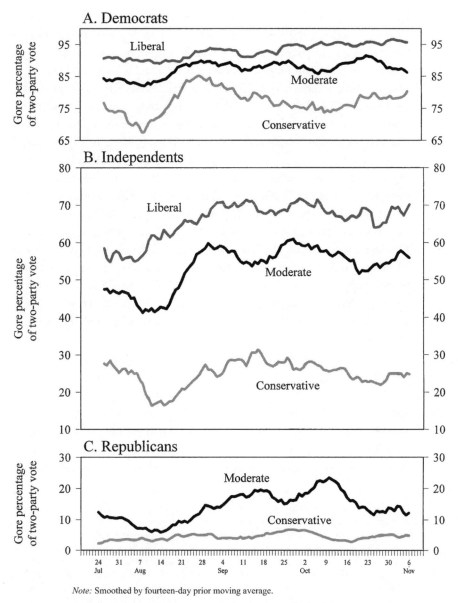

Note: Smoothed by fourteen-day prior moving average.

FIGURE 3.6. Dynamics of Vote Intentions by Party and Ideology.

Late September to Election Day yielded a dramatic widening of certain cleavages. Taking the longer view from July to November, however, the campaign's impact on cleavage widths was modest. Only two gaps widened over the full interval, between blacks and whites and between liberals and conservatives.[19] Otherwise, dynamics simply cut through social and political groups. And one very big group sits outside all this analysis. The largest group in Table 3.1 was moderate Independents, one person in five. Moderate Independents, according to Figure 3.6, were the most mobile group of all. They were especially responsive to the Democratic convention, consistently with the fact that they are collectively further left than they care to admit. The convention permanently shifted them to Gore's side of the ledger.[20] But they also registered subsequent drops and rises in Gore's share with special clarity. They were the most repelled by whatever it was that drove Gore's share down in mid-September. They came back to him in equal measure later that month. They moved clearly away from him after late September and came much of the way back at the end. Given the nature of the group, this can hardly be a story of polarization. It certainly is a story of dynamics.

Conclusions

Balance

To the extent that fundamental factors control candidate choice, the balance among these factors is critical. As it happens, the fundamentals in play *were* evenly balanced, at least with both group size and group

---

[19] Interestingly, these are the two lines of cleavage that Gelman and King (1993) see as widening in their detailed analysis of the 1988 campaign.

The claims in the main text are also confirmed by more controlled analysis. Repeating an estimation like that in Table A3.1 in individual daily samples (to conserve degrees of freedom, party identification and liberal-conservative ideology were treated as continuous, three-category variables, rather than as dummy variables) shows that pseudo-R^2 increases from before the conventions to after, then decreases in September, and increases again in October and November. The individual coefficients that drive this pattern are the ones we would expect: on blacks versus whites (particularly striking for decline and recovery, with the ending values two to two-and-half times as large as the starting ones) and liberals versus conservatives (a steady increase yielding proportionally as great a gain).

[20] This shift is hard to square with the claim by Bartels and Zaller (2001) or by Fiorina et al. (2002) that Gore positioned himself too far left.

distinctiveness taken into account. The primary exception was liberal-conservative ideology, where conservatives outnumbered liberals, to the benefit of George W. Bush. Even this advantage was offset, however, as many self-defined moderates were really liberals at heart.

The Gore and Bush support bases were not just each other's mirror image. Bush was much more a pole of attraction or aversion than was Gore. This helps explain the pattern in Chapter 2, the greater stability in Bush's share in total potential electorate. It is not clear that this is an advantage in a presidential election. Bush might have been able to count on firm support from more persons, but he may have been more limited than Gore in the potential for his share to grow. Gore's support could grow more, but it also could shrink rapidly.

Potential for Movement

The real story about fundamental factors is that they were summarily weak. If the contrast between African Americans and all others matches anything in European studies of partisan cleavage, African Americans are not a bloc on the scale of Catholics or of union movements in the stylized postwar European electorate. Evangelical Protestants are far more numerous than African Americans but the religious gap of which they are one pole is not huge in absolute terms. All told, only four social-group cleavages were big enough to merit graphical treatment and only three groups stood out as plausible bases for campaign mobilization: African Americans, Evangelical Protestants, and union families. Although each group is a somewhat coherent with quite powerful internal lines of communication, collectively the groups hardly constitute the basis for electorate-wide polarization.

More promising, perhaps, are groups defined by partisan and ideological identification. Certainly, the gap between Democratic and Republican identifiers was wide. But what we make of the gap depends on what we make of the party identification measure. The multiquestion indicator idealized by, for example, Keith, Magleby, Nelson, Orr, Westlye, and Wolfinger (1992) is too sensitive to the ebb and flow of candidate fortunes to be credible as a gauge of a fixed factor, of an unmoved mover. The only defensible indicator of long-term commitment is the simple directional indicator, the first question in the traditional NES sequence (and even this indicator is not entirely immune to influence from the campaign). But this indicator leaves a huge middle group.

The same is true for ideological identification. Although self-described moderates lean more toward the liberal side than to the conservative one, they still collectively belong in the middle. In other words, party and ideological identification do not yield exhaustive contrasts: Democrats are very different from Republicans but many voters are neither; liberals are very different from conservatives but many persons are neither. The middle, by definition, is not a place for polarization. Instead, persons in the middle exhibited wide swings in vote intention.

And the blocs at the partisan and ideological poles hardly seem like political communities. Very few self-described party identifiers carry party cards and the parties lack privileged conduits for their persuasive campaigns. This is not entirely true, of course. The African-American community, especially through its churches, gets the news around, as does the union movement for its dwindling band of adherents. On the Republican side, Evangelical denominations do the same. But parties have relatively few direct links to the many Democratic and Republican identifiers who do not belong to one of these groups. Instead, party identifiers are properly seen as aggregates of intentionality not attached to a specifically partisan information network. As later chapters show, party identifiers are biased in candidate perception and are responsive to policy cues originating from their "own" candidate, but they are not especially privileged in receiving those cues in the first place.

Moreover, the direction of swings in the middle group was almost always paralleled in the party and ideology groups on either side. If a candidate's share went up on one side of a partisan or ideological gap, his share tended to go up on the other side as well. The more reinforcement for a person's initial position – for example, if the person was a conservative and a Republican, as opposed to a moderate and a Republican or a conservative and an Independent – the less overall movement such persons exhibited. But the movement that occurred was almost always in the same direction as the movement on the other side or in the middle. However wide the cross-sectional gap between groups, the *dynamics* of vote intention tended to be the same.

If for many persons, party and ideology were reinforcing, for many others they were not. They were more likely to be reinforcing for Republicans than for Democrats, as three out of five Republican identifiers also claimed to be conservative. In contrast, only one Democrat in three claimed to be liberal. This helps account for the greater rootedness of Bush intentions in the social structure, shown by this chapter, and for the general stability in Bush intentions, shown by Chapter 2. But the Republican identification group still exhibits some ideological tension and the Democratic group exhibits a lot. The mere fact of this tension creates a strategic opportunity and a strategic challenge.

An Alternative Reading

We think that the dominant fact about campaign dynamics in 2000 is that they cut through preexisting groups. The campaign did not merely widen preexisting differences; indeed, with two exceptions, preexisting gaps did not widen at all. What moved was the bottom line. But campaign movement could be read another way. Relative to late September, gaps *did* widen; only if we insist that the starting point be late July can we conclude that their was little net impact of the campaign on vote gaps. Gaps narrowed in early September and then, starting in the last week of that month, widened again. Mainly, this widening restored the status quo ante.

This sequence is susceptible to the following interpretation. Al Gore was able to play cards that overrode resistance in normally opposed groups (they remained opposed, just less so than before). This accounts for the closing of gaps between July and September. Then the Bush campaign found a way to undo Gore's temporary advantage and return the electorate to the position dictated by "fundamentals." So although group differences did not widen, a temporary move to narrow them was countered. This could be construed as enlightenment, in the sense intended by Gelman and King (1993). The distraction undone by this enlightenment may have been the product of the campaign itself. But the fundamentalist model of campaigns does not preclude distraction as an interim outcome. It just posits that the success of a distracting move will be only temporary.

This reading may be correct as far as it goes, but it contradicts another reading that also refers to fundamentals. The point at which fundamental gaps begin to widen, according to this chapter's evidence, coincides with the end of the campaign's first postconvention phase. That phase, the August–September period, saw Al Gore enjoying the solid lead that all econometric models forecast for him. The earlier success of these models was the central exhibit in the fundamentalist case. So central was the economy to political judgment that it could override the tawdriness of Monica Lewinsky's fifteen minutes on the stage (Zaller, 1998). On this reading, the termination of the first phase seems more like a *departure* from fundamentals than a reaffirmation of their power.

Both stories about fundamental factors may be true. Chapter 5 will argue that the first postconvention phase delivered a structure of vote intention close to that implied in forecasting models. The nominating conventions burned off "error" in economic judgment and enabled the electorate to give the Democratic candidate his due. Chapter 6 will show that Gore's late September setback was a media phenomenon, with perception of his honesty at the core. The ebb and flow of cleavage widths in this chapter strongly suggests that the campaign first reduced the moral content of choice and then restored it. The lesson should be obvious: fundamentals can yield contradictory indications. The contradictions give scope for strategic choices that do more than uncover some unique, inevitable equilibrium.

Another lesson should also be obvious. To this point in the book, most interpretation of the campaign's fit or lack of fit to predictions based on fundamentals rests on supposition. In this we do not differ from the literature at large, however. The predictive power of the econometric forecasting models was impressive. But for all the success in modeling, election analysts still had only a fragmentary appreciation of the link between the models and the campaign. What we had were powerful and suggestive – and probably mainly correct – intuitions about how things worked. The lack of concrete evidence about the microprocesses that delivered predictive success before 2000 left us floundering when the prediction model finally failed. The rest of this book tries to fill the evidentiary gaps.

The Natural Experiment

One of the most impressive fundamentals was simple geography. Vote differences among states were much larger than would be predicted from differences in states' social, partisan, or ideological composition. Equally striking, these differences persist from election to election, such that each state's 1996 result forecast its 2000 result with remarkable efficiency. These linked facts – the size of differences and their stability – play directly into the logic of the Electoral College, making some states more pivotal than others. The pivotal states may see most of the campaign's action. But in an election like 2000 these pivotal states should also be a microcosm of the whole country. So if we observe perceptual or behavioral differences between the battleground – the states that history has made pivotal – and the others, these differences are likely to stem from the efforts of the Democratic and Republican campaigns, not from factors intrinsic to those places. Divergence in candidate perception, policy opinion, or vote intention would not be the product of "enlightened" preferences. More probably, divergence would stem from how questions were framed by one or the other party's ads – or from the sheer weight of advertising dollars.

4

Ads and News

The Campaign as a Natural Experiment

In a presidential election, not all votes are of equal value. Because the ultimate decision rests with the Electoral College, votes carry more weight in some states than in others. As a result, campaigns face powerful incentives to concentrate their resources geographically. By 2000, only a minority of states comprising only a minority of the electorate were worth campaigning in at all. But these states were something of a microcosm of the country as a whole, and this made the campaign into a natural experiment: One set of voters got the ad and visit "treatment," the other did not.

This chapter starts by examining the allocation of resources by campaigns – of candidates' time and of money spent on advertising. The first task is to identify the primary strategic incentive governing allocation of effort across states – which is more important about a state, its size or the competitiveness of its presidential race? Campaigns also must decide how to distribute ads over time – should they spend resources early or should they store them up for the end? The study of resources culminates with the bottom line, the impact of visits and ads on vote intention. In 2000, ads made a difference at the margin, and the Bush campaign was the beneficiary when it counted most, at the end. This is one piece of evidence about the natural experiment.

Advertising is not the only media component of a campaign. Candidates also made use of the "free" media. Indeed, ads are designed not just to persuade or mobilize voters directly, but also to move the news. Be that as it may, by the end of the 2000 campaign network news leaned the opposite way to the balance in ads: Al Gore's message dominated network news in the last week as fully as George W. Bush's message dominated the ads. This divergence between the ads channel and the news channel strengthens our case about the natural experiment. We can distinguish voters by their relative exposure to ads and to news, respectively. Although news messages can in principle be heard everywhere, citizens can be differentiated by their likelihood of receiving a news message. Ads may be designed and placed to burn through attention and exposure differentials, but because of the Electoral College they are not in fact accessible to all citizens. Did exposure and attention to news insulate against ads? For that matter, did news interest also insulate against the news itself? Did the noise of ads block the news? The answer to each question turns out to be "yes." The analysis sheds light on a body of theory about communications effects – about communications effects in general, but also about the relative power of free and paid media. The analysis also carries heavy political freight. It helps explain how it was possible for Al Gore to win the popular vote but lose the Electoral College.

The Geographic Concentration of Effort

Models of Resource Allocation
Political scientists have remarkably little to say about how presidential campaigns allocate resources under their direct control – the volume of ads and the use of candidates' time. The earliest work, focused on the allocation of candidates' time, emphasized the sheer size of each state, as reflected in its number of Electors (Brams and Davis, 1974). Because of the unit rule, it was argued, large states attract resources out of proportion to their representation in the Electoral College.[1] The critical factor is how likely a state's Electors are to create or break a tie in the College, and this likelihood is more than proportional to the state's share of the total Electoral vote. Colantoni, Levesque, and Ordeshook (1975) subsequently argued that the key factor was not the state's size

---

[1] At present, all but two states assign all their Electoral votes to whichever candidate wins the popular plurality in the state. The exceptions – Maine and Nebraska – use a statewide assignment for two votes (effectively, the Senatorial votes) and district-level assignment for the rest. As a practical matter, these two states also regularly give all their Electoral votes to the statewide plurality winner.

but its competitiveness. Campaigns should channel resources to states that hang in the balance, where changing the minds of one or two percent of the electorate might alter the statewide outcome. The effect of size found by Brams and Davis was the byproduct of historical accident: In the years they studied, 1960 to 1972 inclusive, competitive states tended also to be large.[2] Where size and competitiveness diverge, competitiveness is the more critical factor.

In 2000, both considerations – size and competitiveness – mattered, but their relative influence depended on the resource to be allocated. Figure 4.1 represents the independent contributions made by the two considerations to the campaigns' decisions about how to allocate their resources across states, estimated according to the model proposed by Colantoni and his colleagues.[3] The predictor of competitiveness comes straight out of Chapter 3: Bill Clinton's share of the 1996 two-party vote in the state. A state's competitiveness is the absolute value of the difference between Clinton's percentage in the state and his percentage nationwide, 54.74. The nearer the state's 1996 score to zero, the more competitive the state's race could be expected to be in 2000.[4] By historical standards, the correlation for 2000 between size and competitiveness was weak.[5]

[2] Later work on resource allocation includes Bartels (1985) and, most importantly, Shaw (1999b), whose work has strong affinities with ours.

[3] The parameter estimates appear on Table A4.1. All data for visits and ads in this chapter span the period from Labor Day to Election Day. Although our ad data go back to June, 2000, our visit log started on Labor Day, so consistency drove us to confine ad and visit analyses to this period. As it happens, this a reasonable representation of the heart of the campaign. Later in this chapter we report news coverage from July to Election Day. We justify the inconsistency by appealing to the intrinsic interest of coverage around the conventions. Whenever news *impact* is at issue, however, analysis is conducted as with visits and ads, that is, for the Labor Day–Election Day span.

[4] For reasons that will become clear later in this chapter, we gathered data by Nielsen Designated Market Area (DMA). To construct state-level dependent variables, we aggregated the market-level data to the state. This is a complicated task because, as we will discuss in more detail below, DMAs do not respect state boundaries. Rather than making assumptions about the intended targets of campaign visits when aggregating to the state level, we divide the visits to markets that cross state boundaries among the relevant states. We count a day spent in Spokane, for instance, as .69 of a day in Washington, .28 of a day in Idaho, .02 of a day in Montana, and .01 of a day in Oregon, because those are the proportions of the DMA's population living in each of those states. Because the relevant ad unit in this part of the chapter is the Gross Ratings Point (GRP) and GRPs refer to percentages in the market, each state's portion of a given multi-state DMA receives the total number of GRPs.

[5] The correlation between Electoral vote and competitiveness as defined in the body of the text was about 0.20.

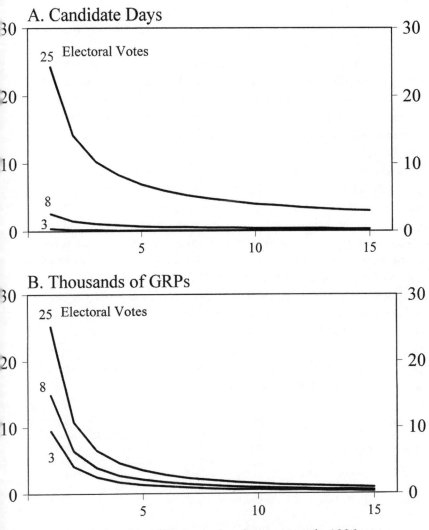

FIGURE 4.1. Impact of Competitiveness and Electoral Vote on Resource Expenditures by States.

Decisions about where to send candidates turned on size and did so more than proportionally.[6] The candidates spent some time even in the uncompetitive states with large electoral votes – states such as California, New York, and Illinois. In part this probably reflects the importance of those states as sources of campaign funds and as centers of news media operations. Among competitive states, the candidates spent much more time in large states than in small ones. Not even a very close race induced the candidates to spend much time in, for instance, New Hampshire.

Advertising, in contrast, was allocated more by competitiveness than by size. Advertising effort is measured not in dollars but in "Gross Ratings Points" (GRPs). If expenditures were expressed in dollars, differences among markets mainly would reflect the simple fact that advertising costs more in large markets than in small ones. To facilitate ready comparison across markets, advertisers often express their purchases of television airtime in GRPs, calculated as the percentage of the residents in a media market who can be expected to see the ad multiplied by the number of times they can be expected to see it. An advertiser who buys 200 GRPs for an ad from a single station, for example, can expect the station to air the ad frequently enough that everyone in the media market will see the ad twice in a week.[7] In effect, GRPs express advertising effort in dollars per capita.

---

[6] Visit data were derived from newspaper reports of the candidates' schedules. A visit was recorded for each location the candidate visited each day, not just where he made public appearances. For days on which a candidate visited more than one location, each received the appropriate fraction. Excluded from these counts are Republican visits to the Waco and Austin markets in Texas, where Bush lived and worked, and the Idaho Falls market in Wyoming, where Cheney lived. Also excluded are Democratic visits to the District of Columbia, where Gore and Lieberman lived most of the time.

[7] In principle, choosing when to air an ad so that every person in the market sees it twice would seem to be a daunting task. For that reason, in part, the process is drastically simplified in practice. The sale of 200 GRPs might obligate a station simply to air an ad ten times during programs that Nielsen had determined to have a rating of twenty – that is, programs watched by twenty percent of the market. The possibility that the twenty percent watching one program might overlap with the 20 percent watching another is not taken into account. In effect, the value (in terms, for instance, of sales of the product being advertised) of exposing 20 percent of the market to the ad ten times is assumed to be equal to the value of exposing 100 percent to the ad twice. Whether this logic, even if true of advertising for products, extends to advertising for presidential candidates is an interesting question, though obviously beyond the scope of this project.

The campaigns aired practically no advertising in uncompetitive states, regardless of their size. But they did advertise in the smallest states – provided they were competitive. Certainly more advertising resources were devoted to the larger competitive states than to the smaller ones, but the difference because of size was much smaller for advertising than for candidates' schedules. Indeed, the size effect was far less than proportional. For instance, competitive states with, say, twenty-five Electoral votes saw just under three times as many GRPs as did similarly competitive states with three Electoral votes. A highly competitive state with three votes saw many more ads than a relatively uncompetitive one with twenty-five.

The contrast between the allocation of time and of ad buys reflected fundamental differences between the two types of resources. The costs of a visit – of the candidate's own time, of transporting the candidate to a state, and of the transactions in arranging appearances – are no less when the candidate visits a small state than when he visits a large one. The cost *per voter* of a slot on the candidate's schedule, therefore, is greater when the candidate visits a small state. To maximize the return on an investment of the candidate's time – the return in terms of exposure, citizens' votes, and, ultimately, Electoral votes – the appropriate strategy is to send the candidate where the most people will see him, either in person or on the local television news. The cost of a GRP of television advertising, in contrast, varies positively with the size of the audience. In contrast with visits, ads cost less in small markets. Indeed, the cost *per voter* of a GRP is roughly constant from market to market. So the price structure of advertising by itself provides no incentive for a campaign to focus its advertising effort, as measured in GRPs, on the largest states. For advertising effort, the controlling consideration is the state's competitiveness.

Geography of Visits

Figure 4.2 depicts the actual geography of visits between Labor Day and Election Day. The presidential and vice presidential candidates flew the length and breadth of the country, but in large portions of it their planes rarely touched down. By undertaking an arduous travel schedule, a candidate obviously focuses on the potential voters who attend campaign events. Of greater concern, however, is the much larger audience the campaign can reach through local television news coverage

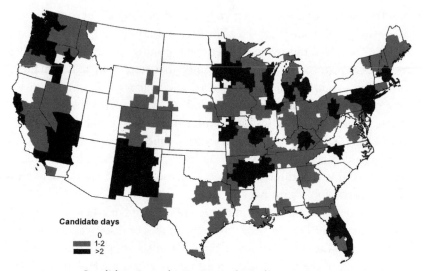

Candidate days
   0
   1-2
   >2

FIGURE 4.2. Candidate Days, by Designated Market Area.

of the candidate's visit. The local news generated by personal appearances and speeches on the stump may be less critical and therefore more favorable to a presidential candidate than network news coverage.[8] In recognition of the importance of the local television news, the geographic units employed for Figure 4.2 are "Designated Market Areas," the 210 areas into which Nielsen Media Research divides the country on the basis of research on television viewing habits.[9]

The candidates visited fewer than half the nation's media markets. They made little effort to appear in the Great Plains, the Rockies, most of the Southwest, and much of the Deep South. Personal campaigning in 2000 was largely confined to the Northeast, the Midwest, the Border South, and the West Coast, plus Florida and New Mexico. Candidates

[8] This is strongly indicated in Just et al. (1996), who find that news tone does not vary much by locale and that the local tone is more positive than the national one. See their Figure 5.10 and accompanying discussion.
[9] Each DMA consists of a group of counties in which the residents tend to view the same television stations. Residents of the counties in the Chicago DMA, for example, spend more time watching Chicago television stations than stations in any other city; the residents of counties adjacent to the Chicago DMA watch Chicago stations less than they watch stations in Milwaukee, Rockford, Champaign, South Bend, and so on. Nielsen adjusts the boundaries of DMAs annually, and we use the ones that applied in 2000.

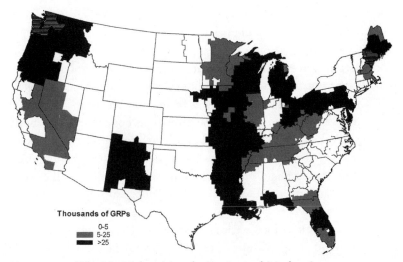

FIGURE 4.3. Television Advertising, by Designated Market Area.

spent more time in large cities than elsewhere. They spent more than eleven days in Philadelphia, more than twelve in Detroit, and nearly ten in Tampa, but just one third of a day each in Johnstown, Lansing, and Fort Myers. So population was clearly a consideration when drawing up the candidates' schedules. Candidates did not absolutely ignore the small markets, however. At least one candidate visited Erie, Traverse City, and Tallahassee, for instance. Indeed, in states where the candidates visited one market, they visited all of them sooner or later. Although states were fairly tightly targeted, major population centers outside the competitive core – New York, Chicago, and Los Angeles in particular – also saw visits.

Geography of Ads

TV advertising, according to Figure 4.3, was sharply focused on competitive states but quite evenly spread across the whole landscape of those states. The figure maps the combined advertising campaigns mounted by the presidential candidates and their associated national committees between the conventions and Election Day 2000.[10]

---

[10] Data on advertising buys were given us by each campaign. For this reason, Figure 4.3 does not include advertising by independent groups. Independent advertising data must be derived from a public source, the Campaign Media Analysis Group (of which more below), and these data do not extend to all DMAs.

The campaigns aired advertising in the same regions their candidates visited. But while the candidates themselves strayed into other areas from time to time, if only briefly, advertising expenditures did not. Within states, advertising expenditures were remarkably uniform: any market that saw advertising saw about as much advertising as every other market in the state. Florida was the major exception, for reasons we come to later in this chapter. The campaigns bought about as much airtime in Yakima as in Seattle, in Lake Charles as in New Orleans, in Wausau as in Milwaukee. The sale of television advertising is organized by market, but strategic decisions about where to allocate the 2000 campaigns' advertising resources were organized in large measure by state.

But making allocation decisions by state still does not guarantee containment of ad effort within strategically pivotal states. The fact that many DMAs cross state boundaries means that some advertising bleeds into strategically unhelpful places. Most common is spillover from a DMA centered in a competitive state into the parts of the DMA that sit in a less competitive state. Missouri was a prime example. Ads in the Kansas City and St. Louis DMAs were seen by many households in eastern Kansas and western Illinois. Ads aimed at Philadelphia leaked into New Jersey and Delaware. Spokane ads were also seen in Idaho and Montana. The other pattern is where access to a competitive state is through a market centered in an uncompetitive one. The prime example is Mobile, Alabama, the principal media center for the Florida panhandle.[11]

Ads by groups nominally independent of parties and candidates but aligned with one of the sides also weighed in the balance, according to Figure 4.4. Data for independent ads must come from another source than the official campaigns, of course, so the figure marks the introduction of the key data source for the rest of this book's advertising analyses. These data were collected by the CMAG, an independent tracking organization that relies on satellite intercepts of open-air broadcasts. In 2000, CMAG captured ad data for the seventy-five largest media markets, which comprised 78 percent of all U.S. TV households and

[11] The map treats Boston this way as well, as the conduit to New Hampshire. Closer inspection reveals that virtually every ad placed in the Boston DMA was placed on WMUR in Manchester, a station with practically no Massachusetts viewers.

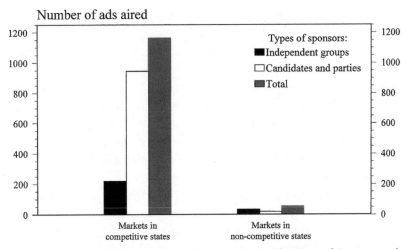

FIGURE 4.4. Average Advertising Volume per Station by Type of Sponsor and Competitiveness of State.

74 percent of the NAES sample. As implied in the first part of this chapter, there was little relationship between a state's size and its competitiveness, so the CMAG data span the full range of strategic importance. All analyses involving CMAG data have as their unit an individual *airing* of an ad.[12] Values in this figure and in later tables and figures represent the number of airings a person would have been able to see had he or she watched TV nonstop. The total number of airings in the DMA is divided by the "effective" number of stations on which ads were played. As the number of plays in a DMA is partly a function of the number of stations, a simple count of plays would misstate the realistic opportunities for a respondent to see an ad. But within the typical DMA, ads are not spread evenly across outlets, so simply dividing ads by the number of stations will not do. We created instead an "effective" number of stations by dividing the total number of plays in the DMA by the number of plays on the station with the largest

---

[12] Most ad plays were thirty seconds long, the classic "spot," but a few were as long as one minute or as short as ten seconds. Between Labor Day and Election Day, 94.8 percent of all airings were of thirty-second ads, 4.9 percent were of sixty-second ads, and 0.3 percent were of either ten-second or fifteen-second ads. Although most sixty-second ads were placed by pro-Bush forces, Democrats placed almost one-quarter of them. All things considered, there seemed to be little point in weighting airings by their length.

volume.[13] The average per DMA is also weighted to reflect the DMA's population relative to other DMAs.

Figure 4.4 presents ad volumes in competitive and uncompetitive states for candidates and parties and for independent groups.[14] As we would expect from earlier in this chapter, the advertising campaign was much heavier in markets in competitive states than in markets in uncompetitive states. Where 1996 results suggested the race would be close, a major television station aired over 1,150 presidential campaign ads between Labor Day and Election Day. In other markets a major station aired about 55 presidential ads, on average.[15] The candidates' campaigns and the parties' national committees sponsored most of those totals: about 950 per station in markets in competitive states, about 20 per station in markets in uncompetitive states. But ads sponsored by independent groups made up a substantial percentage of the total advertising campaign: close to 20 percent in the competitive markets, over 60 percent in the uncompetitive ones.[16]

---

[13] Our measure is somewhat analogous to the "effective number of parties" indicator regularly employed in cross-national studies of parties and elections; see Laakso and Taagepera (1979). The mean value for this indicator is 2.97, indicating that the typical DMA saw ads played on three stations. This fairly represents the center of the distribution, as values for sixty of the seventy-five CMAG DMAs range from 2.25 to 3.75. The most fragmented market in a competitive state was Miami, where ads were spread across 4.1 stations. The most consolidated market was Boston, where, as already mentioned, virtually every ad (3,499 of 3,580) was played on WMUR. In this DMA, we took the additional step of setting the numerator to zero for all respondents residing in Massachusetts. Such persons truly saw no ads, while New Hampshire residents, for whom WMUR was effectively a monopoly outlet, were bombarded.

[14] The state to which each market was assigned for this analysis is the state in which a plurality of the DMA's residents lives. Competitive states are defined as those in which Clinton's percentage of the two-party vote in 1996 differed by less than five percentage points from his national percentage – roughly the median of our continuous measure of competitiveness.

[15] Figure 4.4 understates the effect of competitiveness on allocation decisions made by the campaigns, because most of the ads in DMAs assigned to uncompetitive states were in fact aimed at the substantial minority in the DMA who lived in an adjacent competitive state.

[16] The relatively heavy volume of independent advertising in uncompetitive markets does not necessarily indicate that independent groups were less concerned than the candidates' campaigns with competitiveness. In order to allow for so-called issue ads – those that do not endorse a particular presidential candidate but only a particular policy – we include among the independent ads all ads sponsored by independent groups that did not mention a candidate other than a presidential candidate – that is, that did not mention a House or Senate candidate. But many issue ads presumably

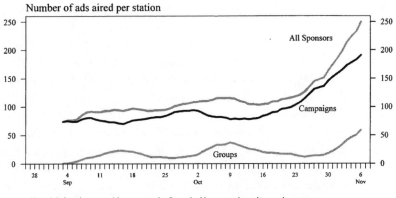

Note: Markets in competitive states only. Smoothed by seven-day prior moving sums.

FIGURE 4.5. Dynamics of Advertising Volume by Type of Sponsor.

Dynamics of Ads

Just as ads were concentrated in space, so were they concentrated in time. Figure 4.5 traces the volumes aired during the week preceding any given date on each major station in markets located in or overlapping states identified as competitive by the 1996 pattern. The unit is the number of ads that a respondent might have been able to see in his or her market area in the week before the date of interview, had he or she watched TV nonstop. This is very similar to taking a seven-day moving average, and so the line is smoothed. Smoothing of some form is necessary, even though the data in the figure are close to a census and there is virtually no noise from sampling. The reason is that ad volumes vary over the days of the week, and in the absence of smoothing, trends can be overwhelmed visually by the weekly cycle. The fact that the cycle is weekly is the main argument for smoothing by seven days.[17] The sum, as opposed to the moving average, strikes us as an intuitively reasonable way to think about ad volumes: how many ads could one have seen in the preceding week? This quantity

were aimed at influencing congressional elections. The best example in 2000 was the large number of ads placed in Nebraska, where the Senate race was close but the presidential race was not.

[17] In producing the impact estimations that we report later in this chapter, we also experimented with other smoothing periods. None dominated the seven-day one.

is, after all, directly related to the unit the spot market processes, the GRP.

The main dynamic feature is a sharp upturn after the last presidential debate. From early September through the third week of October, the total volume increased gradually from about seventy-five ads per station per week to about 110. By the end of October, in contrast, each station was airing 175 ads per week, and in the last week of the campaign each high-volume station broadcast about 250 ads. The presidential campaigns – the candidates' organizations and the national committees – and the independent groups followed somewhat different strategies in allocating their advertising over time. The volume of advertising sponsored by the candidates and parties began to rise immediately after the last presidential debate, with only a slight steepening of the growth path on October 23. Independent advertising did not really grow until the last week. The independent volume rose modestly in mid-September, fell back, grew again around the second debate, and fell back again. To a greater extent than the candidates and parties, then, independent groups hoarded their resources until November. In the last week, the independent advertising volume *trebled*, so that on the last two days before the election, ads sponsored by independent groups represented almost 25 percent of all presidential advertising.

The Balance of Forces

Volume

Figure 4.6 shows that over the whole period, Bush enjoyed a considerable advantage in ads directly placed by candidates and parties. The figure has the same logic as Figure 4.4, indicating the number of ads per station, in this case for stations in competitive states. For ads placed by candidates and parties, the Republican side placed roughly half again as many ads per station as the Gore campaign did. This was offset considerably by independent groups, which placed about twice as many pro-Gore ads as pro-Bush ones. This still left Bush forces with more ads, but not startlingly more (about 20 percent more, in fact).

Most of Bush's advantage accrued at the very end, however. The top panel of Figure 4.7 plots pro-Gore and pro-Bush ad volumes from Labor Day to Election Day in states predicted to be competitive. The bottom panel gives the Gore-Bush difference. Ads directly under candidate

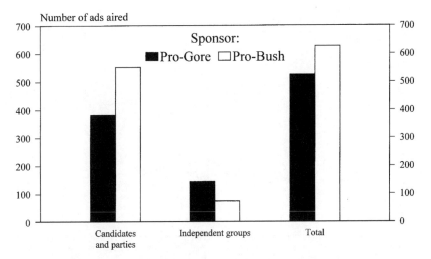

Note: Markets in competitive states only.

FIGURE 4.6. Average Advertising Volume per Station by Type and Party of Sponsor.

and party control are combined with ads by independent groups.[18] For much of September, Gore actually enjoyed an edge (assisted by independent ads). By early October, however, pro-Bush forces took the lead, relinquishing it only briefly after the last debate. Their advantage remained small until the last week. Then both sides increased their outlays sharply, but the shift was far more dramatic for Bush than for Gore. In the last week, a resident of a competitive state was more than half again as likely to see a pro-Bush ad as a pro-Gore one. He or she could have seen about sixty more Bush ads than Gore ones, out of a total of 250 ads.

Impact

Did it matter? Table 4.1 addresses this question by adding visit and ad volumes to the basic estimation described in Chapter 3. This is the only occasion that we refer to the logistic regression estimation without translating coefficients into realistic probability differences.

[18] Party/candidate and independent sources are also combined in the impact estimations below. In earlier work, we kept ad sources separate but found that their impact was almost identical. See Hagen, Johnston, and Jamieson (2002), Table 1.

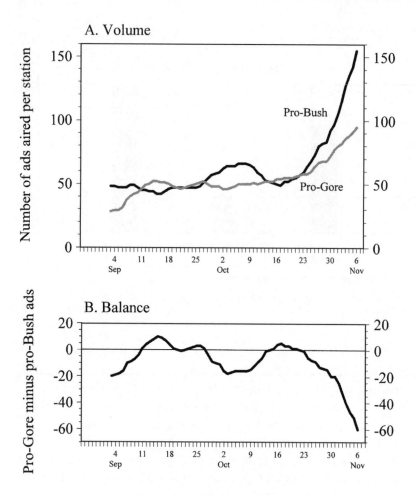

Note: Markets in competitive states only. Smoothed by seven-day moving sums.
FIGURE 4.7. Dynamics of Advertising Balance.

Notwithstanding the general opaqueness of individual coefficients, the table is an efficient way to effect comparisons among alternative avenues of impact. Comparisons are between Gore and Bush, between ads and visits, and between current and lagged values of a variable.

The impact of visits is puzzling, and we can supply no substantive interpretation. The visit variables combine both presidential and vice presidential visits, as preliminary estimations by us indicated that each

TABLE 4.1. *Ad and News Impacts (N=12705)*

	Ads only		Ads + news	
	Gore	Bush	Gore	Bush
Ads – 7-day sums				
current week	0.0053	0.0019	0.0052	0.0019
	(0.0020)	(0.0020)	(0.0020)	(0.0021)
previous week	−0.0011	−0.0015	−0.0011	−0.0015
	(0.0022)	(0.0023)	(0.0022)	(0.0023)
Visits				
Democratic	0.02	0.01	0.02	0.02
	(0.04)	(0.04)	(0.04)	(0.04)
Republican	−0.04	−0.15	−0.05	−0.15
	(0.05)	(0.05)	(0.05)	(0.05)
TV News – 3-day sums				
current 3 days			0.0006	0.0003
			(0.0022)	(0.0023)
previous 3 days			0.0032	−0.0008
			(0.0024)	(0.0025)
Black	0.62	−0.68	0.62	−0.68
	(0.10)	(0.13)	(0.10)	(0.13)
Evangelical	−0.16	0.32	−0.16	0.32
	(0.07)	(0.07)	(0.07)	(0.07)
Union family	0.03	−0.25	0.03	−0.25
	(0.07)	(0.08)	(0.07)	(0.08)
Male	−0.05	0.27	−0.05	0.27
	(0.05)	(0.06)	(0.05)	(0.06)
Democrat	1.65	−0.25	1.65	−0.25
	(0.06)	(0.08)	(0.06)	(0.08)
Republican	−0.07	1.76	−0.07	1.76
	(0.09)	(0.07)	(0.09)	(0.07)
Liberal	−0.08	−0.69	−0.08	−0.69
	(0.06)	(0.08)	(0.06)	(0.08)
Conservative	−0.49	0.71	−0.49	0.71
	(0.07)	(0.06)	(0.07)	(0.06)
1996 Vote	1.21	−1.73	1.22	−1.74
	(0.43)	(0.46)	(0.43)	(0.46)
Constant	0.35	−0.05	0.35	−0.05
	(0.06)	(0.06)	(0.06)	(0.06)
χ^2	6741.71		6745.27	
Pseudo R^2	0.25		0.25	

Estimation by multinomial logistic regression. Asymptotic standard errors in parentheses.

kind of visit had essentially the same impact. Taken at face value, the estimation suggests that the only visits that mattered were by Bush or Cheney, that they mattered only for Bush vote intention, and that their impact was perverse: other things equal, a Bush or Cheney visit made things worse for their own ticket. No obvious controls make this effect go away and we can offer no defensible speculation about the causal mechanisms at work, so we do not dwell on it further.[19]

Impact from ads, in contrast, is consistent and interpretable. By "ads" is meant the cumulative Gore-Bush difference in airings per station in the seven days before the interview (the day of interview plus the six preceding ones) summarized graphically in Figure 4.7. In Table 4.1, however, ads vary across DMAs as well as over time. The estimation thus embodies the natural experiment of 2000, the fact that only some DMAs received the ad "treatment," that some got more of it than others, and that most got none. Two modeling choices require elaboration:

- The choice of the simple arithmetic difference between Bush and Gore ad volumes may seem arbitrary and crude. It is natural to think that ads should have diminishing marginal impact, that beyond some point there is little gain from further repetition of a message. In the laboratory, this may be true. But notwithstanding the campaign's interest as a natural experiment, the setting for the experiment was not in fact a laboratory, it was the real lives of potential voters. Ads are not repeated *ad nauseam* so that an individual finally surrenders just to stop the pain. They are repeated to guarantee that the ad gets seen in the first place – and perhaps a few more times – by an audience that is not motivated to seek it out.[20] Given the general

---

[19] In earlier analyses (Hagen, Johnston, and Jamieson, 2002), several controls were entered specifically to make this perversity disappear. The animating idea of these controls was that Bush and Cheney concentrated their visits in places that naturally favored Gore, thus creating a spurious artifact and masking the visits' true marginal effect. The 1996 vote variable in Table 4.1 carries some of this logic but earlier estimations also included the voting age population of the DMA, on the supposition that within competitive states the metropolitan places that candidates typically visited (Figure 4.1) leaned toward Democrats. This made no difference to the results. Besides, the Bush-Cheney result is not mirrored by a Gore-Lieberman one. As it happens, we are not the only observers to find this perverse effect. In private communication, both Charles Franklin and Daron Shaw report similar findings.

[20] We can also report side evidence on the defensibility of the difference measure. We did experiment with proportional measures, which in effect discount large arithmetic

impenetrability of the audience, more (at least of a resonant message) is better.

• The estimation allows for the possibility that citizens have a memory for ads, that earlier Gore-Bush differences in ad volumes are not merely overwhelmed by differences in the current week. Earlier volumes are represented by the previous week's value for the seven-day difference.[21] This setup addresses competing models of ad cognition: on-line versus memory-based. The more powerful the lag coefficient, the greater the role for memory. Previous ad balances will buffer the impact of current ones, and the more important it will be to get ads out early. The weaker the lag coefficient, the more on-line is ad cognition and the more important is the current ad balance. The history of ads still matters, but only for where it places the current starting point.

The difference in ad volume between Gore and Bush mattered to the vote, and the difference that mattered was that for the current week. The candidate for whom it mattered was Al Gore. Ad volumes mattered hardly, if at all, to the likelihood of choosing George W. Bush. So we have a powerful echo of patterns established earlier in this book: Gore's share was more volatile than Bush's; Bush was the main pole of attraction or aversion for social and ideological groups. The invulnerability of Bush support to ads seems the natural complement to these patterns. Ads moved the balance of intention mainly by mobilizing or demobilizing voters "available" for appeals from the Gore campaign.

The ads that move the balance are the current ones, placed in the week leading up to the day of interview. By implication, the cognitive transmission belt for ad impact would seem to be on-line processing.

---

differences. Such measures do not yield larger or more stable estimates of impact. In preliminary work for Hagen, Johnston, and Jamieson (2002), where independent and party ad impacts were estimated separately, proportional measures yielded a coefficient on party ads that was larger than the coefficient for independent ads by almost exactly the ratio of party to independent ad volumes. The coefficients were telling us that the relationship is linear.

[21] Other setups are imaginable, and Hagen, Johnston, and Jamieson (2002) report one: the cumulative ad difference. This does not outperform the simple lagged value. And it requires us to stipulate when cumulation shall start. Besides, the simple lag corresponds to the canonical representation of memory in time series analysis, the lagged value for the previous time unit. We are particularly grateful to Christopher Wlezien for advice on this issue.

The current week just updates the previous one; the previous week exerts no independent gravitational force. This makes the very last week of the campaign critical, and this of course was when the pro-Bush advantage was most massive. It does not follow that parties should simply decline to advertise in earlier weeks and save it all up for the end. If one side drives support up in earlier weeks, then the other side has that much more ground to make up. But it would be wise to hoard serious resources for the end.[22] In the last week of the 2000 campaign, the Gore campaign was unable to match the sheer volume of Bush ads, both because it lacked the requisite resources from the start and because it spent more on advertising in the early going.

Figure 4.8 translates the disparity in ads into day-by-day predictions. It depicts the impact for each day from the preceding week's Gore-Bush ad difference, relative to what might have happened had ad volumes been equal between sides. As our focus is now on impact, it makes sense to examine the actual battleground for 2000 rather than the potential one indicated by 1996, with special emphasis on the last week. Accordingly, estimated impact is from average ad differences in the thirty-two CMAG DMAs that saw the highest volume of ads at the end. For the most part, these are the same DMAs – identified by 1996 information – that underpin Figure 4.7. By November, however, both campaigns had discerned that some states expected to be competitive were not so in fact. Kentucky is an obvious example. Only the Republicans had any continued interest in California. At the same time, other states thought to be Democratic strongholds were now identified as clearly in play. Minnesota is the best example. The main discrepancy between this figure and Figure 4.7 is that Gore's advantage around the last debate is now revealed as deeper and longer lasting, reflecting the fact that many of the mid-period pro-Bush ads were playing in California.

Predicted values in the figure reflect the fact that Table 4.1 imputes a small (statistically insignificant) perverse effect of ad differences on support for Bush. More important is the large and empirically

---

[22] There is little to say about the over-time stability of the pattern captured by Table 4.1. Given the modest number of days in the data matrix, the sample cannot be split finely by time period without loss of critical longitudinal variance. Suffice it to say that splitting the sample roughly at the halfway point between Labor Day and Election Day yields essentially the same structure of ad effects for each period.

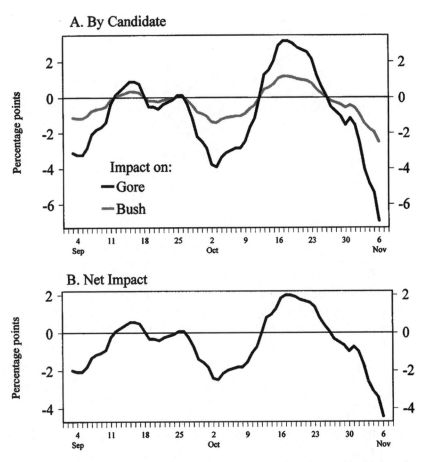

A. By Candidate

Impact on:
— Gore
— Bush

B. Net Impact

Note: Entries indicate estimated percentage-point impact of previous week's ad balance in DMA on current-day vote intentions. Battleground markets only. Derived from estimation in Table 4.1.

FIGURE 4.8. Advertising on Vote Intentions.

straightforward effect on Gore support. Gore helped himself in mid-September and again in mid-October. Most eye-catching, however, is the very end, when the negative ad balance in fiercely contested DMAs – all in or adjacent to states that would be Electoral College pivots – depressed Al Gore's vote share possibly by four points among the least committed persons. The time path of ads does not, of course, coincide with the time path of the vote. The days when the Bush advantage was greatest were also days when Al Gore was staging his final recovery.

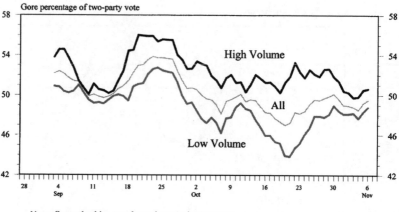

Note: Smoothed by ten-day prior moving average.

FIGURE 4.9. Dynamics of Vote Intentions by Advertising Volume.

So the ad deluge did not absolutely block his recovery nationwide. But Figure 4.8 is the first indication of trouble for Gore in the very states where recovery would have done him the most good.

Figure 4.9 captures this predicament effectively, if crudely. It divides the sample into DMAs with low and high ad volumes. As the figure does not process evidence for any specific DMA, it can include observations from the whole sample, not just the seventy-five DMAs captured in the CMAG data. A high-volume DMA, then, is any of the thirty-two already identified plus any DMA also centered in that state or any DMA broadcasting into it. All others fall in the low-volume category. As with Figure 4.8, the low/high volume difference is driven by the last week, so some "high-volume" DMAs did not in fact see many ads (and some saw none) in September or early October. Smoothing in this figure is aggressive – ten-day moving averages – the better to focus on the contrast between arenas. To bridge this display to the vote dynamics in Chapter 2, the whole-sample line also appears, smoothed the same way as the other lines.[23]

---

[23] The ten-day criterion is driven by the high-volume line, which has the smallest sample sizes – around ninety observations in the typical day. The patterns emphasized in Figure 4.9 are visible with less aggressive smoothing but the critical distinctions between high- and low-volume DMAs tend to be obscured by the bounces induced by campaign stimuli impinging on both groups, by debates in particular.

The first thing to strike the eye may seem counterintuitive: Gore won the high-volume DMAs and lost the low-volume ones. High-volume DMAs were not a perfect microcosm of the United States, and so the natural experiment of 2000 was not all that carefully controlled. The Democratic/Republican ratio among party identifiers was slightly higher and union families were slightly more common, but the high-ad-volume audience also included fewer African Americans. Most critically, perhaps, high-volume DMAs were concentrated in states where Bill Clinton's share of the 1996 two-party vote was 1.25 points above his nationwide share. The other DMAs lay in states where his share was 0.84 points below the national value.

For all that, the critical fact in the endgame is not so much the starting point as the direction of short-term shifts. And the phase transitions identified in Figure 2.1 – also reflected in the "All" line here – are much clearer in the low-volume DMAs. The late-September shift away from Gore is visible in both places, but the total drop was twice as great in the low-volume DMAs. Most important, *the recovery that defined the third phase was visible only in low-volume places.* Gore did make late gains in high-volume places, but on a completely different rhythm and only temporarily. His gain in high-volume places came earlier, around October 23. This gain was quite sudden (so sudden that its abrupt onset burns through the smoothing in the figure) and was sustained for over a week. Then it evaporated completely. It seems reasonable to infer that this pattern reflected the ad advantage Gore had built in mid- to late-October. That advantage disappeared on the 26th, and Bush's advantage became especially pronounced about the time that Gore's earlier gain in the high-volume arena was erased. Gore's gain in low-volume places was slower to be realized but never dissipated. Relative to a starting point of, say, October 30, Gore gained about one point in low-volume areas, but lost over two points in high-volume ones.

The Dynamics of TV News

The dynamics of vote intentions in the portions of the country that saw no ads obviously cannot have been the product of shifts in the ad balance, at least not directly. This section turns, then, to the other facet of the campaign, the "free" media. As with ads, discussion begins with

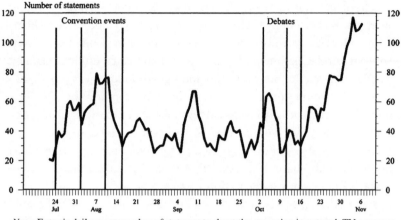

Note: Entry is daily mean number of statements about the campaign in network TV coverage, smoothed by five-day prior moving average.

FIGURE 4.10. Dynamics of Campaign News Volume on Television.

volume and then turns to balance, or "valence." The section concludes with estimations of impact.

Volume

News coverage, like ads, was concentrated toward the end. Apart from short-term bursts around key public events, coverage stayed fairly steady until just after the last debate, as shown in Figure 4.10. By volume of coverage is meant the number of *statements* on a given day. News stories were broken into statements as the first act of coding. A statement is typically one sentence in length, but not always. The governing principles are that a statement be by one source (for example, a reporter, a candidate, a campaign operative, or a private citizen in a "streeter"), about one candidate, and about one topic (for example, an issue or an aspect of the candidate's character). Statements vary in the airtime they represent but there is no correlation between the length of statements and time in the campaign, so variation in the number of statements is a reasonable representation of volumes of coverage. The figure understates attention to conventions and debates, as it does not include special programming for those events. It just indicates that the three networks' core nightly news programs' commitment to the campaign did not increase much at those events. After the debates, however, the volume of core coverage grew markedly. In the last few

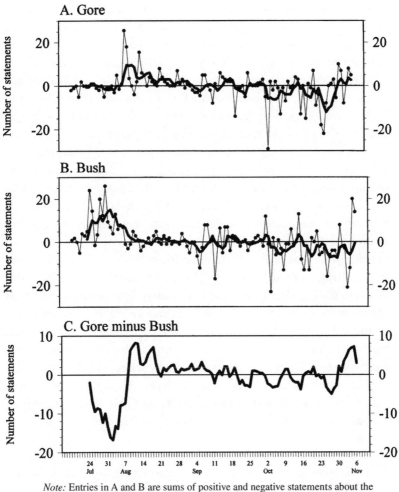

Note: Entries in A and B are sums of positive and negative statements about the candidate. Smoothed values are five-day prior maoving averages. Entries in C are difference between smoothed values in A and B.

FIGURE 4.11. Dynamics of Valences in Television News Coverage.

days, a nightly broadcast gave the campaign over three times as much attention as it had three weeks before.

Valence

Figure 4.11 shows that network coverage became more negative for each candidate, more negative for Gore in particular, as the campaign

wore on. Daily entries in the Gore and Bush panels of the figure are
the sum of positive statements for the candidate minus the sum of
negative statements. The more statements on a given day, the greater
is the scope for positive or negative overall judgment. So the valence
indicator is not a proportionate one; it combines the signal's direction
with its volume.[24] The bottom panel is just the sum of the Gore and
the Bush smoothed lines. Smoothing is by five-day moving averages, in
keeping with this book's standard smoothing criterion.[25]

Most days, coverage of a candidate was neither very negative nor
very positive. The major positive exception for each candidate was
around his party's convention. Around the Republican event, Bush received positive coverage for sixteen of seventeen days. Gore's coverage
at this point was essentially balanced. Gore was less warmly handled
around the Democratic event, but he still received positive (at least
non-negative) coverage for twelve of fourteen days. For each candidate, coverage turned positive well before the convention itself. Bush's
coverage during the Democratic convention, like Gore's earlier, was
essentially balanced. So on each side, valences around the conventions
conform closely to the vote intention pattern in Chapter 2. Thereafter,
coverage tended to be quite balanced, with notable exceptions. But valences also mainly drifted downward. For most days before October 16,
the total number of statements about each candidate was about twenty,
with the net valence usually a small fraction of that total. Coverage of
Bush was more variable, day to day, than coverage of Gore.[26] For both

---

[24] The implication of this measurement choice is clearest when Gore's advantage in the
last week is compared with his advantage in late September. Proportionally, he got
more positive coverage in September than in November, but the number of statements
was smaller in the early period, as Figure 4.10 shows. Because of the sheer volume
of statements in November, the smaller proportionate advantage represents a larger
absolute one. Although this yields a line in the bottom panel that resembles the line of
vote intention less closely than it might, we did not feel that such resemblance was a
proper basis for indicator choice. It would smack of curve-fitting, for one thing. The
decisive consideration is that the arithmetic news valence embodies the same logic as
the indicator of ad balance, and we could see no principled reason for treating the ad
signal one way and the news signal another.

[25] The five-day criterion yields the visually most satisfactory rendering. Shorter periods
make it hard to identify stretches of positivity or negativity, while longer ones mask
important shifts. In impact estimations below, we pool news valence for three days,
for reasons that will become apparent shortly.

[26] Where the standard deviation of daily readings for Gore was 6.9, for Bush it was 7.6.

candidates there were some strikingly negative days, but only for Bush were there also sharply positive ones. Coverage became more volatile as the campaign wore on. In part this reflects a simple increase in the total volume of coverage. But Gore's coverage became more volatile in late September, even before coverage volume increased; the increased variance for Gore reflected mainly some strikingly negative days, on a scale he simply did not experience before September 22. For both candidates, valences became quite steadily more negative, at least until the very end. The trend and the similarity in trend between the candidates suggest that television journalists were obeying Zaller's (2001) "rule of product substitution." According to Zaller:

> . . . the more strenuously politicians challenge journalists for control of news jurisdiction, the more journalists will seek to develop substitute information that the mass audience is willing to accept as news and that gives expression to journalistic voice.
> . . . most of the information that journalists substitute for candidate-supplied information is negative. (p. 255)

The trend was more steeply negative for Gore than for Bush, however. Relative to Bush, Gore enjoyed a prolonged advantage, then lost it. If, after the conventions, the balance between the candidates receded toward neutrality, until late September it still clearly favored Gore. Very suggestively, a dip appears in mid-September but subsequent coverage again generally favored Gore. Starting on September 20, however, coverage of Gore turned negative relative to coverage of Bush. The shift from a generally positive to a generally negative balance for Gore was marked by a strikingly negative day for Gore, September 21, his worst day to that point in the campaign. That day's negative value is not outstanding in the context of the whole campaign. Bush had encountered worse days before this date and Gore would have several worse ones in the weeks to follow. But the September 21 reading stands out as a break in the coverage of Gore. Later chapters show that this moment was pivotal to the entire campaign.

Gore won the networks back at the end, however. In the last week he gained mildly positive coverage while Bush's treatment was quite negative, as on November 3 the story of Bush's 1976 arrest for drunken driving broke. This one-sidedness combined with the large overall volume of coverage (Figure 4.10) gave Gore as great an advantage as he enjoyed around the Democratic convention. The advantage waned at the very end, as campaign coverage concluded with positives about both camps, especially about the Bush side. Notwithstanding this, network news stood in sharp contrast to ads. Where Bush won the ad war at the end, Gore won the news war.

Impact

Once again, did it matter? Prima facie, the answer seems to be Yes. The overall path of news coverage roughly tracks the basic parts of the campaign: Gore ahead from the Democratic convention to late September, Bush ahead from late September until the last week, and Gore gaining an advantage at the end. It is a recurring motif of this book that this news pattern *is* critical to understanding the campaign. But a multivariate estimation of news impact produces only a faint suggestion of the relationship. In Table 4.1 appear news variables coded to parallel the ad variables. One term represents the immediate effect of news valence and the other the lagged effect. But where ad variables pool observations over seven days, news variables pool observations over three. This reflects our sense, from Figure 4.11 and from attention to content in transcripts (reported in detail in later chapters), that the maximum duration of a story is three days.[27]

To the extent that any news effect appears in Table 4.1, it is in the lag term for Gore. Now this *does* comport with the lags in a comparison of Figure 4.11 and Figure 2.1. The downturn for Gore in the news series is September 20 or 21; in the vote series it occurs between the 27th and 28th. The upturn in Gore's net valence lies between October 27 and 28 (his valence line crossed the zero threshold on October 30) and the final upturn in his vote started on the 30th. Given the lack of effect from the current news term, it is hard to interpret this lag as evidence for system memory, however. Rather, it suggests

---

[27] Runs of consecutive positive or negative values in Figure 4.11 are typically even shorter. For Gore from September 1 to the end, the median negative run lasted only one day, while the median positive run lasted two days; the mean for each kind was, respectively 2.0 and 2.3 days. For Bush, the corresponding values were similar: his median positive and negative run each lasted two days; the mean value for each was 2.5 and 1.8 days. In settling on a three-day pooling, we also experimented with alternative specifications, none of which produces much interpretable effect.

that a few days are required for news to be widely diffused in the electorate.[28]

Table 4.1 is also organized to test if news valences carry impact from the balance of ads. This is a crude, message-free test of the proposition that ads orient coverage in the free media, as argued by Jamieson (1992). If ad effects are mediated by the news, ad coefficients should shrink once news terms are controlled. No such shrinkage occurs, so impact from the simple weight of ads is entirely direct. This is hardly a fair test of the hypothesis, to be sure. Jamieson's original claim was about the transfer of content from one channel to the other rather than about simple ad preponderance and news valence. Content effects require narrative, which we begin to supply in the next chapter.

The preliminary reading of news effects is mixed, then. The multivariate evidence is weak to negative. The eyeball test, in contrast, suggests that something is going on. Additionally, the earlier section on ad effects made it clear that the dominant dynamic of the last week – Al Gore's recovery – occurred only where ads could not be seen. If only *faute de mieux*, the trail of evidence leads to network news.

The Missing Link: Interest in the News

Where ads are tightly targeted to particular states, the news is broadcast everywhere. But not everyone watches it. This section, accordingly, turns to exposure and attention to network news as a potential mediator for the ad and news impact (or lack of impact) described earlier in this chapter. Interest in the news is a conditioning variable that could either magnify or dampen impact, according to circumstances. First we describe the intensification of news interest over the campaign. This is interesting in its own right but it also serves to introduce the indicator of news interest. Then we turn to what we might expect news interest to do. The theoretical literature is almost perfectly ambiguous on the matter, so we are largely on our own. When we turn to estimating

---

[28] Analyses that demonstrate a correlation between news and public opinion are open to the charge that, rather than showing that news influences opinion, they show that journalists choose what to write on the basis of what they think people want to hear. The fact that, in our analysis, changes in news valence lead rather than follow changes in the electorate's vote intentions casts doubt on that interpretation in this case.

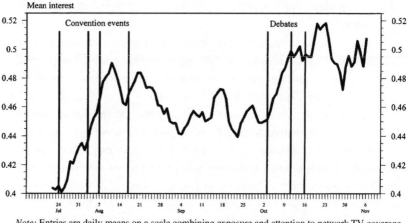

Note: Entries are daily means on a scale combining exposure and attention to network TV coverage, smoothed by five-day prior moving average.

FIGURE 4.12. Dynamics of Interest in the Campaign.

effects, we start, as before, with multivariate evidence and then turn to a simple high-volume/low-volume contrast.

Intensity of Interest

Interest in the campaign grew around major public events and commonly did so in advance of significant increases in either coverage or advertising. Figure 4.12 plots daily means on a measure that combines response to an exposure question and to an attention question, both oriented to network news, by day.[29] On this scale, respondents' interest clearly climbed in the run up to the conventions and during them. It never fell back to preconvention levels, although interest did recede as memory of the conventions faded. Interest rose sharply after the first

---

[29] Exposure is measured by the number of days in the past week the respondent claims to have followed the campaign on network news. Attention is tapped by a question about the amount of attention paid to network news coverage of the campaign. The second item was a companion to the first, asked only of those who followed the campaign for at least one day. Despite their overlap, these items capture complementary elements of overall interest in TV coverage. We asked parallel questions about newspapers, local TV news, radio news, and talk radio, and about discussion with friends and family and with co-workers. Combining exposure and attention for a given channel enhanced the measure. Combining channels did not. In both of these findings, we echo Price and Zaller (1990). The measure is scaled to the 0, 1 interval.

debate and quite a bit after the third one. Then it faded again, perhaps as the debates also faded from memory. In the last week of October, half the interest gain induced by the debates dissipated. In the last week of the campaign, however, interest picked up again and returned to the level prevailing just before the last debate. Comparison of Figure 4.12 with Figures 4.5 and 4.10 indicates that voters were not just passive objects of the volume of news coverage or of ads. They responded autonomously to the logic of the occasion and increased their engagement when key events were imminent. If anything, the campaigns and the networks responded to citizens, to a prior surge in their readiness to engage with the event, not the reverse. In this sense, citizens constructed the event for themselves (Just et al., 1996).

This indicator serves as our conditioning factor for impact from news and ads. In analyses below, we do simple comparisons of high- and low-interest persons, where the former are above the median and the latter are below the median on the combined awareness-interest measure. The median value rises with the gain in interest, roughly on the time path of Figure 4.12. Because of this, we make no claims about whether net gains in interest make the electorate more susceptible or less susceptible to impact from the campaign. At every point, we simply compare the top half with the bottom.

Theoretical Stakes

As the opening chapter reminded us, the literature on interest as a condition for mass media effects yields competing predictions:

- Exposure is a necessary condition for receiving a message and receiving the message is a necessary condition for persuasion. This has been styled the *reception* factor (McGuire, 1968; see also Zaller, 1992). High-interest persons should be more exposed to campaign stimuli in general and might, for that reason, be the more responsive group.
- Exposure over an extended period builds a stock of relevant prior information, which should help in the interpretation of the current message. This should inoculate informed persons against its persuasive content. This is the *yielding* factor. High-interest voters should be more resistant to novel persuasive content, and for that reason, be the less responsive group.

Depending on which factor is dominant, the summary interest-impact relationship could be positive or negative. A message that is intrinsically persuasive but cognitively demanding would evoke a positive relationship between interest and impact. A message that is contestable but that requires some capacity to decode may evoke the opposite relationship; an example would be a demagogic appeal where the subtext is the real text. The joint operation of these two mediators could make the interest-impact relationship curvilinear. This was the argument in, for example, Converse (1962). In the simple dichotomy between high- and low-interest groups, the mediators' joint operation might just erase any differences.

References to persuasive messages naturally lead us to ask, messages from what source? The key distinction in sources is between ads and news, and the literature to date is light on whether the interest-impact interaction is itself conditional on the message's source. What we have is scattered findings: a positive link between interest and impact of news in the 1988 Canadian election (Johnston et al., 1992); a negative relationship between interest and the impact of ads in a U.S. test (Ansolabehere and Iyengar, 1995). The Canadian evidence was gathered in an election fought over a Canada/U.S. free trade agreement (a precursor to the North American Free Trade Agreement [NAFTA]). Although ideology and interest got many voters to one side or the other of the issue, the complexity of the proposed agreement also evoked a quite sophisticated campaign discourse, with voters in the center playing a critical role. The positive interest-impact link may have reflected this discursive complexity. The oppositely signed relationship found by Ansolabehere and Iyengar for ads may reflect the fact that their research setting was a laboratory. This setting controls the "reception" mediator, the probability that the message will be received. This leaves the field open for the impact by the "yielding" mediator, and low-interest respondents have less capacity to resist a message if they but receive it.

Evidence

The first strategy is to take the multivariate model of Table 4.1 and estimate it separately in high- and low-interest groups. The key results appear in Figure 4.13, which takes the ad balance for the last day (that is, the sum of Gore-Bush differences on November 6 and the preceding

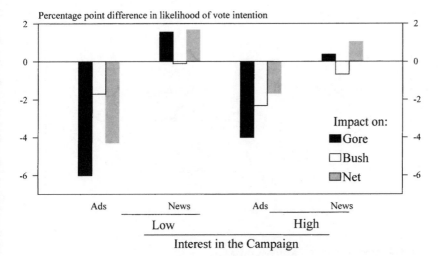

Percentage point difference in likelihood of vote intention

Note: Entries are estimated impact for last day of campaign, based on values in Table A4.2. Interest in the campaign is measured by a scale combining exposure and attention to network TV coverage.

FIGURE 4.13. Advertising and News Impact on Vote Intentions.

six days) and news balance for November 3 (the sum of daily Gore-Bush valences for that day and the two preceding days) and converts them into impact on each of Gore and Bush intentions and into the net effect.[30] The lagged news balance appears in deference to the fact that only it comes close to statistical significance by the conventional criterion.

The principal lesson of the figure is that *news interest neutralizes impact from the mass media,* from *both* news and ads. In the low-interest group, the Bush-Gore asymmetry is sharper and the net effect is larger than implied in the whole-sample estimation of Figure 4.8. In the high-interest group, the impact is quite symmetric and of the "wrong" sign for Bush, such that the net impact in this group is less than half that in the low-interest group. The marginal impact of ads, then, falls almost entirely on persons who get relatively few news messages directly from the network source. But the same is also true for news. Of the news coefficients in Table A4.1, the only one larger than its standard error is the lag term for impact on Gore preferences among low-interest respondents. Taken at face value, this suggests that Gore's positive

[30] The complete estimation can be found in Table 4.2.

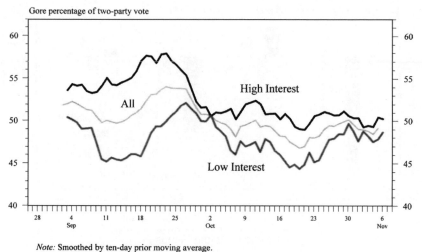

Gore percentage of two-party vote

Note: Smoothed by ten-day prior moving average.

FIGURE 4.14. Dynamics of Vote Intentions by Interest in Campaign.

news readings late in the last week (Wednesday to Friday, in fact) may
have boosted his share in the low-interest group 1.5 points relative to
what it would have been had he neither won nor lost the news battle.[31]
The fact that news effects fall primarily on low-interest citizens may
complement the fact that news effects also register only with a lag.
Low-interest citizens evidently get the news not from TV networks but
from social ones.

  Further confirmation but also some qualification of these claims
comes from Figure 4.14. There is one point at which high-interest
respondents both follow the news and drive the "horse race": the late
September collapse in Gore's lead. Before the collapse, high-interest
persons were much more supportive of Gore. Of course, this was also
a period when TV news was supportive. High-interest persons were
responsible for almost the entire predebate component of the total
collapse. After the first debate, however, the high-interest group was
essentially locked in, leaning slightly toward Gore. All further dynamics
were generated by low-interest persons. They – and only they – reacted
to the debates and then powered Al Gore's comeback.

---

[31] There is a hint of effect on the high-interest side, an estimated impact of about one
    percentage point. But this truly is pushing the interpretive envelope.

Conclusions

The 2000 campaign can be seen through two competing narratives. One narrative featured network news, and all citizens could potentially witness and participate in it. In network news, Al Gore received, on balance, more favorable treatment than George W. Bush from the conventions to late September, less favorable treatment from late September to the last week, and more favorable treatment, once again, at the end. This corresponds to the three phases in Chapter 2. The other, competing narrative was dictated partly by the logic of the Electoral College. Because of the strategic imperatives created by the College, only some states saw any ads. Residents of other states – a majority of the electorate, in fact – were deprived of direct exposure to each side's most targeted and unmediated rhetoric. And the campaign's three phases simply did not register in the chronology of ad balance. Until the last week to ten days, the ad advantage flipped back and forth between the candidates. On average it mildly favored George W. Bush, but for a critical two weeks in mid-October, at the low point of Al Gore's popularity, the Democratic campaign enjoyed a clear lead in ads. At the end, however, the ad advantage shifted decisively to George W. Bush. Crudely, the ad pattern and the news pattern – in October and November, at least – were mirror images.

Of the three phases identified in Chapter 2, only two appeared in "battleground" DMAs. The late September flight from Al Gore that marked the transition between the first two phases was as dramatic in the "battleground" as out. The further drop in mid-October occurred only in low-volume DMAs, however. Where ad volumes – Al Gore's ad volumes in particular at this point – were mounting, the Democratic candidate held his own for the rest of the month. Where no or few ads were aired, his share continued to drop. His postdebate recovery, however, took place only outside the "battleground." Where advertising – now overwhelmingly by Bush – was heavy, there was no recovery; indeed in the last week Gore's share in these places dropped two to three points.

Thus, the natural experiment. In two separate demonstrations, this chapter has shown that campaign stimuli move the bottom line. Which stimuli these were depended on context. One element of context was time. Before October, a news effect evidently had free reign; its impact was felt in places where ads appeared and where they did not. Of course, at this point the volume of ads was still small. Whether or not the smallness of the overall ad volume was important to the September/early October story, to the late October/November story the mounting volume of ads *was* critical. The late barrage evidently blunted the primary dynamic effect of the news, to promote Al Gore's recovery. News awareness may also have blunted ads, at least by one of our tests, but not every one was highly interested in the news.

The natural experiment was also a political reality, of course. If the narrative of Al Gore's late recovery sheds important lessons on how campaigns matter, it is also critical to *ex post* interpretation of the campaign and the election. It allows the Democrats to claim a moral victory. Moral victories do not necessarily translate into Electoral College ones, however. Now, advertising did not by itself give the election the Electoral College to George W. Bush. This chapter presents at least a circumstantial case that the most dramatic shift of the entire campaign, the sudden collapse of Al Gore's handsome September lead, was caused by network news. The news also helped Gore come back, and this is the dynamic that enabled him to win the popular vote. But the Bush campaign's ultimate dominance in ads in DMAs where ads were actually played stalled his comeback in precisely those places. It is satisfying intellectually that the comeback was *not* stalled where ads did not play. Politically, however, that is of no consequence. The places where Republican ads stalled Gore's comeback were the very places that held the key to the Electoral College.

5

The Economy, Clinton, and the First Phase

Why did it matter that Gore lost the ad war? According to standard forecasting models, he was supposed to win handily. The failure of the forecasts has provoked debate about the models and speculation about what, if anything, was special about 2000. This chapter shows that Al Gore ought to have benefited from the robust economy, as forecasting models predicted. The first phase of the general campaign exemplifies what might have happened. Assessments of the economy were as positive as they had been in years. Voters continued to credit the incumbent administration for good times. This combination of factors helped push Al Gore well in front after the conventions. The nominating conventions helped Gore, in that economic perceptions were initially disordered: Democrats were much less optimistic about the economy than Republicans were. But the conventions sorted out key differences, and made the economy a potential major plus for the Democrats. The campaign itself did not alter perceptions further, although the stock market did temporarily. But Gore took no credit for the economy, to the point that his advertisements mentioned it not once. And toward the end, the impact of economic judgments may just have faded away.

The 2000 election may be the exception that proves the rule, first articulated by Gelman and King (1993) and elaborated by Campbell (2000), that the campaign is necessary to remind voters of the correct economic judgment and so realize the predictions made by forecasting models. One side will always have an incentive to emphasize the economy, the in-party in good times, the out-party, in bad times.[1] In the good times of 2000, Al Gore, the obvious beneficiary, said nothing.

Gore may have chosen to say nothing for fear that priming the economy would also prime unhappy memories of Bill Clinton. Gore was right to worry that Clinton might be a drag on the Gore-Lieberman ticket. The Republicans clearly sensed this, as their campaign mentioned Clinton frequently, notwithstanding his high job approval ratings.

The Economy

Failures of Prediction

Forecasting models are an extension of the emphasis on "fundamentals." The fundamentals described in Chapter 3 are mostly fixed for extended periods, so they cannot really account for major shifts between successive elections. But the economy can account for such shifts and the relevant indicators for forecasting are available well in advance of each election. The "economy" typically means year-over-year change in per capita real income. It is commonly supplemented by the state of foreign policy, as indicated, for example, by casualties in military action abroad. Mediating some of this and a force in its own right is the public's general approval of the President's handling of his job, typically as indicated by a question asked monthly by the Gallup organization. Analysis of short-term movement in the Gallup approval rating suggests a critical intermediary role for the media (Brody, 1991). But all these factors are largely fixed in place by the time the general campaign starts.[2]

The models do not necessarily imply that campaigns are irrelevant. Indeed, Gelman and King (1993) argue that campaigns are necessary for fundamental factors to operate. Most years, economic considerations weigh more heavily in vote intention the closer an interview is to Election Day (Bartels, 1997).[3] The campaign supplements

---

[1] Campaigns pretty clearly do respond to this incentive. West (1997) shows that the from 1952 to 1996 the modal category of general-election ads referred to "domestic performance."

[2] The sources for these propositions are legion, but much of the literature is captured in the March 2001 *PS: Political Science and Politics* symposium.

[3] Bartels uses the US National Election Study (NES) over several years, working with the date of interview. Even though NES cases are not released to field in as controlled a way as Annenberg cases were in 2000, Bartels deploys many controls and his point stands.

pre-campaign economic information with current information, especially as late deciders break toward the incumbent in proportion to how well the economy is doing (Campbell, 2000).

The problem is that in 2000 all these considerations should have made Al Gore the landslide victor. The resulting academic confusion and dismay is amply evident in the symposium mentioned in Chapter 1. Among the symposium contributors, Bartels and Zaller (2001) make the boldest claim, that forecasting models had focused on the wrong economic variable all along. Rather than looking at overall economic growth, models should have focused on after-tax income, the preferred indicator in 1970s econometric modeling.[4] The 1999–2000 interval saw the weakest link between total income and disposable income in the postwar period, as economic growth registered more in tax revenue than in take-home pay. Had presidential forecasting models incorporated disposable income, they would have made rather better predictions before 2000 and spectacularly better ones for 2000 itself.

Bartels and Zaller seem to be alone in their opinion.[5] Lewis-Beck and Tien (2001) suggest that some respecification can reduce the prediction error for 2000, but only slightly. Wlezien (2001) is forthright in stating that the campaign is the key to the prediction failure. Three attempts to account for the failure are especially pertinent:

- Campbell (2001), harkening to his own earlier work and to Gelman and King, argues that all forecasting models presuppose that one candidate or the other will put the economy on the agenda. He wonders if Al Gore failed to do so. This chapter shows that Gore did, indeed, fail to take credit for the economy.
- According to Holbrook (2001), forecasting models assume that "economic news" – media coverage of the economy and the reflection of that coverage in respondents' reports of economic satisfaction in surveys – tracks the real economy. If in the past this assumption was justified, it was not in 2000: In that year economic

---

[4] See, for instance, Kramer (1971) and Tufte (1980). Election analyses in that decade focused on the House, as the Presidential time series was not yet long enough for econometric treatment. Presidential analyses at that point were not of elections but of popularity, where quarterly or monthly time series of poll readings could be deployed.

[5] The most scathing reaction to Bartels and Zaller is by Fiorina, Abrams, and Pope (2003), who argue that the Bartels-Zaller claim "does not pass the straight face test," and that the piece is "a brilliantly executed spoof of election forecasting" (164).

news was about as pessimistic as in 1960 and almost as negative as in 1992 and 1980, notwithstanding the most positive survey-based reports of personal finances for the entire postwar period.[6] But this chapter shows that voters in 2000 were very positive in their assessments of the national economy, more optimistic than they had been in years.

- Norpoth (2001) points in a different direction, to Bill Clinton's januslike persona, highly esteemed as a political actor but reviled for his private life. Al Gore may have feared precisely this, and in a way his fears were justified. So this may account for his failure to trumpet the economic successes of the incumbent administration. But in failing to emphasize the positive on the Clinton record, he may have left himself open to Republicans' emphasis on the negative.

The Economy in the Campaign

Strikingly, neither campaign mentioned the economy more than in passing. That the Republicans did not stress the economy is no surprise. In 2000, no suggestion that the economy was performing poorly would have been plausible. In itself, the economy was a major obstacle for Republicans to get around. One device was to attribute the economic expansion to ordinary Americans, not to government action. Another was to suggest that the robust economy set the stage for real choices and that a Republican administration would make better choices. Both themes appear in this Spanish-language ad:

They say that our economy has never been better. And that is thanks to people's hard work. But an area that we need work in is improving education. In Texas, Governor Bush elevated the academic standards and the salary of teachers. And [...] Minority students of Texas are leading the nation in academic progress. Bush in Spanish: For me, education is number 1. Because our children deserve the best.

The most prominent theme, however, was taxes. The growth of the 1990s finally made a debate over taxes possible, such that a candidate

---

[6] The key evidence in Holbrook (2001) is his Figures 1 and 2, pp. 41 and 42. His reports of economic satisfaction come from the Survey of Consumer Finances. His findings suggest that Bartels and Zaller seriously misstate voter psychology in 2000. Holbrook echoes the argument by Hetherington (1996).

could propose tax cuts without necessarily cutting spending on cherished programs. This Bush ad is a classic statement of the case:

You know what Presidents Ronald Reagan and John F. Kennedy have in common? They both understood that cutting the taxes you pay increases government revenue and generates more economic growth. George W. Bush believes the same thing.... Let's compare the Presidential candidates' tax plans. Which tax plan do 300 leading economists support? The Bush plan. Which tax plan benefits all Americans and not just some? The Bush plan. Which plan would completely eliminate income taxes for almost all lower-income working families? The Bush plan. Under which tax plan would the wealthiest of Americans pay a higher percentage of total income taxes? The Bush plan. The Bush plan is simple, fair, and will increase government revenue and continue to grow our economy.... Vote for economic growth. Vote for the Bush tax plan. Our future depends upon it.

Economic performance is implicit in this ad, of course, but the focus of the ad is not on priming the economy as such.

The Democratic ads that mentioned the economy were as oblique as the Republican ones. The Democrats simply did not take credit for the country's economic good fortune. Here is a representative instance:

How much experience does America need? To protect Social Security from those who want to raise the retirement age. To really take on the big drug companies and get affordable prescription drugs. To fight against vouchers that drain money from public schools. To preserve Medicaid and strengthen Medicare. To keep our environment clean and our economy strong. How much experience does America need? All it can get.

The economy is mentioned only in passing. The real purpose of this ad was to dramatize the policy differences between the candidates and to impugn George W. Bush's fitness for the job. The strength of the economy is barely implied.

Economic Perceptions

Notwithstanding Holbrook's (2001) claim that voters misperceived the true state of the economy, Table 5.1 suggests that the electorate was very upbeat. Our question asks about satisfaction with current conditions and is identical to the question regularly used by the Gallup

TABLE 5.1. *Economic Perceptions*

	National Economic Conditions are...
Excellent	17.2
Good	50.6
Only Fair	24.9
Poor	7.3
(N)	(36995)

organization.[7] The percentage believing that the national economic conditions were good or excellent, 67.8, was close to Gallup reports for the same period. The Annenberg and Gallup readings were, in turn, some thirty points higher than in the corresponding months of 1996. In Gallup readings from July to October, 2000 inclusive, the share describing the economy as "good" or "excellent" was 73 percent (more Gallup respondents than Annenberg ones said "excellent"). The average for comparable months in 1996 was 42.3.

What is more, the conventions removed what may have been a systematic perceptual bias working against Democratic candidates. Figure 5.1 plots economic perception by day, controlling party identification.[8] Before the conventions, Democrats were no more positive about the economy than Independents were. Most positive by far were Republicans. At this point, then, invoking the economy might actually have depressed Democrats' support for their own candidate. The Republican convention made all groups more positive. Only with the Democratic convention, however, did Democrats become more like

[7] The measurement choice we faced lay between the NES question about year-over-year change in the economy and the Gallup question about satisfaction with things as they are now. The relentless growth of the U.S. economy in the years up to and including 2000 led us to choose the Gallup question: "How would you rate economic conditions in this country today? Would you say they are excellent, good, only fair or poor?" The Gallup question has the additional advantage of a higher frequency of repetition than the NES question.

We also asked about satisfaction with personal finances. Consistent with the standard finding (exemplified by Kiewiet, 1983), personal finances are overshadowed by national economic perceptions as a factor in the vote. Usually, personal finances did have a statistically significant impact, but its substantive modesty led us to put it aside, the better to focus on the big picture.

[8] The four categories of economic perception are scaled to the -1, $+1$ interval, with intermediate categories set to -0.33, $+0.33$.

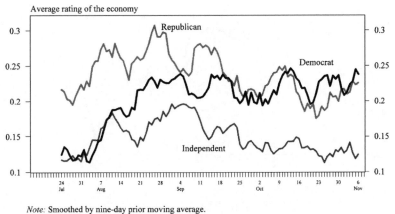

Average rating of the economy

Note: Smoothed by nine-day prior moving average.

FIGURE 5.1. Dynamics of Bias in National Economic Perceptions.

Republicans than like Independents. And the Democratic convention did have a prosperity theme, thanks to Bill Clinton. His speech on the Monday night focused on his legacy, with the economy front and center. Clinton uttered the words "economy" or "economic" eighteen times; "unemployed," "unemployment," and "employment" received four mentions; and "prosperity" was mentioned six times. Gore, in contrast, mentioned the economy four times (typically to say that it was not the issue), unemployment not at all, and prosperity four times.

For the rest of the campaign, partisan bias in economic perceptions was very small. Indeed Republicans remained more positive than Democrats until the second presidential debate. From mid-September on, Independents became steadily less positive, and ended up where they started, much less positive than either partisan group. The good news for Al Gore, however, was that after the conventions opinion on the economy was largely independent of party identification. It was no longer relatively negative among his own natural supporters.

After the conventions, Democratic perceptions did not shift further, certainly not as much as in other groups. It is as if the convention inoculated Democrats against further economic information. Independents and Republicans continued to respond to external forces, however, as judgments became more negative in each group. Republicans' judgments made a considerable recovery toward the end. As far as we can tell, movement in perception was not related to specific campaign events. Figure 5.2, which combines party identification groups,

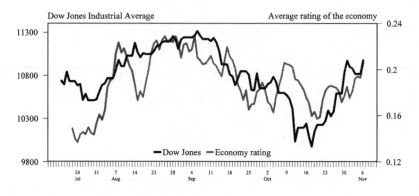

Note: Economic perceptions smoothed by five-day prior moving average.

FIGURE 5.2. The Stock Market and Economic Perceptions.

suggests that the driving force behind some of this movement was the stock market, especially as gauged by the Dow Jones Industrial Average (DJIA).[9] The stock market cannot be the whole story, however. Where the DJIA's August rise was much less dramatic than its September–October fall or its October–November recovery, the opposite was true for economic judgments. Whatever the source of perceptual shifts, the fact that perceptions were at a low point in early October cannot have helped Al Gore. Their recovery later in the month, in contrast, may have helped him. All along, however, the critical fact was that perceptions of the national economy were, by any reasonable standard, very positive.

There is no reason to believe that voters were unwilling to give the Clinton-Gore administration credit for economic good times. On a question about which party is more competent to manage the economy, response was highly partisan, but Independents and others clearly leaned toward the Democrats. A similar question about Bush's and Gore's ability to handle the economy yielded the same pattern. A question about whether government policies over the preceding twelve months helped or hurt the economy yielded highly positive response. Even Republicans said that, on balance, the government was helpful. There is some ambiguity about what the "government" was, perhaps,

---

[9] No other stock market index was as closely aligned to economic perceptions as the DJIA.

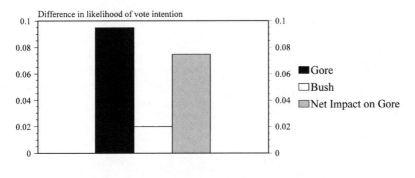

Note: Entries are differences in probability induced by a shift from a "good" to an "excellent" assessment of the economy. Derived from estimation in Table A5.1.

FIGURE 5.3. Positive Economic Perceptions and Vote Intentions.

but the response pattern cannot have been bad news for a Democratic candidate. When asked who deserved more credit for the federal budget surplus, voters were more likely to say the Clinton administration than the Republicans in Congress (although response to this question was also highly partisan).[10]

In short, the stage was set for Al Gore. Economic perceptions were far more positive than they had been for Bill Clinton in 1996. There is little reason to think that citizens discounted the Clinton administration's role in creating this good fortune. And for a time at least, Al Gore reaped the benefit. Figure 5.3 renders the multivariate coefficient on economic judgments in Table A5.1 into plausible impact on vote intention. As in earlier chapters, the graphical rendering is in terms of a shift that an individual might plausibly make. In this case, the height of a bar indicates the gain in probability of choosing a candidate, relative to no-preference, of shifting from seeing the national economy as "good"

---

[10] The questions discussed in the body of the text are, in order:

- Who do you think would do a better job of handling the nation's economy? The Republicans or the Democrats, or wouldn't there be any difference between them?
- Regardless of your choice for president, who do you think would do a better job of keeping the economy strong? George W. Bush or Al Gore?
- Over the past year, would you say that the economic policies of the federal government have made the nation's economy better, worse, or haven't they made much difference either way?
- Who do you think deserves more of the credit for the federal budget surplus? The Clinton administration or the Republicans in Congress?

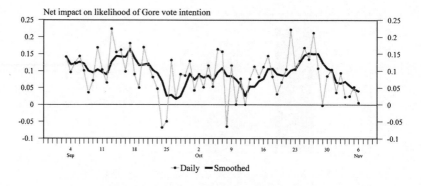

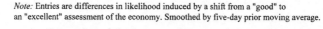

Note: Entries are differences in likelihood induced by a shift from a "good" to
an "excellent" assessment of the economy. Smoothed by five-day prior moving average.

FIGURE 5.4. Dynamics of the Impact of Economic Perceptions.

to seeing it as "excellent."[11] As it happens economic optimism makes
a person more likely to choose a major-party candidate, Bush *or* Gore.
This is consistent with the party identification pattern in Figure 5.1
(although party identification is controlled in the estimation). But optimism helps Gore much more than Bush, appropriately, so his net gain
from such a shift – controlling all background demographic, partisan,
and ideological factors – would have been about seven points.

But this pattern was not sustained over the whole campaign.
Figure 5.4 indicates that the electoral power of the economy ebbed
and flowed, but at the end, ebbed. As this figure introduces another recurring graphical form, it requires some explication. The vertical scale
on the figure is exactly the same as in Figure 5.3, the impact of a shift
from seeing the economy as "good" to seeing it as "excellent." In this
case, the shift is the net one, on Gore relative to Bush (equivalent to the
rightmost bar – "net impact on Gore" – in Figure 5.3). The estimation
in Table A5.1 is repeated for each day's sample of three hundred or
so persons.[12] Inevitably, the daily estimates are rather unstable, as

---

[11] More specifically, this involves setting respondents at the mid-point on all other variables, and then running through the "good" and the "excellent" predictions for each
of Bush and Gore vote intentions, and converting those to probability shifts.

[12] This is not to be confused with the daily impact estimation in Figure 4.8, in which
the operative coefficients came from a single estimation derived for the whole campaign and what varied from day to day were the values of the variable of interest. In
Figure 5.4, values are a fixed hypothetical – start at "good," switch to "excellent" –
but the coefficients of effect are allowed to vary from one day to the next.

befits the small sample size on which they are based. So the figure also presents a smoothed representation, the now-standard five-day moving average.

Figure 5.4 indicates that the economy *wanted* to drive the vote, so to speak. When Gore was riding high in September, the impact of the economy looks to have been part of the reason. Suggestively, there was a localized ebb and flow that coincides with the drop and rise in his support. Right before the end of this phase, the economy ceased to be a factor. The force that surged through the system to deprive him of his lead also may have distracted voters from the traditional relationship. The relationship returned, although not as strongly, in early October. But it ebbed again, possibly after the second debate. It became important again around the last debate, and as important as ever shortly after that event. Its impact peaked around October 25 or 27, and then fell to a nullity. The smoothed line understates the magnitude and finality of the drop. For the last six days, the average net effect was about a four-point shift. Compare that value to the estimate derived in Figure 5.3 for the whole campaign, eight points, or the stretches in Figure 5.4 where the good-to-excellent shift would boost Gore's support fifteen points. It is natural to wonder if the economy would have been so irrelevant at the end if Al Gore had taken credit for it.

The Clinton Factor

Perhaps Bill Clinton was the problem. Mention of the economy might only have invoked memories of Clinton, and too many of these would involve Monica Lewinsky. Clinton's *job* ratings in this period were very high, a mean approval percentage in Gallup polls in this period of 58.9. The average rating for his whole presidency was fifty-five, fourth highest since the start of the Gallup series.[13] Most critically, perhaps, his 2000 rating was ahead of the value, 56.6, for the comparable period in 1996. In this context, then, the data in Table 5.2 are startling. The table gives average ratings for Clinton and for each candidate, originally from a one-hundred-point "feeling thermometer"

---

[13] The three highest, in descending order, were Kennedy, Eisenhower, and George H. W. Bush.

TABLE 5.2. *Clinton and the Candidates*

	July–Nov (N = 37120)		Sept–Nov (N = 19962)	
	Mean	SD	Mean	SD
Clinton	−0.056	0.722	−0.058	0.726
Gore	0.081	0.636	0.101	0.649
Bush	0.142	0.616	0.133	0.628

Entries are means "feeling thermometer" ratings, on a scale centered at 0 and ranging from −1 to +1.

scale, for the whole July–November period and then for the period of most intense campaigning, September to November. For comparability to other indicators in this book, the one-hundred-point thermometer scale has been centered at 0 and compressed to the −1, +1 range. Feeling thermometers evidently are a gauge of personal regard. On the −1, +1 scale, Clinton's mean rating was *negative*. (On the original one-hundred-point scale, he scored lower than fifty.) Of Bush, Gore, and Clinton, Clinton was by quite a margin the least liked. Bush received the most positive readings (the equivalent of fifty-six to fifty-seven degrees on the original scale). Gore was clearly less well liked than Bush, although he did reduce the gap after the conventions. But Clinton was always much further behind Gore than Gore was behind Bush, and his ratings did not change appreciably over the campaign. The fact that Bush was clearly more popular than Gore, yet ultimately won fewer votes than Gore did, reinforces interpretation of differences as primarily reflecting judgment on them as individuals. This interpretation seems even more obvious as an explanation of the difference in mean rating between Gore and Clinton.[14]

A reasonable counterfactual is to imagine what would have happened had Clinton been as positively judged as Gore. Given Gore's own modest thermometer reading, this is hardly an earth-shattering thought experiment. Putting it this way allows us to estimate the extent of Clinton's impact on the Gore-Lieberman ticket.[15] Figure 5.5

[14] Of course, all three ratings are closely associated with the fundamental factors identified in Chapter 3. The point in this chapter concerns differences in mean ratings, which simply cannot be the product of background differences in predisposition.

[15] The idea of imagining leader or candidate counterfactuals seems to have originated with Bean and Mughan (1989) and is the routine strategy in the chapters in King (2002). In the simulation in this book, all other variables are set zero. The probability

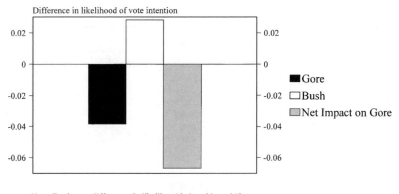

Note: Entries are differences in likelihood induced by a shift from the mean Gore rating to the mean Clinton rating. Derived from estimation in Table A5.1.

FIGURE 5.5. Evaluations of Clinton and Vote Intentions.

gauges the impact of such a counterfactual shift. The sign of the estimation is reversed to make the visual record consistent with the fact that Clinton dragged the Gore-Lieberman ticket down. The net impact would be about 6 points in Gore vote intention. Some of this would have been in demobilizing Gore support and some in direct conversion. Even had the marginal voter been merely indifferent to Clinton (rated him at zero, in our recoded scheme), Gore would have extracted about one more percentage point from the electorate than he did with the real Clinton on the scene.

Fittingly, the Bush campaign did not fail to remind the electorate of Gore's ties to Clinton. Not only did the Republicans mention him far more often than the Democrats did (the Democrats essentially did not mention him), as Table 5.3 indicates, he was a recurring theme in their ads.[16] Overall, almost 30 percent of Republican airings mentioned Clinton. Figure 5.6 shows that about September 25, the Republicans sharply increased their focus on Clinton. By mid-October, half their airings mentioned him by name. This percentage fell back at the end,

of a Gore choice is estimated for someone who rates Gore at the sample mean and then again for someone who rates him at Clinton's value. The same is done for impact on choice of Bush. The difference between each shift is the net impact. Keep in mind that the coefficients driving the simulation are for the effect of *Clinton* ratings.

[16] The unit in Table 5.3 is an "airing," as defined in Chapter 4. Twenty distinct Republican ads mentioned President Clinton.

TABLE 5.3. *Bill Clinton in the Ads (Labor Day to Election Day)*

	Ads played by	
	Democrats and allies	**Republicans and Allies**
Clinton?		
Mention	0.2	29.7
No Mention	99.8%	70.3%
No of airings	85291	100160

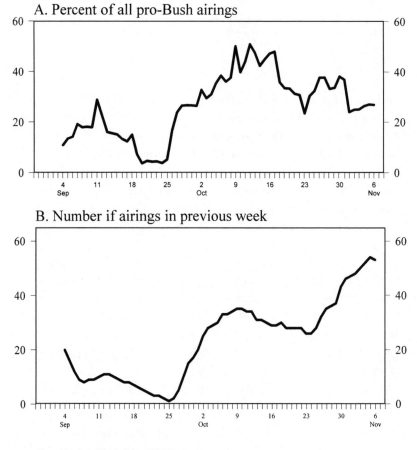

Note: Airings in "Battleground" DMAs.

FIGURE 5.6. Clinton in Republican Ads.

but even so 30 percent of their late airings mentioned him. This lower percentage operated on an enlarged volume of plays, so that in the last week the typical resident of a high-volume DMA could have encountered about fifty spots mentioning Clinton.[17]

Ostensibly, references to Clinton were tied to policy, not to the President's personal foibles. Indeed, most were not to "Clinton," but to "Clinton-Gore," as in:

America's having a recession – an education recession that's hurting our children. Our students rank last in the world in math and physics...[On screen: U.S. Dept. of Education, '98; Al Gore, *Meet the Press*, 12/99]...and most fourth graders in our cities can't read. [On screen: *Education Week*, 01/08/98] The Clinton-Gore education recession: It's failing our kids. But in Texas, George Bush raised standards, and test scores soared. Now Texas leads the nation in academic improvement. Learn more about the Bush Blueprint for accountability, high standards and local control. [On screen: www.EducationBlueprint.com; Paid for by Republican National Committee]

Bracketing Gore with Clinton was obviously necessary to make Gore responsible for Clinton administration failings and to disrupt Gore's own strategy of standing on his own feet. It is striking, nonetheless, that the Republicans placed so much emphasis on Clinton-Gore failures in policy domains that Democrats are thought to "own."[18] Of primary interest here is their non-policy subtext. To the extent that policy is the point of the ads, Clinton-Gore should have been as useful in mid-September as in mid-October, certainly as useful to the Republican cause on September 25 as on September 27. The suddenness of the shift toward Clinton suggests design. The events of the days before the 25th indicated to Republicans that Gore was vulnerable to signals that reminded voters of "slick Willy." The timing of Republican mentions of Clinton seems too closely tied to this vulnerability – signaled by media coverage of Gore's call for release of oil from the nation's petroleum reserve and validated by media interpretations of his story about the drug costs faced by his mother-in-law and her dog – to

---

[17] As before, the number of airings is weighted by the inverse of the effective number of stations in the DMA and by the number of TV households in the DMA.

[18] In addition to education, the Republicans emphasized Medicare, support for nursing homes, and prescription drug prices. Most anti-Clinton-Gore ads on the Republicans' own turf were placed by allied groups not by the Bush campaign itself or by the RNC. Most notable were anti-gun-control ads.

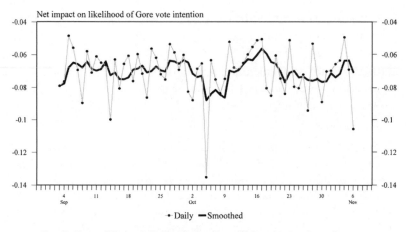

Note: Entries are difference in likelihood induced by a shift from the mean Gore rating to the mean Clinton rating. Smoothed by five-day prior moving average.

FIGURE 5.7. Dynamics of the Impact of Clinton Evaluations.

be a coincidence. The timing also suggests that policy was not the point. The days in question were also critical to judgment on Al Gore's personality, and are a major theme of the next chapter.

In contrast to impact from economic perceptions, impact from opinion on Bill Clinton did not fade, according to Figure 5.7. This figure combines the logic of Figures 5.4 and 5.5. As in Figure 5.5, the vertical axis captures the net impact of the counterfactual shift. As in Figure 5.4, the underlying evidence is from daily reestimations of the basic equation, with a five-day moving average superimposed. Clinton's impact was as great at the end as in early September. There is a strong hint that his influence was greatest right in the period that Gore was losing vital ground. Impact became strikingly more negative after the Bush campaign ramped up its emphasis on Clinton. October 5 stands out as a huge negative outlier and accounts for some of the drop that the smoothing projects onto a larger period. But it does not account for all of the increase in Clinton's impact in this period. So this was a period when association with Clinton was particularly unfortunate for Gore.[19]

---

[19] The same may be true at the end. Certainly the second largest negative reading is for the very last day. It would be folly to make much of this, however.

Conclusions

Al Gore ought to have benefited from the economy. Voters were as enthusiastic about it as they had been in years and they did not appear to deny the Clinton-Gore administration due credit for the good times. But Al Gore declined to claim his share of the credit. At the end, and at earlier critical points when his candidacy was in trouble, the impact of the economy faded.

This is not supposed to happen. The economy should not become less important as the campaign goes on. The evidence from earlier studies is very strong. Bartels (1997) draws upon decades of NES data to show the opposite effect of campaign time – the importance of the economy typically *grows*. Campbell (2000) makes the case that this growth is particularly significant right about the time that we see it shrink. Campbell (2000) and Gelman and King (1993) conjecture that without campaigns, the econometric models might not work as well as they do. Our findings confirm their intuition. The confirmation is the exception that proves the rule, however. The missing link is rhetorical emphasis on the economy. For the economy to be primed by the campaign, one side or the other has to mention it. Conventionally, one side has a strong interest in doing so, and in 2000 this ought to have been the Gore campaign. At the Democratic convention, President Clinton showed the way and arguably helped his successor by getting his natural supporters to abandon their economic pessimism. But Gore declined to pick up the theme and in the weeks that followed mentioned the economy in his ads not once. Although the evidence is circumstantial, his failure to mention the economy may well account for his failure to get credit for it.

It may be a weakness in our case that the effect of the economy did not fade monotonically. Its impact had ebbed and flowed earlier as well. So the drop in economic impact at the end may not have been the specific product of Gore's refusal to emphasize the issue. And there is the general problem in attempting to explain an effect by the absence of a cause. So we should not go out too far on a limb of claiming a strong relationship between Gore's silence and the economy's ultimate lack of impact. What we can say, however, is clear and counterintuitive. First, notwithstanding good economic times, Gore took no credit. Second, in contrast to the typical pattern, the impact of the economy did not increase.

If Gore's failure to mention the economy reflected fear of association with Bill Clinton, there was clearly some basis for this. Net differences in "thermometer" rating evidently indicate personal regard, and by that criterion Bill Clinton was held in very low regard. Clinton's negative ratings by themselves may account for Gore's difficulty in realizing the full political promise of the booming economy, in that they may simply have offset any positive economic impact. But if Al Gore thought that by mentioning very little about the Clinton years he would escape association with bad memories, he had not reckoned with the Bush campaign. Given the published reports of Clinton's popularity as the head of an administration, it is all the more striking that the Republicans chose to attack the president frontally. None of these choices seems inevitable. One can imagine the Bush strategists drawing a different lesson from their congressional colleagues' unsuccessful attempt to impeach Clinton. One can also imagine the Gore strategists concluding that if the Bush campaign insisted on associating him with Clinton, then Gore himself might just as well make the best of the association and take credit for the economy and possibly for his predecessor's other achievements. For Gore, the Clinton legacy was a mixed one and he faced a true dilemma. But he need not have approached the dilemma the way he did.

So a chapter that starts with one of the strongest generalizations in the study of elections, the remarkable predictability of elections, ends with counterfactuals. To the extent that they are plausible, the counterfactuals direct us to the contingency at the core of campaigns. Gelman and King (1993) suppose that both sides know where their strategic interests lie and, sooner or later, find their way to those positions. The failure of the 2000 result to deliver the inevitable casts this supposition in doubt.[20]

---

[20] It also casts an ironic light on Zaller (1998). Zaller argued that Bill Clinton survived the Lewinsky scandal because of the power of "fundamentals," especially the economy. This chapter suggests that Al Gore failed to benefit from the outstanding fundamental of 2000, the robust economy, because of the power of Monica Lewinsky.

6

Candidate Traits and the Second Phase

The first phase of the general-election campaign came to an end when the electorate abruptly revised its estimation of Al Gore's character, of his honesty in particular. Although the shift cannot be attributed to any major public event, it was no accident. The ground was laid, we believe, by themes in Republican ads, including focused attacks on Al Gore in early September. The ad campaign did not register directly with the electorate. Rather, it supplied language that then infused news coverage of Gore in late September, and a series of negative stories about Gore caused many citizens to reevaluate him. This manifested itself in precipitate drops in ratings of various facets of his personality. The deepest drop came in estimations of Gore's honesty, the thematic heart of the Republican ad campaign and of the negative press coverage.

This chapter adds a dynamic twist to accounts of personality in elections. The literature on perceptions of candidates' personality traits is modest but seems to be pointing toward a consensus. Voters make personality comparisons that are not just the residue of prior partisan and ideological commitments, although party and ideology do color personality judgments. And these personality comparisons affect the vote, at least at the margin. But few candidates are outstandingly superior on any evaluative dimension of personality. If they are, this advantage may be offset by relative judgments on another dimension. By the end, this was certainly true of the 2000 election, as Bartels (2002) has already shown. But personality judgments produced the most compelling dynamic of the campaign.

The approach in this chapter is frankly inductive. It begins by laying out evidence from a battery of trait perceptions modeled on those in the NES. Early movement in these perceptions corresponded to shifts in overall popularity. Later movement was differentiated, and reflected the content of the campaign. It then shows that perceptions mattered to the vote, and that the shift in perception accounts for the bulk of the transition from the first to the second phase of the general campaign. Finally, the chapter describes the character themes in the Bush campaign and shows how these themes echoed through news coverage at a critical moment. Comparison of time paths of advertising, news, and vote intention strongly suggests that the news was the key conduit of effect. This is confirmed by comparison of perceptual shifts among high- and low-interest groups. But the content of the news was powerfully affected by the rhetoric in Republican ads. The pattern is a further illustration of an argument originating with Jamieson (1992).

The Perceptual Tradeoff

Al Gore was undone by the collapse of his reputation as a man of character. Among all considerations that were potentially relevant to vote intention and that were not predetermined, only shifts in perceptions of his personality moved at the right time. This is the lesson of Figures 6.1 and 6.2. Figure 6.1 plots daily means for response to "trait" items modeled directly on questions from the NES and originating with Donald Kinder (see, for instance, Kinder, Abelson, and Fiske, 1979, and Kinder, 1986). Survey respondents were given a word or phrase and asked how well it fits the candidate – "extremely well," "quite well," "not too well," or "not well at all." In the Annenberg study, the traits are:

- "really cares about people like me,"
- "honest,"
- "inspiring,"
- "knowledgeable," and
- "provides strong leadership."

The last question was asked for the first time only on August 17. The first two concern the candidate's personal *character* and the last three,

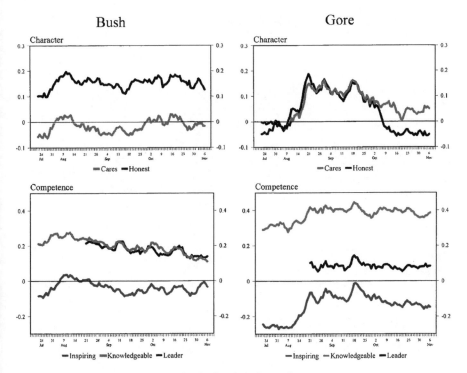

Note: Entries are mean rating, smoothed by five-day prior moving average.

FIGURE 6.1. Dynamics of Candidate Traits.

his *competence* to discharge the duties of the office.[1] In keeping with the convention in this book, response codes are fixed to the −1, +1 interval with higher values indicating more favorable judgments.

The public is able to distinguish among candidates and traits in ways that transcend prior partisanship. Of course, much of the variation across individuals *is* infused with partisan and ideological bias. But differences among candidates in average ratings, trait by trait, are not just projections of background factors nor even of simple popularity. All along, perceptions were more differentiated for Gore than for Bush. All judgments on Gore shifted more – both upward and downward – than

---

[1] The twofold division is argued at length in Johnston et al. (1992), Chapter Six, and in Johnston (2002). The case is basically one of face validity combined with empirical potential for different dynamics between the character and competence domains, a difference that certainly appears in the Annenberg data. That said, response to trait items always seems to be governed mainly by a single, partisan factor.

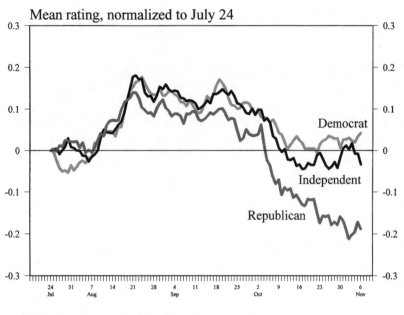

Note: Smoothed by seven-day prior moving average.

FIGURE 6.2. Partisan Bias in Perception of Gore's Honesty.

judgments on Bush did. Where for Bush all trait perceptions tended to exhibit common dynamics, for Gore dynamics were greater for character judgments than for competence ones.

For both candidates before late September, however, dynamics did not vary much from trait to trait. All evaluations of Bush generally moved up during the Republican convention, then all settled back. Thereafter, two of the three competence traits, "knowledgeable" and "inspiring," declined gradually relative to the other three traits. Similarly, all evaluations of Gore jumped with the Democratic convention, drifted down slightly over the following weeks, and moved back up in late September. This September decay and recovery tracks the movement in vote intentions described in Chapter 2. All five Gore indicators peaked on September 18, then all five indicators turned down, never to recover. To this point, dynamics differed between candidates but not among traits. Gore experienced greater evaluative gains and losses than Bush, but the gains and losses were broadly similar across all traits (although a bit more sharply defined for the two character traits than for the three competence ones).

Character and competence judgments diverged after October 3, the day of the first presidential debate. In particular, judgments on Gore's honesty resumed their fall, in contrast to the situation with each other indicator. Judgment on the other character indicator, on how much Al Gore "really cares," dropped later, after the second debate. But it never dropped as far as "honesty" judgments did and less of the damage was permanent. Honesty judgments on Gore, in contrast, ended up lower than they started, and the late September/early October damage was never repaired. Honesty is the only trait on which Al Gore was worse off at the end than at the beginning.

Shifts in perception mostly cut through preexisting bias and so had the potential to go straight to the bottom line of vote intention. Candidate perceptions certainly were biased by prior partisanship. For example, Republicans and Democrats differed, on average, 0.7 of a possible 2.0 points in rating Al Gore for honesty. Independents leaned slightly toward the Republican perception, as a byproduct of a tendency to see both candidates in a bad light. But the trait itself is intrinsically a valence consideration; who would argue for less honesty among public figures? In contrast, most issue questions are positional, in that there really are two sides to the question. So, whatever the bias in starting points, dynamics in trait perceptions are potentially uniform. Figure 6.2 shows that this is mostly true. To sharpen the focus on dynamics, trait ratings are normalized to the same starting point as in Figure 6.1. From late July to early October, shifts were nearly identical between partisan groups. After October 2, Republicans shifted more than the other groups and partisan bias thus increased. The increase had two parts, the first a greater shift right after the first debate and the second a continued slide where Democrats' and Independents' perceptions stabilized. So far, then, the campaign just reinforced a preexisting partisan difference, the sort of polarization we looked for (and mainly did not find) in Chapter 3. All this happened in spite of the fact that the consideration in question was not intrinsically positional. But at least as striking as the increase in polarization are the uniformity of direction and the overall scale of the net shift within partisan groups. Most remarkable is that Democrats shifted their perceptions as much as Independents did. Each group's total drop in Gore ratings was as great as the net widening of the gap between these groups, on one hand, and Republican identifiers, on the other. So the suspicion is confirmed,

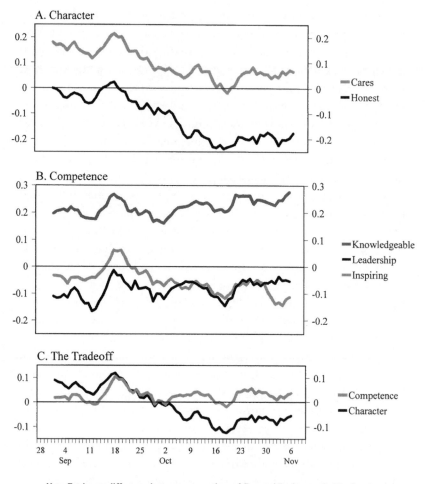

Note: Entries are differences between mean ratings of Gore and Bush, smoothed by five-day prior moving average.

FIGURE 6.3. Dynamics of Differences in Trait Ratings.

shifts in perceptions of candidates' trait have enormous explanatory potential for campaign dynamics.

Figure 6.3 translates trait patterns into a direct comparison between the candidates. The figure concentrates on shifts after the conventions, so as not to be dominated visually by the dynamics around those events. Comparisons are first conducted trait by trait, although traits continue to be grouped. As we know, most, although not all, of the dynamics were produced by shifts in perceptions of Gore. At the peak on September 18, he ranked above Bush on four of the five indicators. For "honest" and "inspiring," the difference was tiny, but for "knowledge-able" and "cares" the advantage was large. Only on "leadership" did Bush never lose his advantage, although even there it was minuscule on the 18th. Thereafter, Gore dropped seriously behind in perceived honesty and slightly behind on "inspiring." His advantage on "really cares" became negligible and for a brief span after the second debate was reversed. Only on "knowledgeable" and "leadership" was his position relative to Bush no worse at the end than in late September.

The bottom panel summarizes the tradeoff faced by the electorate. Here the individual trait items have been combined to form two dimensions – character and competence. Where by late September Gore was apparently advantaged on both evaluative dimensions, at the end he was ahead on only one – competence – and not by much. He was behind on the other – character – again not by much, but seemingly by more than he was ahead on competence. Relative values on each dimension are somewhat arbitrary, particularly as they depend on the specific trait ratings included in the survey. But the existence of a trade-off comports with a commonsense view of the situation. And the dynamical divergence between dimensions is *not* an artifact of choice of component items. The fact that the divergence was driven by honesty judgments in particular reinforces a substantive interpretation of the event. Intuitively speaking, honesty lies at the core of character.

The shift in character perception was a major factor in distinguishing between the first and the second phases, as indicated by Figure 6.4. This figure takes the coefficients in Table A6.1 and translates them into impact estimations.[2] Our setup follows the model of Rahn, Aldrich, Borgida, and Sullivan (1990), who make a spirited argument that citizens engage in pairwise comparison when choosing and that a model expressed in differences between candidates is the correct one. Rahn et al. also argue for separate representation of competence and what they call "personal qualities," and we follow suit.[3] Coefficients in

---

[2] Issues are the topic of the next chapter but we feel compelled to include them at this stage and let Table A6.1 stand as our representation of the final stage. Like Bartels (2002) we do not feel comfortable insisting on a specific order between issue position and candidate assessment, in the manner of Miller and Shanks (1996).

[3] Johnston et al. (1992) use the competence/character summation in their study of the 1988 Canadian campaign, the clearest precursor for the design of the Annenberg study. Other studies, notably Miller and Shanks (1996) and Bartels (2002), leave the trait battery disaggregated.

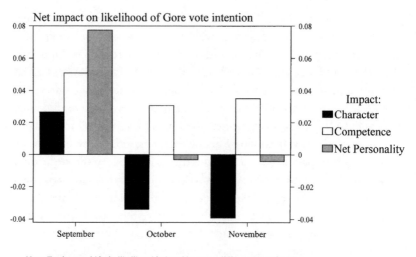

Net impact on likelihood of Gore vote intention

Note: Entries are shifts in likelihood induced by mean difference in trait ratings in the indicated month. Derived from estimations in Table A6.1.

FIGURE 6.4. Trait Ratings and Vote Intentions.

Table A6.1 allow the structure of impact to shift between phases, although structural variation from phase to phase appears to be small. In translating Table A6.1 coefficients into estimates of actual impact, we use the average value on the perceived Gore – Bush trait difference for each period. A positive value indicates that Gore was seen more favorably than Bush, a negative value, that Bush was seen more positively than Gore. Another way of thinking about the value is the distance covered if an individual starts by seeing the candidates as identical and then moves to distinguish one from the other. That shift – from a neutral to a differentiated perception – generates the probability impacts in Figure 6.4.[4] In effect, each month's value is being compared with the entirely plausible counterfactual that the candidates are rated identically on the dimension.

In September, relative to everything else – demographics, party identification, ideology, judgment on the Clinton record, and issues – trait

---

[4] The estimation controls all the fundamental factors identified in Chapters 3 and 5 as well as three issue variables. It appears to suggest that the marginal impact of competence outweighs that of character. In Johnston et al. (2003), however, we find with a disaggregated estimation – five traits represented separately – at four of the five trait differences have very similar coefficients but "knowledgeable," part of this book's competence indicator, has a rather weaker effect than the others.

perceptions boosted Gore's support; they provided an additional reason to vote for him. In October, this remained true only for judgments on his competence, and even competence judgments helped Gore less than in September.[5] Character judgments, in contrast, dragged him down. The critical comparison is between September and October values. Where in September character considerations added between two and three points to his share of vote intentions, in October, they subtracted a like amount, perhaps more.[6] In November, the tradeoff became a little sharper. Gore's character disadvantage remained stable and large, but his competence advantage grew slightly; the latter reflects increasing doubts about Bush's leadership qualities and his knowledge (see Figure 6.1).

The basic stability of the system that translated perception into vote intention is confirmed by Figure 6.5. This figure is closely parallel to Figure 5.4. First an estimation model like that in Table A6.1 was reestimated for each day of interviewing.[7] Then fixed values for competence and for character were run through each day's coefficients. As differences in perception of the candidates roughly stabilized after the last debate, the fixed values chosen are the average post-debates difference, the period of the maximum tradeoff. Running that value through daily coefficients produces an "as if" simulation: how much of the difference between, say, September and November is the result of shifts in coefficients? To the extent that the coefficient pattern is stable, the difference in vote intention must be the result of shifts in variables, not in parameters.

The figure confirms that the critical shifts were in the variables. There is a hint that character and competence each made slightly less

---

[5] Gore's edge in perceived competence shrank; the shift was just not as dramatic as the outright reversal on the character dimension (see Figure 6.3). The coefficient on competence in Table A6.1 also shrank, reducing the value of any advantage.

[6] Notwithstanding the presence of obvious controls in Table A6.1, we still suspect that the estimates of effect for any period, and of changes in net effect between periods, are too high. Most likely this is because cross-sectional bias in perception, mainly driven by partisanship and ideology, is leaking into the coefficients. See Johnston et al. (2003) for an unsuccessful attempt to purge the estimation of extraneous cross-sectional factors. Point estimates of impact should probably be discounted, although by how much we do not know.

[7] Because some of the issue questions were asked only of half-samples, the issue components of Table A6.1 were dropped for the daily estimations.

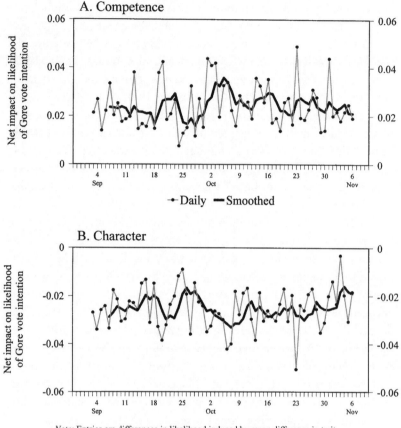

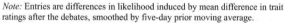

Note: Entries are differences in likelihood induced by mean difference in trait ratings after the debates, smoothed by five-day prior moving average.

FIGURE 6.5. Dynamics of the Impact of Trait Ratings.

difference for Gore at the end. There is also a suggestion that both dimensions had their greatest impact right in the period that Gore's character ratings were making the fatal plunge. But these are side stories. Most important is not that one or the other factor was primed, but that character perceptions themselves shifted dramatically. What the campaign did was *persuade* a large body of citizens to alter their perception of Gore.

By the end, of course, the net effect of character and competence was barely discernible. On Election Day, perceived personality traits could not have had a big effect on the outcome, as one dimension almost exactly offset the other.[8] *Dynamically*, however, shifts in trait perceptions were the most important single story of the campaign. They produced a dramatic reversal of fortune, induced a transition between campaign phases, and put Al Gore well behind his opponent. The reversal was largely attributable to the collapse of his reputation as a person of character.

Ads, News, and Character

What undid his reputation? This section makes a circumstantial case along the following lines. The Republican ad campaign made character a central theme. Most of this was implicit, largely through claims about education policy, and usually Gore was not mentioned by name. In early September, however, Republican ads made direct attacks on Gore's campaign finance record and accused him of lies and exaggerations. Just as these direct attacks were withdrawn from the field, a media storm erupted around Gore. The media storm preceded by a matter of days the downturn in Gore's trait ratings. His performance in the first debate was also vulnerable to interpretation along lines of character, and indeed television coverage followed suit. So if the episode was initiated by ads, the transmission belt for impact was television news.

In an indirect attack on Clinton and Gore, Republican ads regularly illustrated a theme of integrity and accountability. Certain words recurred with remarkable frequency in ads that received very heavy play: *trust, accountability* and *accountable, responsibility* and *responsible, standards, discipline, moral, character, tough* (as in choices), *right* (as in correct), and *values*. Here is an omnibus ad that illustrates the theme (emphasis added):

BUSH: I believe we need to encourage *personal responsibility* so people are *accountable* for their actions. And I believe in government that is *responsible* to the people. That's the difference in philosophy between my opponent and me. He *trusts* government, I *trust* you. I *trust* you to invest some of your own Social Security money for higher returns. I *trust* local people to run their own schools. In return for federal money, I will insist on performance. And if schools

---

[8] Bartels's (2002) Election Day estimation for net effects in 2000 also gives Bush a slight advantage, the smallest net advantage or disadvantage in any race from 1980 to 2000 but the most consequential.

continue to fail, we will give parents different options. I *trust* you with some of the budget surplus. I believe one-fourth of the surplus should go back to the people who pay the bills. My opponent proposes targeted tax cuts only for those he calls the "right people." And that means half of all income-tax payers get nothing at all. We should help people live their lives, but not run them. Because when we *trust* individuals, when we respect local control of schools, when we empower communities, together we can ignite America's spirit.

A less specific but similarly inclusive ad that lays special emphasis on moral strenuousness is the following (emphasis added):

BUSH: This is a moment in history when we have a chance to focus on *tough* problems. It's not always popular to say "Our children can't read," or "Social Security needs improving," or "We have a budget surplus and a deficit in *values*." But those are the *right things* to say. And *the right way* to make American better for everyone is to be bold and decisive, to unite instead of divide.

Particularly prominent was an emphasis on education. Not only did this address deep-seated parental concerns in a way that did not capitulate to Democrats' emphasis on spending, it invoked images of raising children, an absolutely central arena for moral issues. The most widely played ad of this genre was:

BUSH: If we really want to make sure no child gets left behind in America, we need the courage to raise *standards* in our schools. We need more *accountability* and more *discipline*. And we need to stop promoting failing children to the next grade and giving up on them. ANNOUNCER: George Bush raised *standards*. Tests scores soared. Texas leads the country in academic improvement. BUSH: It's easy just to spend more. Let's start by *expecting more.* ANNOUNCER: Learn more about the Bush Blueprint for *accountability, high standards*, and local control.

Figure 6.6 portrays the focus and scale of Republican advertising on this theme. Altogether, fourteen discrete ads employed at least one of the words listed above at least once and many of them more than once. Any play of such an ad counts toward the values in the figure. The top panel shows the percentage of all Republican ads on a given day represented by these fourteen ads, indicated by the line labeled "implicit mentions."[9] This rendering is insensitive, of course, to the overall volume of ads; that is a matter for the bottom panel.

[9] All the ads in question were placed by the Bush-Cheney campaign, by the RNC, or by a state Republican Party.

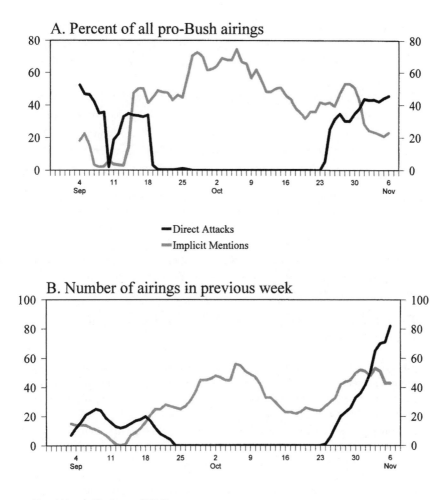

Note: Airings in "Battleground" DMAs.

FIGURE 6.6. Character in Republican Ads.

The figure confirms that this was a major Republican emphasis. From Labor Day to Election Day 39.6 percent all Republican ad airings involved one of these fourteen ads. In late September, the Bush campaign featured the theme in over 70 percent of all airings. Emphasis then drifted back to roughly the whole-campaign average of about two ads in five. Proportionally speaking, the emphasis dropped even further at the very end. But absolute volumes of emphasis, as the bottom panel reveals, rarely dropped. Panel B shows that the volume devoted to implicit character themes grew after mid-September, fell back in mid-October, then grew again. In the last week, a resident of a high-volume DMA might have encountered more than forty "implicit" character spots.

After the implicit campaign primed association with Clinton's moral defects and increased the general salience of the category, the Bush campaign also mounted explicit attacks on Al Gore's character. One episode filled the early September lull in "implicit" character ads. This attack used two ads to call up episodes from Gore's biography:

[Image of Gore on television in kitchen] WOMAN: There's Al Gore, reinventing himself on television again. Like I'm not going to notice? Who's he going to be today? The Al Gore who raises campaign money at a Buddhist temple, or the one who now promises campaign finance reform? Really. Al Gore: claiming credit for things he didn't even do. AL GORE [audio from television]: I took the initiative in creating the Internet. WOMAN: Yeah, and I invented the remote control, too. Another round of this and I'll sell my television.

The other ad explicitly juxtaposes Gore's character and the issue of accountability in schools:

[Image of Al Gore on television in kitchen] ANNOUNCER: Al Gore's promising campaign finance reform. Can I believe him? Because of Gore's last fund-raising campaign, twenty-two people have been indicted, twelve convicted, seventy took the Fifth Amendment, and eighteen witnesses fled the country. Now Al Gore is promising more accountability in our schools. And that sounds good – until you find out he doesn't require any real testing. And no testing means no accountability. Just more politics from Al Gore.

In the first week of September, these two ads attacking Gore directly constituted one half or more of all Republican plays. In the following week, the concentration was slightly smaller. The peak of the attack roughly coincided with a trough in Democratic share of vote intentions and with the temporary decline in Gore's personality ratings. Nonetheless, when the ads left the air, Gore's star was in the ascendant.

No sooner did the Republicans' direct attacks stop but the media picked up the thread. As Chapter 4 indicated, before September 20, Gore enjoyed a nearly unbroken television news advantage over Bush, and Gore's worst day was also Bush's worst day. This was the 12th, when attention was lavished on a Republican ad said to have contained a subliminal "rat" theme. The airtime given over to playing the ad itself during newscasts registered as negative coverage of the Gore

campaign, but criticism of the Bush side easily outweighed the negative impression the news conveyed about Gore. The real turning of the
news tide dates from the 21st, Gore's worst day to that point and the
first of five consecutive nonpositive days.

Arguably, the story began on the 18th, and not on television. On
September 18 the *Boston Globe* published a critical account of an
August 28 Tallahassee, Florida, speech by Gore. Gore claimed that
his mother-in-law paid three times as much for arthritis medicine for
herself as Gore paid for the same medicine for his dog. The *Globe*
revealed that Gore could not confirm that either his mother-in-law
or his dog actually took the medicine. The cost comparison reflected
data from a study by congressional Democrats. The story went national on the 19th, as major papers reported a comment by Bush
communications director, Karen Hughes. The *USA Today* passage is
representative:

As Bush flew from Texas to Little Rock, his communications director, Karen
Hughes, called reporters' attention to a story in Monday's *Boston Globe*. The
article said Gore stretched the truth last month when he said his mother-in-
law pays three times as much for the same arthritis medicine his dog uses. The
Globe said that it was not clear that either Margaret Ann Aitcheson or Shiloh,
the dog, takes the drug, Lodine, and that the costs Gore cited came not from
his family's bills but from a House Democratic study.

Kym Spell, a Gore spokeswoman, said both Aitcheson and the dog were pre-
scribed Lodine; she called the *Globe* story "inaccurate." GOP vice presidential
candidate Dick Cheney issued a statement calling the news story "disturbing
in the sense that it looks like another Al Gore invention."

In none of the newspapers was this headline news and in none of
them did the story make the lead. In every case, it was a revelation
saved for late in the daily digest of campaign news. The headline for
the *USA Today* digest, for instance, was "Bush pitches 'Blueprint' to
women, middle class." Nor did the story make it to television that day.
Television news for the 19th focused on the gender gap and on Bush's
appearance on the Oprah Winfrey show.

The next day was entirely different. In the *New York Times* and *USA
Today* the story received separate treatment and its own headline. In
the *Times* the headline read: "THE 2000 CAMPAIGN; THE REPUBLICAN
RUNNING MATE; In Harshest Attack Yet, Cheney Accuses Gore of Fab-
rications." In *USA Today*, the headline read "Gore campaign faces
questions about anecdotes; Republicans say he's 'making up stories'

after his comments on price of medicine." As the story gained prominence it was also transformed. Continuing the previous day's theme, it was cast as a character issue by Republican attackers. Questions were also being asked about the core claim, that the drug cost more for humans than for dogs. One possibility was that the wholesale price for dogs was being compared to the retail price for humans. Another possibility was that the difference was in dosages. In any case, Gore was now shown as misleading twice over in a single anecdote. A second anecdote fleshed out the implications of the first one. Just as Gore told a fabrication about his mother-in-law, so did he make up a childhood recollection:

On Monday, addressing a Teamsters meeting, Gore spoke of childhood lullabies and then sang, "Look for the union label..." That song was written in 1975, when Gore was twenty-seven.[10]

Much of the narrative drive for the newspaper stories came from speeches by Bush and Cheney that hammered the point home. Also on the 20th, the story broke through to network television, as the *CBS Evening News* repeated the point that the cost comparison was based on a congressional report, not personal experience.

The 21st was the day of the firestorm. Newspapers aired the various possible avenues of deception and Gore's attempt to shift the discussion back to the cost of prescription drugs. More prominent, however, was another issue, the rising price of fuel and Al Gore's call for President Clinton to release oil from the Strategic Petroleum Reserve.[11] Gore attempted to frame the issue in terms of monopolistic pricing by oil companies that in turn were closely tied to Bush and Cheney, but newspapers and television received the proposal highly critically. They pointed out that Gore himself had come out *against* the idea

---

[10] The excerpt is from the already-cited *USA Today* article.
[11] The call was foreshadowed in a *Times* story the previous day, a story that focused mainly on the mother-in-law anecdote. The story's last paragraph shifted focus:

The campaign was eager to move on to other subjects. Mr. Gore said today in an interview with Fox News that on Thursday he would address the increase in the price of heating oil, no doubt affording him the opportunity to discuss Mr. Bush's ties to the oil industry. "The profits of the big oil companies have skyrocketed just at the time when the American people have been paying these gigantic price increases," Mr. Gore told Fox. "I'm going to be making a major policy speech tomorrow outlining a specific course of action."

eight months earlier. On CBS, correspondent John Roberts said, "Eight months ago, Al Gore dismissed the idea. Today, seven weeks to the election, it's suddenly sound policy." Also prominently featured were earlier disagreements inside the Clinton administration, particularly opposition by Treasury Secretary Larry Summers. On the *NBC Nightly News*, Lisa Myers reported:

> Even most of the president's economic team has opposed it. In a memo last week, Treasury Secretary Lawrence Summers writes that he and Fed Chairman Alan Greenspan agree it would be, quote, "a major and substantial policy mistake." But today Summers toes the line, says Gore's limited action, only five million barrels, might be appropriate.

Republicans argued that this was just politics, an attempt to deflect criticism from the Clinton administration's lack of an energy policy. Especially telling was the claim that Al Gore would do or say anything to win. And the proposal followed suspiciously closely on the prescription drug controversy. From NBC:

> CLAIRE SHIPMAN: Gore may be looking for political cover, but he's also hoping that his oil announcement will provide a change of subject from what has been his worst week in a month and a half.
> CHRIS LEHANE (Gore Spokesman): I think he was making a pretty simple point.
> SHIPMAN: First, a blow-up on the issue of health care. Questions about whether Gore misstated the costs of arthritis medication for both his mother-in-law and his dog.
> GORE: It costs her $108 per month. It costs $37.80 a month for a dog.
> SHIPMAN: In fact, it seems Gore did not take those numbers from personal experience, but from a congressional report on drug prices. The Gore campaign says the general idea is right, but citing privacy issues, won't give the actual numbers.
> GORE: Well, the-the issue is not her, the issue is what seniors around the country are paying.
> SHIPMAN: Why is this important?
> BILL TURQUE (*Newsweek*): He has had a tendency over the years to take a pretty good story and try to make it a little better by embellishing, adding, sort of stretching it beyond where the facts would take it.
> SHIPMAN: And then questions about this.
> GORE: I still remember the lullabies that I heard as a child, "Look for the union label..."

SHIPMAN: But that union song was written in the 1970s, when Gore was in his mid-twenties. Gore says he was obviously joking. Reporters are also grumbling that it's been hard to get answers from Gore. He hasn't held a full-scale news conference in two months.

Although the next day, the 22nd, did not yield coverage as uniformly negative, the story was kept alive by President Clinton's decision to release some of the reserve. Comment, including excerpts from the Bush campaign, reiterated claims of policy confusion inside the administration and electoral motivation on both Clinton's and Gore's parts. And CBS updated a story that cast further doubt on Al Gore's probity:

DAN RATHER, anchor: Some just-recovered White House e-mails deal with what Vice President Gore has long acknowledged are past mistakes in fund-raising activities. This includes the fund-raiser he attended in 1996 at a Buddhist temple in Los Angeles. The new e-mails suggest Gore staffers at least were well aware it was a fund-raiser. The Gore campaign says the e-mails contain, quote, "nothing new."

The news storm coincided with the shift in Gore's trait ratings. Figure 6.7 juxtaposes ad, news, and trait perception shifts in real time. The ad line in the top two panels is essentially the line from the lower panel in Figure 6.6 turned upside down for visual effect, to convey negativity. The line is a moving average rather than a cumulative sum, to facilitate comparison with the line for trait perception. Because the ad line, consistent with earlier chapters, pools information from seven days, we use the same number of days for the other three lines. The news line is essentially the same as in the top panel of Figure 4.11, although now with a much higher aspect ratio for the smoothed line. The trait perception is the line for Gore's honesty. Although, it is a useful simplification to talk about general character perceptions, the greatest damage in this period was done to his honesty ratings, hence our focus on that trait in particular.

Advertising concentration on Gore's character predated the permanent turn in perceptions of his honesty by about two weeks. A lag this long seems inconsistent with the one-week time horizon established in Chapter 4 for ad effects. That said, there may be a short-term effect from the ads, in that Gore's trait ratings fell and rose roughly in step with the ad campaign. So did the news valence, in part as some of the

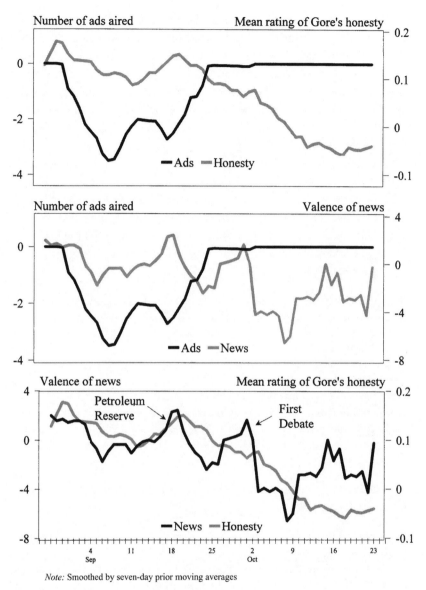

Note: Smoothed by seven-day prior moving averages

FIGURE 6.7. Ads, News, and Honesty.

news in this period consisted of reports about the ads. A combination of intense Republican attacks on Gore's character combined with reporting of the ads may account for the September dip and rise in his support.

The late September crash in perceptions of Gore, in contrast, can only be a story about news, at least in terms of direct cause and effect. The sharp drop in Gore's news valence predated the first drop in his honesty ratings by exactly one day. This drop in valence reflects the interpretation of the Petroleum Reserve issue as pandering played against the backdrop of stories about Al Gore and his mother-in-law and dog. News valences for Gore then recovered, although not all the way to the previous level.

The first debate brought more trouble for Gore. Tellingly, Gore's negative television news numbers for October 4, the day after the debate, were his worst of the entire campaign.[12] And the dominant theme was his character. Once again, the story went, Gore embellished the facts and then was caught. His claim to have accompanied the Federal Emergency Management chief to view brush fires in Texas was one misstatement. From the *CBS Evening News*:

BOB SCHIEFFER: Both occasionally fudged facts. Bush incorrectly claimed Gore's primary campaign cost more than his. When Bush brought up these fires that swept south Texas, Gore recalled going there with the Federal Emergency Management chief.
GORE: (From debate) I accompanied James Lee Witt down to Texas when those fires broke out.
SCHIEFFER: Today Gore said, 'Maybe not.'
GORE: (From *Good Morning America*) I was there in Texas, in Houston, with the head of the Texas Emergency Management folks and with all the Federal Emergency Management folks. If James Lee was there before or after, then, you know, I got that wrong then.

This created an opening for replaying a Bush character attack directly from the debate:

SCHIEFFER: Mostly they talked issues, but several times, Bush questioned Gore's character.
BUSH: (From debate) You know, going to a Buddhist temple and then claiming it wasn't a fund-raiser is just not my view of responsibility.

CBS also played a sequence in which Gore tried to extend his speaking time, to the visible exasperation of moderator Jim Lehrer. NBC

---

[12] That day was also bad for Bush. Comments about Bush were not about his character, however; they tended to focus on policy.

ended its analysis with the "Truth Squad." The segment criticized both candidates but the most telling blows landed on the Vice President. The strongest criticisms of Bush were that he seemed to have changed his position on the "abortion pill," RU-486, and that he was wrong when he suggested that Gore had the numbers wrong on his tax cut proposals. Gore, in contrast, was portrayed as positively deceptive on spending:

LISA MYERS: But Gore appears to have been misleading about his own priorities, seeming to minimize his new spending plans.
GORE: For every dollar that I propose in spending for things like education and health care, I will put another dollar into middle class tax cuts.
MYERS: According to an independent analysis, that's not true. It finds that for every dollar Gore devotes to tax cuts he proposes more than $3 in new spending, some $1.4 trillion.
CAROL COX WAIT (Committee for Responsible Federal Budget): It is the largest expansion of government since the Great Society program and LBJ.

Then he was accused of mischaracterizing his own statements about Governor Bush:

MYERS: Also not true, this Gore statement.
GORE: I have actually not questioned Governor Bush's experience, I have questioned his proposals.
MYERS: In fact, Gore and his aides repeatedly questioned Bush's qualifications. Gore himself asking, "Does he have the experience to be president?"

The NBC segment also included the debate's two "embellishments." One was Gore's claim about accompanying James Lee Witt to the Texas brush fires. The other was about crowding in a Florida classroom:

MYERS: Also challenged, Gore's dramatic story about the need for more money for school construction, describing a letter from a father in Sarasota, Florida, whose fifteen-year-old daughter has to stand in class.
GORE: She is the thirty-sixth student in that classroom, sent me a picture of her in the classroom. They can't squeeze another desk in for her, so she has to stand during class.
MYERS: Today the Sarasota superintendent says Gore is right about overcrowding but wrong about the student. She did have to stand but only for one day.
WILMA HAMILTON (Sarasota, Florida, School Superintendent): On her first day in science, she did stand in the back, and the second day when the custodians were made aware that another desk was needed, one was moved in and it was available to her.

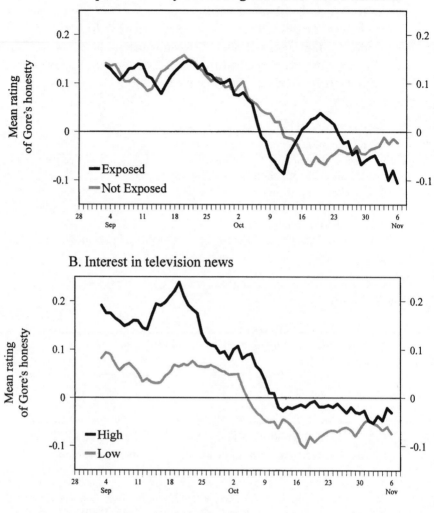

A. Exposure to early advertising attacks on Gore's character

B. Interest in television news

Note: Smoothed by seven-day prior moving average.

FIGURE 6.8. Gore Honesty Ratings by Ad and News Exposure.

In sum, commentary on Gore's debate performance was infused with discussion of character, of honesty in particular. It seems entirely reasonable to infer that the debate was instrumental in the further drop in the public's judgment on that particular trait. All this said, as Figure 2.2 indicated, the first debate had no effect on vote intentions. The debate's importance stems from its reinforcement of a trend in underlying factors that could only hurt Al Gore in the long run.

In terms of direct effect on perceptions of Gore, television news carries the strongest presumption. The timing of news valences was right, in the sense that two sharply negative days for Gore preceded drops in his honesty ratings by exactly one day. The timing of ad concentration was wrong, in that the ad hit preceded shifts in honesty ratings by too many days. Further evidence appears in Figure 6.8. The figure splits the sample in two ways, to consider ads and news as alternative avenues of effect. To test the possibility that the Republican attacks on Al Gore did it, the sample was split between DMAs that saw any of the direct attack ads portrayed in Figure 6.6 and DMAs that saw none, with Gore's honesty rating plotted for each. (Plots of the other traits would make the same point.) To the extent that the ad channel did the job directly, Gore's ratings should drop earlier and possibly further among those exposed to the ads than among those not exposed. The evidence suggests that, until October 3 at least, no such difference appears. In contrast, news attention and exposure *did* make a big difference. In the bottom panel the sample is split at the median on television interest measure introduced in Chapter 4. Before the 21st, the highly exposed and attentive gave Gore much higher ratings than did their opposite numbers. Then precipitately after the 21st, the high-interest group converged on low-interest ones. No interpretable movement appears in the low exposure/attention group. By the eve of the first debate, the exposure/attention difference was essentially nil.[13]

Conclusions

This chapter uncovers the central causal dynamic in the transition from the general-election campaign's first phase to its second. This is the dramatic reevaluation of Al Gore's character, especially his honesty. The evaluation began on a specific day, was accomplished in a clearly defined sequence and reasonably short time, and was never reversed. As these character perceptions shifted, their causal power did not shift, not in any enduring sense. So the total sequence is quite simple and is a

---

[13] This echoes the vote intention pattern in Chapter 4.

dramatic example of campaign persuasion. It permanently transformed the terms of competition to Al Gore's disadvantage.

The apparent irreversibility of the shift lends weight to an on-line processing model of campaign cognition, a pattern of occasional updating with no moderating induced by considerations called up from memory. This is not to say that all campaign processes are like this. Certainly, the patterns in Chapter 2 suggest a complex overlay of processes, some of which do exhibit fading of impulses. But Chapter 2's identification of a basic change of phase, from one of clear Gore advantage to one of Bush advantage, seems vindicated. What changed was a fundamental consideration – a "driver," in consultants' parlance.

The shift was built upon stylized facts about Gore that go back at least to 1996 and that resurfaced in his primary struggle against Bill Bradley. Scripts about Gore as someone with a shady fund-raising history, who would do anything to win, and who was prone to exaggeration were already in circulation. The Republicans brought these stories to the forefront of their campaign in September. When a news story about Gore's tendencies broke, the Republican campaign made sure that the rest of the press caught it. When Gore, hoping to pre-empt charges that he and Clinton were indifferent to the cost of heating, asked the President to release inventory from the Strategic Petroleum Reserve, the old script had already been primed and was swiftly invoked. Shifts in perception of his character followed shortly. To that point in the campaign, our indicators of candidates' trait perceptions all seemed to move together (even though they presented a fairly differentiated picture cross-sectionally). But after this late September moment, perceptions of Al Gore's character took on a sharply different dynamic from perceptions of his competence. Perceptions of his honesty were especially mobile at the transition, always downwards. The main conduit for stimuli on this matter was television news. In this, however, the 2000 campaign illustrated a key point in Jamieson (1992). Just as in her 1988 examples, in 2000 the news echoed and amplified a message handed to them by ads, in this case, Republican ads.

The critical ads played in early September. But Figure 6.6 shows that there was a second character blast, detonated in the last two weeks. This renewed emphasis neither persuaded voters further about Gore's perfidy nor primed negative perceptions already in place. Figure 6.1 shows that all the damage had already been done before these ads appeared. Figure 6.5 suggests that, if anything, both character and competence carried less weight at the end. Those ads may have had a different intent, however. Where the first round of character attacks said nothing about issues current to the 2000 campaign, the second, late-campaign round was also about Gore's own attacks on key Bush policy proposals. Personality perceptions were clearly part of the late-campaign story, as the old script was now being used to discredit Gore's attacks on Bush's plan for Social Security. This takes us into the realm of issues.

7

Social Security and the Third Phase

In the last weeks of the campaign, Al Gore staged a recovery, one fueled in large part by a single issue. That issues provided the impetus is itself a remarkable fact. George W. Bush tried from the start to occupy the center in issue perceptions, especially on the New Deal/Great Society agenda traditionally owned by the Democrats. It was not obvious that a Republican candidate could capture traditionally Democratic ground, for such a strategy runs contrary to predictions from theories of "issue ownership" (Simon 2002). But the Gore campaign evidently concluded that Bush had succeeded, for Gore came to see his task as pushing Bush back to the ideological right, perceptually speaking. In particular, Gore sought to persuade voters that a key Bush proposal, a plan to reform Social Security, far from securing the program's future, profoundly threatened it. Gore succeeded, but only incompletely.

What this chapter shows is the specific manifestation among issues of the tug-of-war between news and ads described in general terms in Chapter 4. The account begins with each side's initial rhetoric on the issue. At the Republican convention, Bush delineated his plan for Social Security in some detail; at the Democratic convention, Gore voiced his opposition. But for some time thereafter, neither side devoted much attention to the issue, at least in advertising. At the first debate, that changed as Gore launched an energetic attack on the Bush proposal. Gore continued his critique in television advertising and, in the end, by virtually taking over the network news. In the end he did win over the opinion of a substantial fraction of the electorate; as he did so, he also succeeded in making the issue more important, through a combination of priming and learning, in addition to basic persuasion. All this occurred notwithstanding the persistent operation of cognitive bias in issue perception. What ultimately turned back the Gore recovery was not a psychological process that minimized the effect of the campaign, but rather the campaign itself, as in the last week the Bush campaign concentrated its advertising on Social Security, linked the Gore critique to the character theme described in Chapter 6, and controlled the resources necessary to air more than twice as many Social Security-themed ads as the Gore campaign in the crucial media markets.

Early Exchanges

In the 1990s, Bill Clinton seized the center of U.S. politics. Republicans, in contrast, allowed themselves to be pushed to the right-wing fringe. Their disastrous 1992 convention was dominated by the cultural right, and in 1996 candidate Bob Dole was cast as a menacing figure. George W. Bush and his handlers were determined to position their candidate closer to the center, to label him a "compassionate conservative." As Mark McKinnon, director of media for the Bush campaign, put it:

> ...when you looked at the issue matrix on this election, all the issues that people typically cared about were Democratic issues: education, Social Security, health care. So, we knew that while we probably couldn't win on those issues, we had to at least keep them close. Fortunately we had a candidate who had been talking about those issues, not just in this campaign but for years as governor in Texas. So there was a platform there, and a history. Our strategy was to stay close on those issues. Those were the issues Bob Dole had been wiped out on by 20 or more points. (quoted in Jamieson and Waldman 2001, pp. 145–6)

The Republican plans for health care, Social Security, or education were certainly different from Democratic ones. But they were also constructed to portray George W. Bush as different from other Republicans, as not fundamentally opposed to the legacy of the New Deal and the Great Society.

In contrast to the 1996 campaign, which cast Dole as an opponent of an active federal government, the Bush campaign angled for the centrist track. Simply by addressing the issues and offering proposals,

Bush signaled that he accepted the legitimacy of government interven-
tion in each area. This is not to say that the Bush positions were just
echoes of Democratic positions. On each issue the campaign emphasized the characteristically Republican theme of choice, and contrasted
their candidate's respect for individuals and communities with the al-
leged Democratic preference for a government that dictates to private
citizens.

Thus Social Security ranked high on the agenda of the Bush general-
election campaign from its start. A distinctive feature of the Bush campaign was that it aired advertising heavily over the summer, placing
ads in a number of states between the completion of the primaries on
June 12 and the Republican convention that began July 31. Social Security was among the issues most prominently featured in those ads.
Among the ads aired most frequently during the summer was one that
laid out, in seven brief sentences, the Bush plan:

BUSH: Government has made a commitment, and you have made your plans.
These promises will be honored.
ANNOUNCER: George Bush's plan strengthens Social Security. It guarantees
everyone at or near retirement every dollar of their benefits. No cut in Social
Security. And the Bush plan gives younger workers a choice to put their Social
Security in sound investments they control for higher returns.
BUSH: This generation will save Social Security.

This ad aired heavily in the middle two weeks of June and again in the
week prior to the Republican convention.

In his speech to the convention in early August, accepting his party's
nomination, Bush spoke at length about his plan for Social Security.

We will strengthen Social Security and Medicare for the greatest generation
and for generations to come.... Social Security has been called the third rail
of American politics, the one you're not supposed to touch because it might
shock you. But if you don't touch it, you cannot fix it. And I intend to fix it.
To the seniors in this country, you earned your benefits, you made your plans,
and President George W. Bush will keep the promise of Social Security. No
changes, no reductions, no way.
Our opponents will say otherwise. This is their last parting ploy, and don't
believe a word of it. Now is the time – now is the time for Republicans and
Democrats to end the politics of fear and save Social Security together.
For younger workers we will give you the option, your choice, to put part
of your payroll taxes into sound, responsible investments. This will mean a

higher return on your money and, over thirty or forty years, a nest egg to help your retirement or to pass on to your children. When this money is in your name, in your account, it's just not a program, it's your property. Now is the time to give American workers security and independence that no politician can ever take away.

The Bush proposal, then, had two main elements, appealing to two different constituencies. One element affirmed Bush's commitment to the system, encouraging retirees and those near retirement to trust him. The other was an innovation, promising workers more control over their Social Security contributions and inviting contributors to invest part of their contributions in the stock market.

Following the convention, however, the Bush campaign pulled back from Social Security somewhat. Only two of the Bush ads aired heavily in the late summer raised the issue, and neither dealt in the specifics of the Bush proposal. One ad, aired in late July and early August, mentioned the program only in passing, suggesting that Bush's willingness to offer a plan revealed the strength of his character, in implicit contrast to Gore's.

BUSH: This is a moment in history when we have a chance to focus on tough problems. It's not always popular to say, "Our children can't read," or "Social Security needs improving," or "We have a budget surplus and a deficit of values." But those are the right things to say, and the right way to make America better for everyone is be bold and decisive, to unite instead of divide. Now is the time to do the hard things.

Another ad took up the issue at greater length, using footage from the candidate's acceptance speech, but included only the passage promising to maintain the program, not the innovation.

BUSH: We will strengthen Social Security and Medicare for the greatest generation and for generations to come. I believe great decisions are made with care, made with conviction. We will make prescription drugs available and affordable for every senior who needs them. You earned your benefits. You made your plans. And President George W. Bush will keep the promise of Social Security. No changes. No reductions. No way.

This ad aired from late August through mid-September. From then until a week after the first debate, the Bush campaign aired no advertising that mentioned Social Security at all. From the point of view of the Bush campaign, it seems, the political benefits of touting the Bush proposal had been more or less exhausted.

In his acceptance speech Al Gore, too, made mention of Social Security several times, both to offer, at least in generalities, his own proposal for reform and to criticize the Bush proposal. Like Bush, Gore sought to assure voters of his commitment to maintaining the program, saying "we will save and strengthen Social Security and Medicare, not only for this generation but for generations to come" and "We will balance the budget every year and dedicate the budget surplus first to saving Social Security." In a longer passage Gore sought to distinguish his reform proposal from Bush's in more detail:

I'll fight for a new tax freeway to help you save and build a bigger nest egg for your retirement. I'm talking about something extra that you can save and invest for yourself, something that will supplement Social Security, not be subtracted from it. But I will not go along with any proposal to strip one dollar out of every six dollars from the Social Security trust fund and privatize the Social Security that you're counting on. That's Social Security minus. Our plan is Social Security plus.

Later he reaffirmed his opposition to using a surplus in the Social Security fund for other purposes, introducing into the lexicon the term "lockbox."

Putting both Social Security and Medicare in an iron-clad lockbox where the politicians can't touch them, to me, that kind of common sense is a family value. Hands off Medicare and Social Security trust fund money. I'll veto anything that spends it for anything other than Social Security and Medicare.

In short, Gore sought to cast suspicion on Bush's proposal, labeling it an attempt to "privatize" the program, and to claim for himself the mantle of protector of Social Security.

After the convention, however, the Gore campaign invested even fewer advertising resources in Social Security than the Bush campaign. Only one ad sponsored by the Gore campaign and aired between mid-August and early October mentioned Social Security. It was mainly a biographical ad, only touching upon the issue, and it was not aired with great frequency.

ANNOUNCER: 1969. America in turmoil. Al Gore graduates college. His father, a U.S. Senator, opposes the Vietnam War. Al Gore has his doubts but enlists in the Army. When he comes home from Vietnam, the last thing he thinks he'll ever do is enter politics. He starts a family with Tipper, becomes an investigative reporter. Then Al Gore decided that to change what was wrong in America, he had to fight for what was right. He ran for Congress, held some of the first hearings on cleaning up toxic waste, made the environment his cause, broke with his own party to support the Gulf War, fought to reform welfare with work requirements and time limits. His fight now is to ensure that prosperity enriches all our families – not just the few, strengthen Social Security, take on big drug companies to guarantee prescription drugs for seniors, hold schools accountable for results, tax cuts for working families and the middle class. Al Gore – married thirty years, father of four, fighting for us.

Even ignoring the disparity in the attention paid to Social Security within particular ads, the difference in emphasis between the parties is clear. Between the close of the Democratic convention on August 14 and the first presidential debate on October 3, 26 percent of Republican ads mentioned Social Security, while just 8 percent of Democratic ads did so.

A sharp advertising attack on the ground of Social Security was directed at Bush during this period by the AFL-CIO:

STEVE JENNINGS (history teacher, San Antonio, Texas): I didn't expect to get rich when I went into teaching but I did expect to have a decent retirement fund. When George W. Bush first ran he promised not to cut our retirement fund. Then he went and raided it because he wanted to pay for other things. ANNOUNCER: Now, George W. Bush says he'll protect Social Security while pushing a massive tax cut. But studies show Bush's plan would lead to benefit cuts and increase in the retirement age or both.

This ad foreshadowed the Gore campaign's frontal assault launched in October. But it was not aired frequently. Including the ads sponsored by allied organizations only increases to ten the percentage of pro-Gore advertising that mentioned Social Security between the conventions and the debates. At this point, only an allied group, not the Gore campaign itself, appeared to see Social Security as a potentially weak plank in the Bush platform.

The "Free Media"

In October Gore placed Social Security back on the campaign's agenda, launching his own assault on the Bush proposal for reform. The first exchanges of this period reached the electorate through the so-called "free media." Gore returned to his earlier critique, and then refined it, in the presidential debates. Soon after, the conflict made the evening news.

The Debates

With the debates, Gore began to portray the Bush platform as a Trojan horse, a threat to the Social Security system it purported to reform. When, in the first debate, the candidates were invited to specify their differences over Social Security, Gore focused immediately on the drain on the system represented by Governor Bush's stock-market proposal.

I'm also opposed to a plan that diverts one out of every six dollars away from the Social Security trust fund. You know, Social Security is a trust fund that pays the checks this year with the money that's paid into Social Security this year. The governor wants to divert one dollar out of every six dollars off into the stock market, which means that he would drain one trillion dollars out of the Social Security trust fund in this generation, over the next ten years. And Social Security, under that approach, would go bankrupt within this generation.

His leading adviser on this plan actually said that would be OK because then the Social Security trust fund could start borrowing. It would borrow up to three trillion dollars.

Now Social Security has never done that, and I don't think it should do that. I think it should stay in a lockbox, and I'll tell you this: I will veto anything that takes money out of Social Security for privatization or anything else other than Social Security.

Bush's rebuttal reiterated the theme established in his ads: reassurance to the old; the prospect of an investment opportunity for the young. He asked older voters to trust him and assured younger voters that he trusts them.

So for those of you who he wants to scare into the voting booth to vote for him, hear me be loud and clear: A promise made will be a promise kept. And you bet we want to allow younger workers to take some of their own money. See, that's the difference of opinion. The vice president thinks it's the government's money. The payroll taxes are your money. You ought to put it in prudent, safe investments so that one trillion dollars over the next ten years grows to be three trillion dollars. The money stays within the Social Security system. It's a part of the Social Security system. He keeps claiming it's going to be out of

Social Security. It's your money, it's a part of your retirement benefits. It's a fundamental difference between what we believe.

I want you to have your own asset that you can call your own. I want you to have an asset that you can pass on from one generation to the next. I want to get a better rate of return for your own money than the paltry two percent that the current Social Security trust gets today. So Mr. Greenspan missed an opportunity to say there is a third way, and that is to get a better rate of return on the Social Security monies coming into the trust. There's 2.3 trillion dollars of surplus that we can use to make sure younger workers have a Social Security plan in the future, if we're smart, if we trust workers and if we understand the power of the compounding rate of interest.

This provoked Gore to reiterate the initial point, this time making explicit the risk to younger voters of putting contributions into the stock market. To drive home the point, Gore concluded by addressing Bush directly:

Here's the difference. I give a new incentive for younger workers to save their own money and invest their own money, but not at the expense of Social Security; on top of Social Security. My plan is Social Security plus. The governor's plan is Social Security minus. Your future benefits would be cut by the amount that's diverted into the stock market, and if you make bad investments, that's too bad. But even before then, the problem hits, because the money contributed to Social Security this year is an entitlement. That's how it works. And the money is used to pay the benefits for seniors this year. If you cut the amount going in, one dollar out of every six dollars, then you have to cut the value of each check by one dollar out of every six dollars, unless you come up with the money from somewhere else.

I would like to know from the governor – I know we're not supposed to ask each other questions, but I'd be interested in knowing – does that one trillion dollars come from the trust fund, or does it come from the rest of the budget?

Social Security received only passing mention in the second debate, which was devoted to issues of foreign policy, but it was critical to the third one. In responding to the very last question in the last debate, about trust in the political process,[1] the vice president baited the governor in these terms:

[1] The questioner, Thomas Fisher, asked, "My sixth-grade class at St. Claire School wanted to ask, of all these promises you guys are making and all the pledges, will you keep them when you're in office?"

Let me tell you about one of the governor's [promises]. He has promised a trillion dollars out of the Social Security trust fund for young working adults to invest and save on their own, but he's promised seniors that their Social Security benefits will not be cut and he's promised the same trillion dollars to them. So this is the "Show Me" state; reminds the line from the movie, "Show me the money." Which one of those promises will you keep and which will you break, Governor?

Bush took his turn, adding to his previous remarks to younger voters a warning about the long-term financial stability of Social Security without reform and an assurance that investing contributions in the stock market would yield more money for retirement:

...one of my promises is going to be Social Security reform. And you bet we need to take a trillion dollars out of that 2.4 trillion dollar surplus. Now remember, Social Security revenue exceeds expenses up until 2015. People are going to get paid. But if you're a younger worker, if you're younger, you better hope this country thinks differently. Otherwise you're going to be faced with huge payroll taxes or reduced benefits. And you bet we're going to take a trillion dollars of your own money and let you invest it under safe guidelines so you get a better rate of return on the money than the paltry two percent that the federal government gets for you today. That's one of my promises.

Gore returned immediately to his theme, taking another tack to explaining that a worker's contributions are used to pay current retirees, not saved for his or her own retirement:

I'd like to respond to what the governor just said, because the trillion dollars that has been promised to young people has also been promised to older people, and you cannot keep both promises. If you're in your mid-forties, under the governor's plan, Social Security will be bankrupt by the time you retire, if he takes it out of the Social Security trust fund. Under my plan, its solvency will be extended until you're one hundred. Now that is the difference. And the governor may not want to answer that question. He may want to call it a high school debating trick. But let me tell you this. This election is not about debating tricks. It is about your future. The reason Social Security – he says it gets two percent. You know, it's not a bank account that just pays back money that's invested. It's also used to give your mothers and fathers the Social Security checks that they live on. If you take one trillion dollars out of that Social Security trust fund, how are the checks going to be – how are you going to keep faith with the seniors?

So the line of attack was established: Gore maintained that Bush was promising the same massive sum of money to two different groups; the losers in the deception would be current retirees; apart from its substantive policy significance, the proposal cast doubt on Bush's own integrity.

Network News

The debates jump-started network news attention to the topic, according to Figure 7.1. As in earlier chapters, coverage is indexed by the number of statements – in this chapter, however, statements specifically

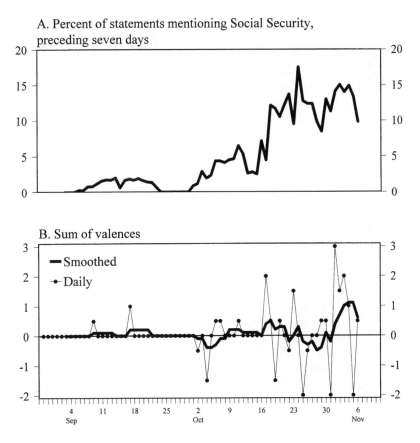

A. Percent of statements mentioning Social Security, preceding seven days

B. Sum of valences

Note: Smoothed by five-day prior moving average.

FIGURE 7.1. Television News Coverage of Social Security Investment in the Stock Market.

on the issue of Social Security. There is a hint that network television started to follow the issue just before the first debate. The debate did move coverage up, however, such that about 5 percent of all campaign-related statements broadcast in the week that followed concerned some aspect of Social Security. That volume of coverage made Social Security quite important but hardly a dominating issue in early October. The third debate, however, induced a further surge in coverage. On the 18th, two days after the debate, the volume of coverage was 12 percent, and coverage continued to climb gradually to the end of the campaign, to a level reached only briefly by a handful of issues during the previous two months.

Gore initially derived no particular direct advantage from increased network attention, according to the bottom panel of Figure 7.1. Coverage following the first debate favored Bush, then slipped back toward balance. The third debate started a period of wide day-to-day swings, as the campaigns alternated attack and rebuttal. In fact, Social Security coverage contributed to some of Al Gore's worst news days of the entire campaign. Some of this was direct reporting of the new negative Gore ads and of the stump rhetoric they provoked from Bush. The NBC report on October 26 was typical of that coverage:

TOM BROKAW, anchor: As for Governor Bush, he had some high-powered help today on the campaign trail and a more pointed commentary on the vice president. NBC's David Gregory is with the vice president tonight in Pittsburgh. David?

DAVID GREGORY (reporting): Well, Tom, making it abundantly clear that the Clinton-Gore scandals of the past eight years will be a major theme in the closing days of this campaign, today Governor Bush does attack Vice President Gore, says he's been a failed leader and Bush promises that if he's elected Americans will once again be able to respect their government. Bush today campaigning in the tough battleground state of Pennsylvania, alongside the popular retired General Colin Powell. And Bush again strongly hints that, if elected, Powell will be a member of his cabinet. Now, today's address focuses on quote, "responsible leadership," and how, on issues like Social Security and Medicare, the Clinton-Gore administration has failed to provide it.

BUSH: They are going out as they came in. Their guide, the nightly polls; their goal, the morning headlines; their legacy, the fruitless search for a legacy.

With two weeks remaining in the campaign, the news about Social Security was more favorable to Bush than Gore.

During the last week, however, Gore got several highly positive news days, three consecutive days as positive on Social Security as any in the campaign. This was mainly a result of the fact that Gore dominated the *NBC Nightly News* for a time each evening from October 30 through November 3. NBC offered both candidates multiple-day interviews with Tom Brokaw. Gore was interviewed live for five nights running, while Bush agreed to appear only once, on tape, effectively conceding several minutes of national news control to his opponent for four nights. All told, Gore drew positive treatment on Social Security, relative to Bush, five of the last six days. His best single day was November 2, when his NBC interview was devoted entirely to the issue, but his message echoed around all three network newsrooms at least two more days. News coverage about Social Security favored one candidate over the other more during the last week than at any other time during the campaign, and it favored Al Gore.

Advertising Attack and Counterattack

Three days after the first debate, on October 6, the Gore campaign began a serious commitment to Social Security themes. The evidence appears in Figure 7.2. Before the 6th, as we have seen, pro-Gore ads

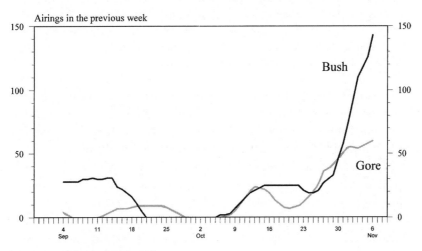

Note: High-volume DMAs only.

FIGURE 7.2. Advertising about Social Security by Sponsor.

mentioning Social Security were rare. In mid-October, in contrast, a resident of a market where advertising was concentrated might have seen twenty-five Gore ads that mentioned Social Security. (Of course, that resident could have seen at least as many Bush ads on the same subject.) The first to air raised the issue in the context of attacking the Bush tax-cut proposal:

ANNOUNCER: The facts on George W. Bush's 1.6 trillion dollar tax-cut promise? Almost half goes to the richest one percent. What trickles down? An average of sixty-two cents a day for most tax payers. Bush gives almost half to the richest one percent, leaving sixty-two cents to trickle down to us. Al Gore builds on a foundation of fiscal discipline. Pay down the nation's debt. Protect Social Security and Medicare. A ten-thousand-dollar-a-year tax deduction for college tuition. Because the middle classes earn more than trickle down.

This ad aired between the first and third debates. After the third debate Gore began to air ads focused exclusively on the Bush proposal for Social Security. One new ad appeared on the 17th, the night of the debate, citing for corroboration a bastion of support for Republican candidates:

ANNOUNCER: What would George W. Bush's plan do to Social Security? He's promising to take a trillion dollars out of Social Security so younger workers can invest in private accounts. Sounds good. The problem is Bush has promised the same money to pay seniors their current benefits. The *Wall Street Journal* shows he can't keep both promises. Which promise is he going to break? George W. Bush. His promises threaten Social Security.

The Gore campaign looked to turn Bush's rhetoric against him. In appealing to seniors to trust him, the Republican had chosen to describe his commitment to maintaining Social Security as a "promise," implicitly contrasting the value of his word with that of Gore's (and Clinton's). "President George W. Bush will keep the promise of Social Security," Bush said in his acceptance speech, and a Bush ad featured that passage of the speech. "A promise made will be a promise kept," Bush said in the first debate. Now the Gore campaign used the word "promise" five times in a thirty-second ad. Like the critique in the debates, Gore's advertising attack targeted more than Bush's policy proposal; it called into question Bush's integrity.

As the volume of advertising ramped up, Gore invoked various sources of expertise. One ad, aired heavily in late October, drew upon academic economists:

ANNOUNCER: Eight Nobel Laureates, top economics experts in America have reviewed George W. Bush's plans. Bush promises the same one trillion dollars of Social Security to younger workers and the elderly at the same time. He uses the surplus on a tax-cut promise, half going to those making over three hundred thousand dollars. Eight Nobel Laureates conclude George W. Bush's promises more than exhaust the surplus, increasing interest rates and the deficit. The Bush Plan does not add up.

Another invoked a former Social Security Commissioner:

BUSH: For those who are retired or near retirement there will be no changes at all in your Social Security.
BALL: My name is Bob Ball, and I was the Social Security Commissioner under three presidents – two Democrats and a Republican. I've looked at Governor Bush's plan. He takes one trillion dollars out of Social Security for savings accounts. But Social Security is counting on that money to pay benefits. His plan simply doesn't add up and would undermine Social Security.

After the third debate, Social Security surfaced in 40 percent of Democratic ads. Social Security was by no means the only theme, of course. Tax cuts carried about the same weight and health care carried even more. But tax cuts and health care were as common early in the campaign as late. The critical thing about Social Security is that it weighed so heavily in Democratic advertising only at the end.

The Republicans responded. The Bush advertising campaign returned to Social Security as a central theme in mid-October and pulled out the stops in the last week. After the third debate, 60 percent of Bush ads mentioned Social Security. And the volume of Republican ads, as we have seen, intensified dramatically. In the last week of the campaign, as a result, a resident of a high-volume media market could have seen over twice as many Bush ads as Gore ads on the issue. In the week leading up to Election Day, the typical station in a high-volume location aired about 140 Social Security spots (Figure 7.2).

In contrast to the ads the Republicans aired early in the campaign, the Bush campaign's strategy on Social Security in the closing weeks was a defensive one. Republican ads now linked the issue to their own well-established character theme. Some of the ads made the link at a fairly abstract level, in terms of the general need to encourage responsibility for one's actions and of the appropriate place for collective and individual action. The primary ad carrying these themes was this one, which went up after the first debate:

BUSH: I believe we need to encourage personal responsibility so people are accountable for their actions. And I believe in government that is responsible to the people. That's the difference in philosophy between my opponent and me. He trusts government, I trust you. I trust you to invest some of your own Social Security money for higher returns. I trust local people to run their own schools. I trust you with some of the budget surplus. We should help people live their lives, but not run them. I'm asking for your vote.

Before this ad went on the air, mentions of the Bush proposal for investment of Social Security contributions in the stock market alluded mainly to higher returns to the fund, an echo both of the policy debate and of younger voters' relatively great exposure to the stock market. Now the language focused on trust.

After the third debate, the Bush advertising, like the Gore advertising, became more aggressive. The general theme of accountability was subordinate to focused attacks on Al Gore that juxtaposed his biography with his pronouncements on this particular issue. The only subtlety in the Bush ad aired most frequently in the last week of the campaign was that it did not actually use the word "lie."

ANNOUNCER: Why does Al Gore say one thing when the truth is another? His attack on Bush's Social Security plan? Exaggerations. The truth? Nonpartisan analysis confirms George Bush's plan sets aside 2.4 trillion dollars to strengthen Social Security. Newspapers say Gore has a problem telling the truth. Now Gore promises smaller government. But Gore's actually proposing three times the new spending President Clinton proposed. Why does Al Gore say one thing when the truth is another?

The last ad introduced into the campaign by the Bush side explicitly referred back to the story that had figured so critically in Gore's drop in the polls in late September.

ANNOUNCER: Remember when Al Gore said his mother-in-law's prescriptions cost more than his dog's? His own maid said the story was made up. Now Al Gore is bending the truth again. The press calls Gore's Social Security attacks nonsense. Governor Bush sets aside 2.4 trillion dollars to strengthen Social Security and pay all benefits.

GORE: There has never been a time in this campaign when I have said something that I know to be untrue. There's never been a time when I have said something untrue.

ANNOUNCER: Really?

These ads, and a handful of others like them, powered much of the dramatic upturn in Social Security advertising at the end of the campaign (Figure 7.2). As Figure 6.6 indicated, Al Gore's personal failings were the centerpiece for almost half of all late Republican plays. Such ads made up 62 percent of all Social Security plays, which in turn dominated the issue landscape. Of *all* Republican plays, these ads represented 40 percent.[2]

Dynamics of Voter Perception

Bush's proposal on Social Security was new to presidential politics. At the campaign's outset, no doubt, few people knew much about it, and many did not know where the candidates stood. Asked in July, prior to the conventions, whether Bush "favors or opposes allowing workers to invest some of their Social Security contributions in the stock market," one quarter of the electorate did not know, and one fifth thought he opposed the plan – notwithstanding the advertising that the Bush campaign already had done. Gore was even further out of focus, perhaps in part because he himself was proposing a scheme for Social Security involving private investment, just not one that diverted money from the current flow of contributions. One quarter did not know Gore's position, and one third believed Gore favored Bush's plan.

Such circumstances are fertile ground for cognitive bias of the sort originally discovered in the seminal study of the 1948 election. Lazarsfeld and his Columbia School colleagues (Berelson et al. 1954) found during that campaign that large numbers of voters whose own view of the Taft-Hartley Act was at odds with that of their party's candidate systematically misconstrued the candidate's position, believing him instead to hold the view they themselves held. This variant of cognitive bias, rooted in the impulse to minimize the psychological tension triggered by recognizing disagreement with a candidate one supports, has come to be called *projection* (Brody and Page, 1972).

---

[2] Social Security mentions outnumber Gore mentions by about 1.6:1, as comparison of the Figures 7.2 and 6.6 indicates. But essentially every Republican spot that mentioned Gore was also a Social Security spot.

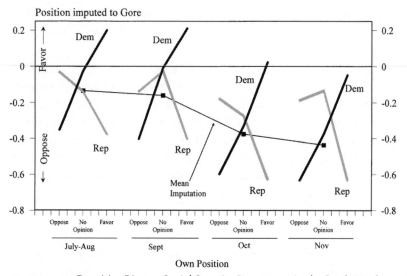

FIGURE 7.3. Cognitive Bias on Social Security Investment in the Stock Market.

Projection was rife in the public's perceptions of Gore's position on Social Security in the summer of 2000. Figure 7.3 presents the position attributed to Gore, conditional on respondents' own positions on the issue and their party identification, in four periods. For each party identification group and in each time period, imputations to Gore operated to minimize cognitive tension. Democrats tended to project their own position onto Gore: those who opposed allowing private investment of Social Security contributions tended to see Gore as opposing the proposal as well, while those who favored the proposal believed that Gore also favored it. Republicans, in contrast, emphasized the difference between themselves and Gore: those who opposed their own candidate's proposal were far less likely than those who supported it to believe that Gore opposed it; they were biased toward reversing the candidates' positions. The pattern, in short, echoes the Columbia studies of social bias in cognition. With Gore in 2000 as with Harry Truman in 1948, perceptions display evidence of assimilation or contrast, depending up the perceiver's party. Democrats assimilate their candidate to their position even when they disagree with him. Republicans assert the contrast with Gore even when they favor his position. What is more, the pattern never disappears; the bias is as strong at the end of the campaign as at the beginning.

Put into motion, the pervasiveness of cognitive bias provides a psychological foundation for the "minimal effects" view of political campaigns. To the extent that the public systematically misperceives the campaign, believing their party's candidate to agree with them regardless of what the candidate says and regardless of their own position, to that extent the scope for the campaign to affect perceptions and ultimately vote intentions will be limited. To the extent that it conserves long-standing tendencies, cognitive bias will blunt campaign dynamics.

But cognitive bias does not foreclose campaign effects altogether. Democrats and Republicans, supporters and opponents of the Bush proposal – all were more likely on average in October and November than earlier to see that Gore opposed the Bush proposal. Figure 7.3 also plots the average position attributed to Gore by the electorate as a whole; this is the line labeled "mean imputation." Even as the pattern of assimilation and contrast remained strong, many more people perceived Gore's position correctly at the end of the campaign than at the beginning.

The decisive moment in cognition was the first debate. Figure 7.4 traces movement in perceptions of the candidates' positions over the campaign. Gore was already moving further to the opposition side

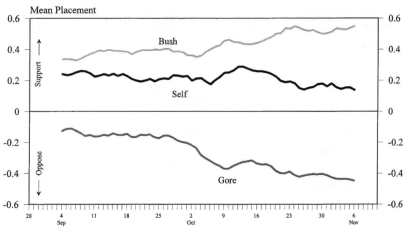

Note: Smoothed by seven-day prior moving averages.

FIGURE 7.4. Candidate and Voter Positions on Social Security Investment in the Stock Market.

in the public's perception prior to that date – October 3 – but the days immediately after the debate saw the swiftest shift. Of the total movement in Gore's perceived location, about two-thirds took place in the week immediately following the first debate. There appears to have been drift toward misperception between the second and third debates. But the third debate halted the drift, and further clarification occurred in the last month, as the ad campaigns became furious. October also was critical to perceptions of Bush. His support for the plan was always more clearly perceived than Gore's opposition, but Bush's position, too, became clearer to the electorate in October, especially after the first debate. The total shift toward clarity for Bush was about two-thirds that for Gore; about half the total shift for Bush was induced by the first debate.

Thus the events and initiatives of the late campaign dramatically clarified the stakes in the election. The critical moments were the debates, where Gore made a point of dramatizing his difference with Bush. This is not to say that it is watching the debates by itself that altered the public's perceptions; too few people actually watched the debates for direct exposure alone to have brought upon shifts on this scale. But the positions voiced in the debates reverberated through the news, where the information was accessible to much larger numbers. In general, it does not appear that the ad onslaught was all that vital to the clarification of the candidates' positions. The early advertising on the subject of Social Security predated the period of greatest clarification, and the explosion of advertising in late October occurred after the learning had taken place. To some extent, the ad campaigns were as much symptom as cause: They indicated the shift in the overall rhetorical posture of each campaign. Had the ads not been aired in the last three weeks, however, it may be that many voters would have forgotten the information brought out by the debates. This may be the implication of the temporary reversal in the clarification of the candidates' positions between the first and third debates; the second debate, on foreign policy, did not give Gore a chance to reiterate the difference between sides, and the information about Social Security was not reinforced by much advertising. Taken together, however, the forces of the 2000 campaign helped to teach the public where both candidates stood on the issue of investing Social Security contributions in the stock market.

Dynamics of Voter Opinion

What the public learned from the campaign about where the candidate's stood need not have been good news for Gore, because Bush's proposal was quite popular. In July, 58 percent favored allowing workers to invest some of their Social Security contributions in the stock market, and just 34 percent opposed the idea. If the only effect of Gore's attack had been to inform the electorate that he opposed it, the campaign's decision to mount the attack could only have lost him votes, not won them. For the strategy to work, the Gore campaign needed not only to convey to the public their candidate's position, but also to educate the public about the issue. Gore needed to persuade the electorate – a substantial fraction of it, at least – to adopt his position.

In the electorate as a whole, Gore's efforts at persuasion met with quite modest success. In fact, the initial movement in the electorate's own position, following the first debate, was toward Bush's position, not Gore's (Figure 7.4). From mid-October onward, however, the electorate moved perceptibly and persistently, if not dramatically, away from Bush's proposal. From Labor Day to Election Day, the public as a whole grew less supportive of Bush's plan for Social Security by 0.1 on the scale from -1 to 1.

Treating the electorate as a whole masks the fact that Gore's success was highly conditional. Figure 7.5 shows the trajectories of opinion separately for Republicans, Democrats, and Independents. The campaign did not move Republican identifiers toward Gore's position at all, but toward Bush's. Most of this shift had occurred by mid-October, mainly as undecided Republicans learned the Republican position. After the last debate there was some drift among Republicans toward Gore's position, but it was entirely reversed in the last week.

Like Republicans, but to a much greater extent, Democrats moved toward their own candidate's position. Nearly all of the change among Democrats was accomplished in the two and a half weeks between the final debate and Election Day: A slight plurality of Democrats favored the Bush proposal in mid-October, but a sizeable plurality opposed the proposal in early November. Democrats exhibited nothing like the unanimity of Republicans on the other side. But the campaign clearly did alter the views of many Democrats on Bush's Social Security proposal. For explaining the dynamics of vote intentions in the last weeks

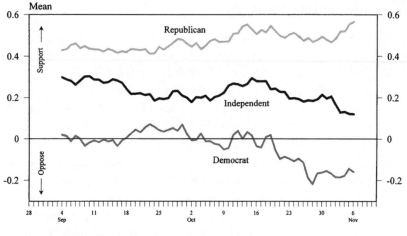

Note: Smoothed by nine-day prior moving averages.

FIGURE 7.5. Voter Positions on Social Security Investment in the Stock Market by Party Identification.

of the campaign, in any case, the critical features are the direction and magnitude of the change.

The campaign encouraged partisans on both sides, then, to adopt the policy position of their party's candidate. This movement toward conformity with predispositions has been termed *self-persuasion* (Brody and Page, 1972). Its character, like projection, is essentially conservative: it contributes to election outcomes that reproduce the balance of partisanship in the electorate. But self-persuasion is not the only process through which the preferences of the electorate on Social Security policy were altered by the campaign, for over the last three weeks of the campaign Independents also moved toward Gore's position. On Election Day a plurality of Independents continued to support the Bush proposal. And Independents did not move as swiftly as Democrats after the last debate; their largest single shift occurred in the last week. But their overall shift from mid-October to the end rivaled that exhibited by Democrats. The evidence seems clear that the Gore campaign in the closing weeks succeeded in persuading a substantial fraction of the critical, uncommitted portion of the electorate to reject the Bush proposal on Social Security.

Combining the electorate's preferences on Social Security with their perceptions of the candidates' positions yields a clearer picture of the

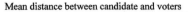
Mean distance between candidate and voters

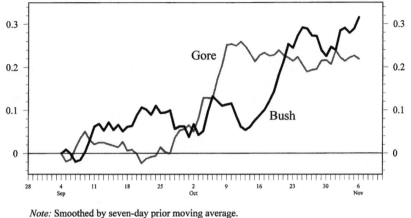

Note: Smoothed by seven-day prior moving average.

FIGURE 7.6. Dynamics of Candidate Distances on Social Security.

timing of the changes the campaign induced in the policy distances between the candidates and the public. Figure 7.6 traces the distances between respondents' and candidates' positions, emphasizing the dynamic pattern at the expense of the cross-sectional one by scaling the lines for both candidates to start at the same point. The initial clarification of Gore's position, induced by the first debate, mainly dramatized to many that on Social Security Gore was further from them than they had thought. The first debate increased the distance between Gore and the electorate by 0.25 points on a −1, +1 scale. In mid-October, Bush was no worse off than he had been in mid-September. Gore, in contrast, was much worse off, as he had succeeded only in highlighting how far he was from the center of opinion.

Following the last debate, however, dynamics reversed. The gap for Bush expanded greatly while the gap between Gore remained constant or even narrowed slightly. As we have seen, the distance between Bush and the electorate grew for two reasons. Bush's own position became clear to yet more people, not all of whom approved it. And the number sharing his position dropped. Gore finally succeeded in dragging the center toward his position. The gap between Gore and the center of the electorate remained larger in an absolute sense, as a majority of the public still favored the Bush position. Dynamically speaking, however, Gore's gambit succeeded. Relative to the eve of the last debate, support for his position grew.

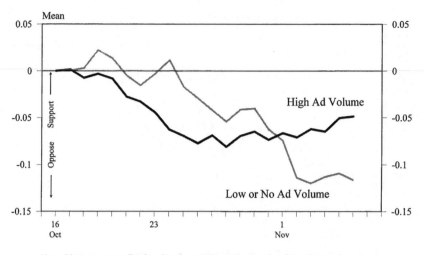

Note: Lines are normalized to October 16. Smoothed by nine-day prior moving average.

FIGURE 7.7. Voter Positions on Social Security Investment in the Stock Market by Ad Volume in DMA.

Shifts in voters' opinions on Social Security did not occur in equal measure across the entire electorate, however, and the disparity under-scores the importance of advertising in explaining the ultimate outcome of the 2000 election. Figure 7.7 controls for potential exposure to campaign advertising during the period of critical shifts in opinion, from the last debate to the end of the campaign, classifying respondents according to the volume of advertising aired in their media market in the last week.[3] For the first ten days following the last debate, as the network news came to focus on Social Security and two campaigns were airing roughly equal volumes of advertising, the movement to-ward Gore's position was quite comparable in timing and distance in low- and high-volume markets. But on October 28, as the Bush campaign sharply ramped up its outlays on Social Security ads (Figure 7.2), the trajectories in high- and low-volume markets diverged. Outside the ad battleground, opinion continued to move generally in Gore's direction. Inside the ad battleground – that is, in the media markets that saw heavy advertising, twice as much of it pro-Bush as pro-Gore – the

---

[3] The smoothing function is now a nine-day prior moving average, as the issue questions were asked of half samples only, and these half samples are split further roughly in half.

movement of opinion on Social Security was reversed, turning back toward Bush's position. Over the last ten days of the campaign, about two-thirds of the postdebate shift toward Gore's position was erased in the high-volume markets.

The divergence between markets inside and outside the battleground makes a *prima facie* case for the influence of advertising on opinion, even in the late stages of a campaign, when the balance of advertising resources heavily favors one side over the other. The Bush campaign's advertising blitz in the last ten days drew some voters back to the Bush position on Social Security. And because the strategy for allocating advertising resources dictates that advertising be concentrated on competitive markets, the voters drawn back to the Bush position lived in the markets that mattered most: markets in the states where the race was closest.

Impact on the Vote

As Social Security opinion moved, so did it become more important to the vote. Figure 7.8 takes coefficients from Table A6.1 and converts them into an estimated effect on Gore's share of an opinion shift from neutrality on the Bush plan to outright opposition. As in earlier simulations, a wide swath of other considerations is controlled and the estimated shift in probability applies to respondents otherwise

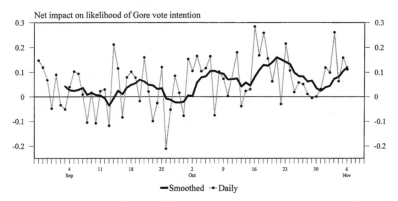

Note: Entries are differences in likelihood induced by a shift from neutrality to opposition to Social Security investment in the stock market. Smoothed by seven-day prior moving average.

FIGURE 7.8. Dynamics of the Impact of Voter Positions on Social Security.

uncommitted to a side. As for simulations earlier in this book, both the daily estimate and a smoothed value appear.[4]

Before the debates, the issue had essentially no impact on vote intentions. Positive days outnumber negative ones, but the smoothed line is only barely above the zero-impact horizon. The issue's impact jumped after the first debate, receded slightly, then jumped again after the last debate. This exactly tracks the content of each debate, which saw a big emphasis on Social Security in the first, none in the second, and an even bigger emphasis in the third. At the peak, a shift from neutral to one side would shift the likelihood of a Gore vote intention by 0.3 (daily tracking) or 0.16 (smoothed tracking), either way a huge movement.

But the impact of the issue then declined. By the beginning of the campaign's last week, the estimated effect was as small as on most days before October. As with evidence in Figure 7.4 for perceptions of the candidates and, to a weaker extent, with the evidence in Figure 7.5 for voters' own positions, the pattern testifies to the power of the debates. But where debates permanently altered perceptions and positions, debates' priming of the issue did not last. The power of Social Security as a consideration in candidate choice seemed greatest right after a debate focused on the question. But absent reinforcement of the debate's message, the impact of the issue faded. Citizens' opinions did not move back to the predebate position, nor did they forget where candidates stand. They just became less likely to make the link between end and means.

In the last week, however, Social Security came back to the fore. Between October 31 and November 1, the issue-vote link began to strengthen. It may have peaked on the 3rd, but the last six readings are all clearly positive and the average reading across those six is slightly higher than that indicated for the last day, November 6. It seems safe to conclude that opinion on George W. Bush's plan for Social Security was as important at the end as at all but one earlier point in the campaign, the days just after the third debate. On the eve of the election, a shift

---

[4] With only half samples available for issue estimations, smoothing is by seven-day prior moving average, rather than the usual five-days. The list of independent variables had to be reduced relative to the full model of Table A6.1. The "Black" variable was dropped as some days had no African-American respondents or, more often, none who expressed an intention to vote for Bush. Party identification and liberal-conservative ideology were entered as interval variables with three categories, rather than as dummy variables for sides.

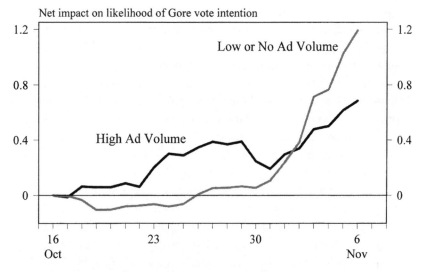

Net impact on likelihood of Gore vote intention

FIGURE 7.9. Effect of Persuasion and Priming on Change in Gore Share of Vote Intentions by Ad Volume.

Note: Entries are differences in likelihood induced by actual net changes both in opinion on Social Security and in estimated impact. Smoothed by nine-day prior moving average.

from neutrality on the Bush proposal to opposition was worth about 0.12 in the likelihood of a Gore vote, other things equal.

The shift implicit in the analysis to this point is hypothetical. At any given moment, in fact, such a conversion from neutrality to opposition to the Bush plan is quite unlikely. But the late campaign featured not just priming of the issue-vote link but also persuasion on the issue. Figure 7.9 attempts to map actual movement in Social Security opinion (Figure 7.7) through the dynamic pattern of impact (Figure 7.8). The mapping spans the period from the last debate to the end, the vital period of pro-Gore opinion movement. It shows an estimated shift in the likelihood of support for Gore relative to support for Bush from a starting point of October 16.[5] Note that the priming component

---

[5] Each day's mean from the smoothed tracking of Figure 7.7 was entered as the value for the Social Security variable in multinomial logistic regression and a notional Gore vote probability relative to Bush was calculated using that day's coefficients from the estimations underlying Figure 7.8. The probabilities were further smoothed and then normalized to the 12 October starting value. Of course, no respondent actually has the mean value. Real values are always −1, 0, or +1. The estimation would yield the same results, however, if we did separate estimations for each of the categories and merged the results weighted for each category's daily share.

underlying the figure distinguishes days from each other but not high-volume DMAs from low-volume ones. We attempted to rerun the exercise in Figure 7.8 separately for high- and low-ad volume places, but estimates were just too unstable to report. The difference between DMAs rests mainly on the persuasion component indicated by Figure 7.7, in any case. And the whole exercise is mainly indicative, to convey a sense of the likely timing and plausible magnitudes of effect.

The numbers that come out of this simulation may seem small, but so was Gore's total recovery – although it was ultimately critical, given the closeness of the election. All told, the combination of persuasion and priming may have been worth over one percentage point in Gore's share of the popular vote in media markets that saw little advertising. All of this occurred during the last two weeks of the campaign, but over those weeks Gore's gains were remarkably consistent in the markets where few ads were aired. More telling, from our perspective, is the difference due to advertising. Over the first ten days following the last debate, Gore gained even more ground in the markets where advertising was heaviest than in those where advertising was light. Over the last ten days of the campaign, however, when the Bush advantage in ads was at its peak, the Gore advance was repelled.

Conclusions

From the beginning of the general-election campaign – even before, in some sense – George W. Bush attempted to position himself, perceptually speaking, close to the center of the electorate on key domestic policy questions. He did so by adopting and emphasizing positions in domains traditionally "owned" by Democrats. Late in the campaign, when Al Gore looked for opportunities to regain the position he had lost in September, he refocused his rhetoric on pushing voters' perceptions of Bush back to the right. Gore won back a critical slice of voters by playing a New Deal card about the defense of Social Security. The particular card was a hard one to play, for it required attacking a plan that Bush had styled as saving the program, not undermining it. Making the point required Gore to discuss complex questions, or at least to find simple examples to make the point. At first, he succeeded in doing little more than teach voters how far apart he and most of them were. At the end, however, he did move opinion as well as prime the issue, and this helped him pull out a plurality of the popular vote. Unfortunately for Gore, these processes worked most effectively in states that were already precommitted to one candidate or the other. In closely competitive states, the Bush campaign's advertising on this vital issue completely swamped Gore's. At the end, a voter in the battleground was two-and-a-half times as likely to encounter a Bush ad on Social Security as a Gore one. This blocked Gore's attempts at persuasion on the issue. For this reason he lost the vote in the Electoral College.

The narrative raises at least two theoretical questions worthy of further consideration. One is whether the phenomenon that we repeatedly refer to as priming really was priming, or whether the process was mainly learning. To the extent that it was really learning, then the event was mainly an exercise in enlightenment, in Gelman and King's (1993) sense. To the extent that it was really priming, then the event seems more susceptible to a strategic interpretation. The second question concerns the direction of persuasion. No persuasion ran contrary to predisposition, not in the aggregate at least. This seems like a limitation on the event's strategic potential. Or is it?

To the extent that Gore helped himself by emphasizing Social Security, was the effect one of *priming* or *learning*? The distinction may be murky, for learning can be the result of priming, of sheer repetition of a candidate's argument. But if learning about an issue does result from priming and if the link between that issue and the vote strengthens, then the priming component in the story, although empirically critical, is normatively incidental. The critical fact is that voters did learn about, and thus were enabled to act on a means-ends relationship. It is clear that respondents on balance improved their cognition of the candidates' positions on the very question candidates emphasized. In part, no doubt, this is a consequence of the novelty, at least in terms of presidential elections, of Bush's proposal to allow workers to invest some of their Social Security contributions in the stock market; in many other issue areas – too many to show the evidence here – the electorate learned little about where the candidates stood.[6]

---

[6] One other exception is perception of Gore's position on the death penalty. A majority of respondents began by imputing opposition to Gore. This remained the case until the last debate, when Gore made clear his support for the death penalty. Immediately, the balance of perception shifted modestly but clearly toward accuracy.

Improvement in perception of candidates' positions occurred notwithstanding persistence of self-directed cognitive bias, the sort of bias that early on formed part of the "minimal effects" trope. The bias prevented neither learning of positions nor persuasion contingent on that learning. As learning and persuasion occurred, the bias – although undiminished in impact among those susceptible to it – became less important in the aggregate, for the number susceptible to it shrank. And there was a rough correspondence between the time path of this learning and the growth in impact from Social Security opinion. The first learning gains came after the first debate, and so did the first gain in impact from opinion. The second gain in learning and impact came after the third debate. Thus far, then, the process is best thought of as one of enlightenment: As the perceived policy distance between the candidates grows, so should the impact of the policy dimension also grow.

But gains in awareness of candidates were neither necessary nor sufficient for a policy question to grow or remain important. Awareness of candidates' positions, once enhanced, did not evanesce much. But the impact that seemed to flow from that enhanced awareness did shrink. As each debate receded from memory, the opinion-vote link shrank considerably. Voters could still call up candidates' positions but they no longer connected them to the vote. At the end, they reconnected them, but not because of late gains in learning. There was relatively little net gain in awareness after the last debate. Citizens reinstituted the connection, we must infer, because the campaigns – Gore's campaign, at least – urged them to. There appears to be a role for simple weight of emphasis, quite apart from any impact that emphasis might have on awareness. Well understood differences can lie dormant.

The notion that campaign effects are thwarted by voters' predispositions presumes that everybody has one. This seems implausible in light of the chronically weak opinionation in the electorate, of the presence of many Independents and ideological moderates, and of the general weakness of the system's social-structural foundation. In the end, Gore moved opinion among Independents as much as he did opinion among partisans. It took longer for Independents to get his message (another aspect of the whole process' highly contingent nature), but when they ultimately did, their movement was the vital final step in the reconstitution of Gore's popular plurality. Obviously, much can depend on just how many moderates or Independents there really are. But opinion movement in this group is not plausibly described as motivated self-persuasion.

Among partisans, little persuasion on the Social Security issue occurred that was contrary to predisposition. Democrats moved toward Gore's position on Social Security; Republicans did not. The campaign resolved cognitive tension by moving one set of respondents toward an issue position consistent with their party identification. In a sense, this represents polarization on a "fundamental," to go back to the language of Chapter 3. The process has all the flavor of cognitive dissonance reduction, where attitude change follows, rather than directs, behavioral commitment. All this said, the attitude change was clearly necessary for some respondents to bring behavioral intention in line with the long-standing party preference. Moreover, it is not hard to imagine Gore's attempt at persuasion failing, such that a critical fraction of Democrats would have remained drawn to Bush. The Social Security issue was complex and Gore struggled to find the language to express his objections to Bush's proposal. It is an entirely plausible counterfactual that Gore would choose not to dramatize the difference between Bush and himself, but to minimize it. Gore did, after all, have a Social Security–stock market plan of his own. And what if there had been no third debate, thus no further occasion for Gore to reinforce his message on Social Security (until the last week at least)? The tracking of cognition suggests that the third debate was a vital extra step in Gore's priming and persuasive efforts. Strategically speaking, the first debate would not have sufficed. So even to the extent that *self*-persuasion, in Brody's and Page's (1972) sense, dominated, the actual mechanics of the process were arduous, far from guaranteed of their result. The outcome of the 2000 election was contingent upon the campaigns' strategic choices.

8

Conclusions

The degree of contingency and the scope for rhetoric in elections seem greater than allowed by most mainstream political science research. This is true even though most propositions in the mainstream about the impact of "fundamentals," of forces outside the grip of campaigns, are also true. Sophisticated analyses of fundamental forces concede that real campaign dynamics exist, that movement in vote intention is not just "error" ultimately banished as individuals find their way to predetermined positions. But the standing political science claim is that, by Election Day, these dynamics deliver – indeed, are necessary to deliver – a highly predictable result. The dynamics do not alter the course of history. For 2000 at least, we see the opposite: The power of fundamentals did not block the operation of highly contingent forces of strategic play and counter play. These contingent forces were more than just the midwives of a history whose causal source lay elsewhere. They also made the history.

Our claim has three parts. The first is about "fundamentals," about how Al Gore's access to some fundamental considerations was blocked even as George W. Bush moved to take away Gore's advantage in others. The second is that the divergence between the popular vote and the Electoral vote was no accident; it reflected a divergence between the campaigns. Third, strategic deployment of resources is critical at the margin, and an even balance in resources and skill cannot be taken for granted.

The outcome should never have been so close. The fundamental forces in play should have handed Al Gore a comfortable victory. Although sociodemographic, partisan, and ideological factors were closely balanced, the economy seemed robust. But the good news for Gore about the economy was neutralized by bad news about another aspect of the previous administration, Bill Clinton's moral failings. Character flaws became a theme in evaluation of Al Gore himself. At the same time, George W. Bush may have succeeded in making himself seem more centrist than his Republican predecessors and so reduced Gore's advantage on issues. On Social Security in particular, Bush was the first Republican ever to make a structural proposal that won majority approval. Gore was never able to overturn that majority but he ultimately reduced it enough to win the popular vote.

But George W. Bush won the Electoral College. Gore carried the popular vote because in the final weeks he won the news war. Bush won the Electoral College because in the same period he won the ad war. Through the debates and, finally, through network news, Gore succeeded in getting his attack on Bush's plan for Social Security heard by a key segment of the electorate. In places that saw few or no ads, Al Gore won voters back. But in places that saw large volumes of ads, the opposite was true. Gore lost ground and Bush gained ground in those places because the news message that favored Gore on Social Security was overwhelmed by ads that mainly favored the Bush position.

Ads favored the Bush position because money talks. In the last week, the Republican campaign aired many more ads than the Democratic campaign. This was in part because pro-Bush forces had more resources all along, but also because the Bush side husbanded its resources and saved them for deployment when it mattered most in 2000, at the end. Moreover, the Bush side recognized that Gore was gaining ground on the Social Security issue and moved to thwart him. They concentrated their ads on the issue, mainly to attack Gore's credibility on the message. Although Gore chose this ground to make his comeback – and in the domain of rhetoric maneuvered deftly – the Social Security messages that actually got repeated *ad infinitum* originated with the Bush campaign.

These are bold claims, and highly general ones. To get to them, we had to wind a course through thickets of data and analysis. Specific, subsidiary points were necessary to underpin the validity of the general arguments. At the same time, the claims raise other questions about elections themselves and about possibilities for further analysis.

Recapitulation in Detail

The Shape of Vote Dynamics
The first point where the struggle between necessity and contingency surfaces is in the ultimate dependent variable, the vote. The total picture of vote dynamics is a complicated overlay of quite evanescent shifts, of systematic patterns that keep candidates' shares within bounds and ultimately narrow the race, on one hand, and of shifts that endure and mark off true phases, on the other. That phases exist is one indicator of electoral contingency. If one side can move the basic terms of competition in its favor, the other cannot assume that autonomic forces will restore the earlier pattern. The disadvantaged side needs to make a strategic move of its own, with no guarantee of success. Although the amplitude of vote swings seems to shrink toward the end of the campaign, the shrinkage is not smooth. Apart from the discontinuity after the conventions, it may even be an illusion. There is little evidence that gaps between key political groups widen as the campaign progresses. Some gaps are wide from the start, but only for a few group differences was there much further widening. And the width of initial gaps did not much inhibit short-term movement in vote intention. If a candidate's share grew (or shrank) on one side of a gap, it tended to grow (or shrink) on the other side as well. Groups in the center were the most malleable of all, unsurprisingly. The existence of a sizeable, mobile middle is itself an important facilitator of campaign effects.

Allocation of Resources
Since one element of electoral fundamentals is geography, mapping this geography – identifying the locations that will be critical to victory or defeat in the Electoral College – is a test of campaign skill. Both sides benefit from the geographic pattern's stability and both find their way to competitive places with roughly equal efficiency. Allocation in space is not the only challenge, however. So is the allocation of resources over time. The balance of spending affects vote shares at the margin and the balance that counts, at least in 2000, is the one in the current week.

By implication, spending in the week immediately before Election Day is most critical of all. But a party cannot spend only at the end, lest it allow itself to fall too far behind. The task, in short, is an optimization problem. Solving it is an opportunity for skill – and for mistakes. The Gore campaign may have spent too much too soon.

Candidates also work the news media. Indeed, their appearances on the stump and many of their ads are designed more to affect the content of news coverage than to persuade or mobilize the potential voters who actually see the candidate or the ad. This is true even for debates, notwithstanding the size of their audiences. How television news treated each candidate did seem to matter, although effects are not easy to pin down. But if broadcast news is "free" for campaigners and is credible for many citizens, its effect is arguably *too* pervasive. It moves votes in places that are not pivotal in the Electoral College, yet in the pivotal places its impact can be blocked by the sheer weight of ads.

The Burden of Recent History

The area that has been most often characterized as a domain of necessity, the impact of the economy, also stands revealed as subject to contingency. Both Gelman and King (1993) and Campbell (2000) argue that the campaign is necessary to prime fundamentals, with the economy as a case in point. The heart of the standard claim is that one side or the other will always have a stake in priming the economy, and each side will know who that is: the in-party in good times, the out-party in bad times. The 2000 election may be the exception that proves the rule. Neither side mentioned the economy, and its effect seemed to evaporate at the end, to Al Gore's disadvantage. Whether or not one accepts the claim about shrinkage of economic impact, there is no denying that Al Gore failed to prime the economy as an electoral issue.

Gore may have feared that priming the economy would call up memories of Bill Clinton. On standard retrospective voting models, however, this too ought to have been a good thing. Clinton's popularity by the regularly cited Gallup indicator was very high. But the standard indicator did not capture Clinton's standing as a human being. Judgment on Clinton's person was highly negative and in this respect he was a drag on the Gore-Lieberman ticket. It appears, then, that voters reach beyond judgments of managerial or political competence, and also judge a President's character. This may seem commonsensical, but it lies outside forecasting models. A candidate who clearly would benefit, other things equal, from taking credit for the economy may be blocked in his practical ability to do so. As an electoral consideration, the economy is thus not automatically available.

Executive Fitness and Interpretive Credibility

Character judgments also apply to a candidate, whether or not that person is an incumbent. Certainly, reevaluation of Al Gore's character was the most dramatic single shift in the 2000 campaign. The shift in character perception marked the transition from the first phase, with Gore ahead, to the second phase, with Gore fighting for his life. This is as far from the world of "fundamentals" as it is possible to imagine. Very few voters would ever have met Al Gore. Very few would have any basis for direct, personal assessment of the man. For almost every citizen, evaluation of the Democratic nominee would depend on the frame placed around him. Would he get to frame himself, or would the task fall to the Bush campaign? The same question applies to George W. Bush himself, obviously.

If the language of framing takes us across the disciplinary aisle, to the study of political communication, it also takes us to a place where rhetorical skill is critical. Mainstream political science models of campaigns posit that skill – like other resources – is roughly evenly balanced between sides. Evidence from 2000 calls this assumption about skill into question.[1] Our reading of the Bush campaign is that it found a rhetoric that worked, where Al Gore's campaign, for the most part, did not. The Bush campaign deployed a modest investment in character attacks to create a frame that it then handed to the news media. Al Gore no doubt assisted his opponents by, for example, careless storytelling before the glare of television cameras in the first debate, but that too goes to questions of skill.

Not only are candidate traits a field for potential framing effects, they also perfectly illustrate an electorally-relevant consideration that

---

[1] In this, 2000 may recapitulate 1988. The 1988 result is the largest residual in forecasting models, a point made by Fiorina et al. (2003). All models forecast a Republican victory but none predicted so one-sided a win.

stands outside the basic logic of mainstream models. In those models, part of the reason the economy is important is that it is a *valence* factor. Voters act as if economic growth is unequivocally good; the only question is how much growth has occurred. Variation in economic growth then cuts through pre-existing electoral forces, and so is a powerful source of inter-election shifts. But the economy is practically the only valence factor that forecasting models admit. (Because they are forecasting models, it is practically the only one they *can* admit.) The rest of the action among fundamentals is *positional*: each question has sides, the campaign moves voters to the "correct" side, and such movement is largely offsetting. This simply cannot be true of voters' perceptions of candidates. Of course, candidate perception is infused with partisan and ideological bias. And a campaign can reinforce this bias; the 2000 one certainly did. But bias in perception of candidate personality is just that, bias. As such, it is rather like error. Any trait that a candidate might possess is in itself either good for everybody or bad for everybody; it cannot be good for some and bad for others. In the face of a sufficiently powerful signal, even voters disposed to the candidate may be given pause. This clearly happened in 2000, and when it did, the impact was critical, as the effect of any valence factor should be.

The Battle for the Center

Issues are inherently positional. Policy questions have at least two sides, which in turn can align with ongoing party and ideological coalitions. So the domain of issues is also, potentially, a domain of polarization along pre-existing lines. To the extent that issue polarization – the widening of gaps between groups on opposite sides of a question – occurs, scope for major dynamic induction will be limited, as shifts will be offsetting.

But why should we expect any issue polarization in a campaign? The image of choice that currently dominates rational-actor modeling of elections implies that campaigns should, if anything, reduce issue polarization and so expand the scope for net shifts in vote intention. On this view, voters choose the candidate closest to them on key issues regardless of whether that candidate is to voter's left or right; voters choose, that is, on the basis of simple "proximity." As a result, the vote-maximizing issue or ideological location for each candidate in two-candidate competition is that of the median voter on the dimension, that is, the same location for each party (Downs, 1957). Under these conditions, with the candidates competing for the same ground, issue polarization seems improbable.

Theory can also be mobilized for the opposite expectation, however. This includes modifications to the standard Downsian model to take into account activists (Aldrich, 1983) or fear of invasion from an ideological flank (Palfrey, 1984) as well the more wholesale reconceptualization associated with "directional" theory (Rabinowitz and Macdonald, 1989). Moreover, all this theorizing assumes that candidates talk only about themselves. But candidates talk about each other, and sometimes one candidate will talk about a second candidate's representation of the first candidate's issue positions. When a candidate talks about the other side, the intent is to widen perceived policy gaps.

The 2000 campaign mainly featured a struggle for the center, but it also illustrates how difficult and convoluted that struggle can be. Every one of the possibilities just canvassed in theories of party location found a correspondence in candidates' actual behavior. The Bush side entered with what strikes us as a workably centrist strategy. On Social Security, the Bush plan was presented as saving the system, not as affronting its basic legitimacy. On prescription drugs, the Bush plan certainly had a Republican flavor in its reliance on private insurers but the mere fact that the plan existed was a centrist move. It signaled an un-Republican willingness to spend public money on the welfare state. The Gore side's populist rhetoric may in one sense have rekindled class war but the rhetoric attempted to place the overwhelming majority of citizens on one side of that war. Besides, Gore deployed the rhetoric as much to characterize Bush as to place himself. As Chapter 7 shows, Gore spent much of the campaign trying to push perception of Bush to the right. As Gore gained traction in this effort, the Bush campaign pushed back. It did so by interweaving issue substance with claims about personality, in particular about Gore's credibility. If Gore lied about the Internet or about his mother-in-law, why should anybody believe his claims about the Bush plan for Social Security?

In sum, there is no satisfactory master theory that predicts what candidates will actually do. Theory has been mobilized for competing predictions and it is not hard to imagine other complications. All of the possibilities seem to have been realized in 2000. The theoretical field is, in a word, muddy. In this respect, theory reflects history.[2]

The Requirement for Skill

Narratives and theory that plausibly combine centrist and non-centrist strategies describe a landscape on which strategic and rhetorical skill is at a premium. The guidebooks give contradictory directions. Candidates must develop sensitive search mechanisms and learn to operate in a "fog of war." Skill is necessary in the deployment of resources, in confronting the recent past, in framing the presentation of personality, and in navigating the issue terrain. Mainstream electoral research presumes that skill is in adequate supply for each side. The challenges are presumed to be part of common knowledge in the community of consultants and advisors. Each side knows its high cards, knows when to play them, and has time to react to the other side.

In fact, this is all supposition. The supposition is driven, we suspect, by the recurring success of the simple forecasting model.[3] The failure of the forecast in 2000 should be humbling. But moving beyond supposition to look closely at the strategic landscape, at the deployment of resources, and at the structure of perception and opinion is also humbling. The task before each candidate was daunting. George W. Bush had to overcome a dark legacy of 1990s Republican rhetoric that failed in the Presidential context and looked to be failing in the Congressional one. For all his advantages, Bush was the product of a weak-governor system and had a short resumé. Al Gore, although positioned in principle to benefit from the robust economy, was burdened by the moral failings of his otherwise remarkably competent predecessor, and his own biography was not without blemish. We think the narrative reveals choices by sides that are strategically problematic, especially on the Gore side.[4] Recovery from mistakes was not guaranteed.

[2] To add a further complication, none of the theorizing admits institutional detail that might be relevant to the issue agenda, such as the existence of the Electoral College.

[3] Arguably, the suppositional claim about equal skill commits the fallacy of affirming the consequent. If equal skill yields equilibrium outcomes, and equilibrium outcomes are successfully forecast, then successful forecasts indicate equal skill.

[4] Lest we get carried away in characterizing a skill differential, we must acknowledge that the Bush side also wasted resources at the end. They spend large sums in a handful of markets in the utterly uncompetitive state of California. Had they deployed these resources in closely fought states, our estimations suggest they might have won the

The Nature of Campaign Communications

Links between Ads and News

As the campaigns grappled with these challenges, they worked with a complex media system to try to make ads and news work together. Sometimes ads and news did work together. At other times they worked at odds. One task for ads was to transmit rhetoric to the news. The Republican move that put Al Gore on the defensive in late September exemplifies this. The Republicans put up a set of character attacks early in the month, and then abruptly stopped them. The ads did seem to go to a real point of vulnerability for Gore, as subsequent events revealed. But if ads find a weak point, why stop them? Intuition suggests that actually playing them was no longer necessary, for the ads had done their work of creating rhetorical content for news. The news stories, starting with the recycled account of Gore's month-old speech in Tallahassee, may not have been the result solely of newsroom initiative. It is natural to wonder what or who brought the story back up. Whatever the route by which the story broke, the Republican campaign was poised with a rhetorical strategy to help the newsroom out. Much of the content of the news in the critical late September period consisted of Republican figures repeating the words of their earlier ads. Soon enough, reporters were also using those words. In this instance, ads and news worked together substantively, creating a powerful signal – or so we infer from the magnitude of the electorate's reaction.

Also important is the simple valence of ads and news, whether each channel systematically favors one side over the other and whether the two channels favor the same side. In the late September episode, the ads-news nexus was mainly substantive, in the rhetoric of stories. The sheer volume of ads at that point was not great by the standard of the following month. Ads at least did not detract from possible impact by the news. Later in the campaign, tension between news and ads increased. In the news, Gore gained as decisive an edge in the last week as either side had enjoyed at any point after the conventions. This was partly by default, as George W. Bush declined to make himself more than minimally available for interviews on the *NBC Nightly News*. Instead, the Bush campaign focused its energy on countering Al Gore's

popular vote as well as the Electoral vote, and won the latter more handily. Why these resources were merely incinerated in places like Los Angeles remains an explanatory puzzle, but it is a puzzle for another book.

apparently successful attempt to deconstruct the Bush plan for Social Security with a massive ad campaign specifically on the issue. The advertising blitz neutralized the news and won back many citizens who had earlier responded positively to Gore's arguments.

Campaigns and the Quality of Electoral Choice

This hardly seems like enlightenment. Whatever the merits of arguments for and against the Bush plan for Social Security, battleground states and media markets cannot differ much from non-battleground places taken all together in their objective stakes in an issue. By definition, the battleground consists of places toward the middle of an overall distribution of political preference. In 2000, when the whole nation was closely divided, the balance of interests in the most competitive states was close to the balance in the rest of the country, just not to the balance in any single nonbattleground state. This is what makes the campaign, in the context of an efficient spot market for ads, a natural experiment. It appears that in this instance the experimental "treatment" worked, as the sheer weight of Republican ads produced a dynamical difference between "treatment" and "control" markets. Such differences are strong *prima facie* indicators of the successful execution of strategy.

The news signal pointed in the other direction. When the signal was not jammed by ads, it produced dynamics in vote intention and in attitudes that also pointed in the opposite direction. But this is not reassuring either. It is as if the mobile sector of the electorate responds to the last thing it hears. This is, of course, consistent with the on-line perspective on political cognition, a perspective that implies an electorate vulnerable to strategically motivated campaign effects. We are not required to take a position on the quality of either the ad signal or the news signal to express unease with the fact that the electorate seems persuasible by each.

Some Open Questions

Personal versus Impersonal Influence
In one sense, the book documents impact from the mass media. Both news and ads move the electorate, and news and ads interact in interesting and sensible ways. Our book is a further vindication of

the argument in Mutz (1998) that a system of impersonal influence has come into existence. Like her, we show that the balance of media content is a critical quantity. But if we have established that messages originating in impersonal media find their way into the electorate and move it, we present no evidence about the avenue of impact. It may not be surprising that the citizens most affected by ads were the least exposed and attentive to the news. But the same citizens – the ones least interested in the news – were also the most responsive to news and debates, at least they were from October on. Did these citizens get the news directly from television, despite the fact that they were relatively unlikely to seek it out? Or did they get it only to the extent that they attached themselves to discussion networks? If face-to-face discussion proves to be critical, then Katz and Lazarsfeld's (1955) identification of the two-step flow of social influence continues to be valid – but with a twist. The message is now less likely to be blunted than it once was.

Ads: Quantity and Quality

We make a strong claim about the simple volume of ads. By our account, had Al Gore saved up more resources for the last week and seriously closed the ad gap in pivotal states, he would have won. The account presupposes that each side adopted a persuasive message; all that mattered was how widely and deeply the messages could be diffused. That the Bush message was persuasive follows from the fact that its wider diffusion boosted his vote share. Our inference that Gore's ad message, when he finally settled on it, was persuasive follows from the apparent effectiveness of his *news* message, for his ad message and his news message were the same. There is no reason to assume that messages will always be appropriate. Our own sense is that Gore's ads acquired a useful focus only toward the end. So the finding about impact from simple ad volume may not be universally applicable.

Other Possible Effects of Ads

We establish that Bush won the ad war and that this mattered to opinion on the key issue and to the vote. But our model of ad impact is very crude. It assumes that resistance to ad content is no different at the end than earlier. Change in ad volumes might change other relationships in the domain, but this book only scratches the surface of those possibilities. It is an open question whether the Republican ad barrage weakened the link between Social Security opinion and the vote, or strengthened it. What about the link between perception of candidates' personalities and the vote? The *prima facie* indication from Chapter 6 is that ads did not alter this link, but the chapter did not compare processes between high and low ad-volume places. Did the ads strengthen or weaken links between candidate perception and issue position? What about effect of ads on the the link between "fundamentals" and the vote? Perhaps the election's demographic and ideological foundations are strongest where ads are most ubiquitous. Perhaps the opposite is true. And the link between ads and news has only begun to be explored. We note that the sound of ads seemed to block the sound of news. But ads may also stimulate news interest. If they do so, they might conceivably breed resistance to their own persuasive intent.

Political Cognition

We make much of phases in the 2000 campaign, as symptoms of electoral persuasibility and of the centrality of on-line processing. But not all dynamics produce phases and not all response to novel stimuli is online; there is also ample evidence of memory. It is one thing to say that memory-based and on-line cognition coexist, it is another to sort out why and how they do. We supply evidence that some of the coexistence hinges on differences among individuals in processing capacity; some persons have longer memories than others, as Zaller (1992) strongly implies. But the coexistence is as much between events and campaign moments as between different kinds of individuals. Clearly we need a theory that sorts events or campaign stimuli according to their processing requirements.

Campaigns in Competitive Context

Unquestionably, all of this matters in a race like the 2000 one, with its razor-thin popular and Electoral vote margins. In 2000, the most trivial of campaign induction would have mattered to the result. In the more typical election, according to Campbell (2000), the most massive imaginable effect could hardly make any difference to the identity of the winner. For many years, presidential elections have not usually been close. But is 2000 a harbinger? In presidential elections, the technology of campaigns has evolved to the point where neither side airs any

appreciable advertising nationally; the intense concentration of resources in markets where the contest is closest itself may make presidential elections closer overall. Moreover, the stable postwar pattern
of divided government, with each party quite comfortably dominant
in one elected branch but clearly subordinate in the other, may have
given way to a pattern in which each branch is closely contested. To
the extent this is true, then understanding campaign dynamics will be
vital to understanding the future course of U.S. electoral history.

Then again, was 2000 fated to be close? To come back to where this
book started, forecasting models said the opposite. The typical forecast
placed Gore some eight points ahead of George W. Bush. Our own
data indicate that in late September Gore's margin was about where
the forecasts said it should be, eight points. In most elections, this
lead would have seemed insurmountable. Campbell's (2000) review of
postwar elections suggests that Gore would lose ground but, given the
late date of this eight-point lead, still win decisively. What no account
predicted is that a lead of eight points would disappear overnight.
The inference is obvious: the election was close because the campaign
made it so.

Appendix Tables

TABLE A3.1. *The Basic Structure of Vote Intention*

	Social Structure		+ Party and Ideology	
	Gore	Bush	Gore	Bush
Black	0.72	−1.04	0.47	−0.72
	(0.05)	(0.07)	(0.05)	(0.07)
Evangelical	−0.33	0.60	−0.21	0.31
	(0.03)	(0.03)	(0.04)	(0.03)
Union family	0.19	−0.30	0.08	−0.17
	(0.04)	(0.04)	(0.04)	(0.04)
Male	−0.19	0.30	−0.04	0.26
	(0.03)	(0.03)	(0.03)	(0.03)
Democrat			1.33	−0.54
			(0.03)	(0.04)
Republican			−0.57	1.34
			(0.05)	(0.04)
Liberal			−0.10	−1.04
			(0.05)	(0.07)
Conservative			−0.94	0.65
			(0.06)	(0.05)
1996 Vote			1.05	−1.51
			(0.23)	(0.24)
Constant	0.38	0.16	0.01	−0.21
	(0.02)	(0.02)	(0.03)	(0.03)
Pseudo R^2	0.04		0.21	
χ^2	3231.1		15920.43	
N	35299		34993	

Estimation by multinomial logistic regression. Standard errors in parentheses.

TABLE A4.1. *Influences on Allocation of Campaign Resources*

	Candidate days	GRPs
Electoral votes (β)	1.956	0.460
	(0.349)	(0.562)
Deviation from Clinton national	−0.779	−1.226
percentage in 1996 (γ)	(0.225)	(0.357)
Constant	−3.104	8.652
	(0.913)	(1.477)
R^2	0.555	0.248
Standard error of estimate	1.689	2.738

Entries are ordinary least-squares estimates, with standard errors in parentheses, of parameters of model of campaign resource allocations based on that of Colantoni, Levesque, and Ordeshook (1975): $Tj + \delta_j = CE_j^{\beta} D_j^{\gamma}$, where R_j is the quantity of resources devoted to state j, δ_j is a minor adjustment added when $T_j = 0$, C is a constant, E_j is the electoral vote of state j, and D_j is the deviation of Clinton's share of the two-party vote in 1996 from his national percentage.

TABLE A4.2. *Ad and News Impacts Conditional on Media Interest*

	Low Interest		High Interest	
	Gore	Bush	Gore	Bush
Ads – 7-day sums				
current week	0.0059	0.0017	0.0044	0.0023
	(0.0026)	(0.0027)	(0.0030)	(0.0032)
previous week	0.0011	0.0007	−0.0030	−0.0040
	(0.0030)	(0.0031)	(0.0034)	(0.0035)
Visits				
Democratic	0.0016	0.0019	−0.0025	−0.0030
	(0.0030)	(0.0030)	(0.0035)	(0.0037)
Republican	0.0041	−0.0003	0.0011	−0.0018
	(0.0032)	(0.0033)	(0.0037)	(0.0039)
TV News – 3-day sums				
current 3 days	0.0016	0.0019	−0.0025	−0.0030
	(0.0030)	(0.0030)	(0.0035)	(0.0037)
previous 3 days	0.0041	−0.0003	0.0011	−0.0018
	(0.32)	(0.0033)	(0.0037)	(0.0039)
Black	0.58	−0.43	0.64	−0.98
	(0.13)	(0.17)	(0.15)	(0.21)
Evangelical	−0.13	0.32	−0.20	0.35
	(0.09)	(0.09)	(0.11)	(0.11)
Union family	0.05	−0.25	−0.06	−0.31
	(0.09)	(0.10)	(0.11)	(0.12)
Male	−0.03	0.25	−0.05	0.32
	(0.07)	(0.07)	(0.08)	(0.09)
Democrat	1.59	−1.80	0.99	−1.60
	(0.57)	(0.60)	(0.67)	(0.72)
Republican	1.57	−0.14	1.67	−0.44
	(0.08)	(0.11)	(0.10)	(0.13)
Liberal	−0.08	1.71	−0.13	1.74
	(0.12)	(0.09)	(0.13)	(0.11)
Conservative	−0.03	−0.61	−0.06	−0.75
	(0.08)	(0.10)	(0.10)	(0.13)
1996 Vote	−0.36	0.65	−0.59	0.80
	(0.09)	(0.08)	(0.11)	(0.10)
Constant	0.07	−0.21	0.72	0.19
	(0.08)	(0.08)	(0.09)	(0.10)
χ^2	2936.63		3767.54	
Pseudo R^2	0.21		0.30	
N	6398		6211	

Estimation by multinomial logistic regression. Standard errors in parentheses.

TABLE A5.1. *The Economy, Clinton, and the Vote*

	Economy Only		Economy + Clinton	
	Gore	Bush	Gore	Bush
National Economy	0.63	0.12	0.50	0.18
	(0.04)	(0.04)	(0.04)	(0.04)
Clinton rating			0.99	−0.73
			(0.04)	(0.04)
Black	0.71	−0.70	0.32	−0.32
	(0.08)	(0.11)	(0.08)	(0.12)
Evangelical	−0.14	0.36	−0.07	0.29
	(0.05)	(0.05)	(0.06)	(0.05)
Union family	0.12	−0.18	0.12	−0.18
	(0.06)	(0.06)	(0.06)	(0.07)
Male	−0.15	0.27	−0.18	0.29
	(0.05)	(0.05)	(0.05)	(0.05)
Democrat	0.57	−2.17	0.10	−1.75
	(0.34)	(0.36)	(0.35)	(0.37)
Republican	1.56	−0.30	1.37	−0.10
	(0.05)	(0.06)	(0.05)	(0.07)
Liberal	−0.14	1.75	0.08	1.63
	(0.07)	(0.06)	(0.08)	(0.06)
Conservative	−0.02	−0.68	−0.13	−0.60
	(0.05)	(0.06)	(0.05)	(0.07)
1996 Vote	−0.45	0.61	−0.36	0.45
	(0.06)	(0.05)	(0.06)	(0.05)
Constant	0.23	−0.06	0.17	−0.23
	(0.05)	(0.05)	(0.05)	(0.05)
Pseudo R^2	0.26		0.32	
χ^2	9942.41		12271.91	
N	18707		18644	

Estimation by multinomial logistic regression. Standard errors in parentheses.

TABLE A6.1. *Character, Issues, and the Vote*

	3–27 Sept		28 Sept–16 Oct		17 Oct–6 Nov	
	Gore	Bush	Gore	Bush	Gore	Bush
Competence	1.89	−2.41	2.08	−2.86	1.72	−2.43
	(0.24)	(0.26)	(0.29)	(0.32)	(0.29)	(0.33)
Character	1.52	−2.13	1.74	−2.11	1.43	−2.17
	(0.22)	(0.23)	(0.26)	(0.27)	(0.27)	(0.29)
SS Stock Mkt	0.04	−0.08	0.10	−0.15	0.11	−0.21
	(0.06)	(0.06)	(0.07)	(0.08)	(0.07)	(0.08)
Taxes	0.13	0.02	0.11	0.06	0.19	−0.08
	(0.09)	(0.09)	(0.11)	(0.12)	(0.11)	(0.12)
Abortion	0.01	−0.03	−0.01	−0.15	0.10	−0.07
	(0.06)	(0.06)	(0.08)	(0.08)	(0.08)	(0.08)
Black	0.47	−0.02	0.34	0.07	0.24	−0.58
	(0.21)	(0.28)	(0.26)	(0.37)	(0.22)	(0.31)
Evangelical	0.08	0.35	0.08	0.12	0.08	−0.03
	(0.13)	(0.13)	(0.16)	(0.16)	(0.17)	(0.17)
Union Family	0.08	0.01	0.27	0.34	−0.19	−0.47
	(0.14)	(0.16)	(0.17)	(0.20)	(0.17)	(0.20)
Male	−0.06	0.25	−0.05	0.13	−0.22	−0.18
	(0.11)	(0.11)	(0.13)	(0.14)	(0.14)	(0.14)
1996 Vote	−0.81	−1.42	−1.74	−1.65	−0.00	−1.28
in State	(0.75)	(0.83)	(1.05)	(1.15)	(1.08)	(1.16)
Democrat	1.25	0.31	1.32	0.12	1.16	−0.05
	(0.12)	(0.16)	(0.15)	(0.20)	(0.15)	(0.20)
Republican	0.11	1.38	0.18	1.53	0.47	1.27
	(0.18)	(0.14)	(0.22)	(0.17)	(0.23)	(0.18)
Liberal	−0.41	−0.47	−0.62	−0.77	−0.19	−0.73
	(0.13)	(0.16)	(0.15)	(0.20)	(0.16)	(0.20)
Conservative	−0.29	0.05	−0.55	0.11	−0.05	0.07
	(0.14)	(0.13)	(0.17)	(0.16)	(0.17)	(0.16)
Nat'l Economy	0.37	0.12	0.12	0.05	0.29	0.19
	(0.11)	(0.11)	(0.12)	(0.13)	(0.13)	(0.14)
Clinton	0.80	−0.05	0.57	−0.03	0.84	0.02
	(0.09)	(0.09)	(0.11)	(0.12)	(0.12)	(0.12)
Constant	−0.26	−0.53	−0.28	−0.56	−0.40	−0.05
	(0.12)	(0.13)	(0.15)	(0.16)	(0.16)	(0.16)
Pseudo R^2	0.45		0.49		0.50	
χ^2	3693.46		2943.19		2794.92	
N	3934		2868		2744	

Estimation by multinomial logistic regression. Standard errors in parentheses.

References

Achen, Christopher H. 1992. "Social Psychology, Demographic Variables, and Linear Regression: Breaking the Iron Triangle in Voting Research." *Political Behaviour* 14: 195–211.

Aldrich, John H. 1983. "A Downsian Spatial Model with Party Activism." *American Political Science Review* 77: 974–90.

Allsop, Dee, and Herbert Weisberg. 1988. "Measuring Change in Party Identification in an Election Campaign." *American Journal of Political Science* 32: 996–1017.

Ansolabehere, Stephen, Shanto Iyengar, Adam Simon, and Nicholas Valentino. 1994. "Does Attack Advertising Demobilize the Electorate?" *American Political Science Review* 88: 829–38.

Ansolabehere, Stephen, and Shanto Iyengar. 1994. "Riding the Wave and Claiming Ownership over Issues: The Joint Effects of Advertising and News Coverage in Campaigns." *Public Opinion Quarterly* 58: 335–57.

Ansolabehere, Stephen, and Shanto Iyengar. 1995. *Going Negative: How Political Advertising Shrinks and Polarizes the Electorate*. New York: Free Press.

Ansolabehere, Stephen D., Shanto Iyengar, and Adam Simon. 1999. "Replicating Experiments Using Aggregate and Survey Data: The Case of Negative Advertising and Turnout." *American Political Science Review* 93: 901–10.

Bartels, Larry M. 1985. "Resource Allocation in a Presidential Campaign." *Journal of Politics* 47: 928–36.

———. 1996. "Uninformed Votes: Information Effects in Presidential Elections." *American Journal of Political Science*, 40: 194–230.

———. 1997. "How Campaigns Matter." Princeton University: unpublished manuscript.

———. 1998. "Electoral Continuity and Change, 1868–1996." *Electoral Studies* 17: 301–26.

———. 2000. "Partisanship and Voting Behavior, 1952–1996." *American Journal of Political Science* 44: 35–50.

———. 2002. "The Impact of Candidate Traits in American Presidential Elections," in Anthony King, ed., *Leaders' Personalities and the Outcomes of Democratic Elections*. Oxford: Oxford University Press.

Bartels, Larry M., and John Zaller. "Presidential Vote Models: A Recount." 2001. *PS: Political Science and Politics* 34: 9–20.

Bean, Clive, and Anthony Mughan. 1989. "Leadership Effects in Parliamentary Elections in Australia and Britain." *American Political Science Review* 83: 1165–79.

Berelson Bernard R., Paul F. Lazarsfeld, and William N. McPhee. 1954. *Voting*. Chicago: University of Chicago Press.

Biocca, Frank, ed. 1991. *Television and Political Advertising, Volume 1: Psychological Processes*. Hillsdale, NJ: Erlbaum.

Brady, Henry E., and Paul M. Sniderman. 1985. "Attitude Attribution: A Group Basis for Political Reasoning." *American Political Science Review* 79: 1061–78.

Brams, Steven J., and Morton D. Davis. 1974. "The 3/2's Rule in Presidential Campaigning." *American Political Science Review* 68: 113–34.

Brody, Richard A. 1991. *Assessing the President: The Media, Elite Opinion, and Public Support*. Stanford, CA: Stanford University Press.

Brody, Richard A., and Benjamin I. Page. 1972. "Comment: The Assessment of Policy Voting." *American Political Science Review* 66: 450–58.

Brody, Richard A., and Lawrence S. Rothenberg. 1988. "The Instability of Partisanship: An Analysis of the 1980 Presidential Election." *British Journal of Political Science* 18: 445–65.

Campbell, Angus, Philip E. Converse, Warren E. Miller, and Donald E. Stokes. 1960. *The American Voter*. New York: Wiley.

Campbell, James E. 2000. *The American Campaign: U.S. Presidential Campaigns and the National Vote*. College Station: Texas A&M University Press.

———. 2001. "The Referendum that Didn't Happen: The Forecasts of the 2000 Presidential Election." *PS: Political Science and Politics* 34: 33–4.

Chaffee, Steven H. 1975. "Asking New Questions about Communication and Politics," in Steven H. Chaffee, ed., *Political Communication*. Beverly Hills, Calif.: Sage (Sage Annual Reviews of Communication Research, Volume 4): 13–20.

Colantoni, Claude S., Terrence J. Levesque, and Peter C. Ordeshook. 1975. "Campaign Resource Allocations Under the Electoral College." *American Political Science Review* 69: 141–54.

Conover, Pamela J. and Stanley Feldman. 1989. "Candidate Perceptions in an Ambiguous World: Campaigns, Cues, and Inference Processes." *American Journal of Political Science* 33: 917–40.

Converse, Philip E. 1962. "Information Flow and the Stability of Partisan Attitudes." *Public Opinion Quarterly* 26: 587–99.

———. 1964. "The Nature of Belief Systems in Mass Publics." In *Ideology and Discontent*, ed. David E. Apter. New York: Free Press.

DiPalma, Giuseppe, and Herbert McClosky. 1970. "Personality and Conformity: The Learning of Political Attitudes." *American Political Science Review* 64: 1054–73.

Downs, Anthony. 1957. *An Economic Theory of Democracy*. New York: Harper and Row.

Erbring, Lutz, Edie Goldenberg, and Arthur Miller. 1980. "Front-Page News and Real-World Cues: A New Look at Agenda-Setting by the Media." *American Journal of Political Science* 24: 16–49.

Festinger, Leon. 1957. *A Theory of Cognitive Dissonance*. Stanford, CA: Stanford University Press.

Finkel, Steven E. 1993. "Reexamining the 'Minimal Effects' Model in Recent Presidential Elections." *Journal of Politics* 55: 1–21.

Finkel, Steven E., and John G. Geer. 1998. "A Spot Check: Casting Doubt on the Demobilizing Effect of Attack Advertising." *American Journal of Political Science* 42: 573–95.

Fiorina, Morris, Samuel Abrams, and Jeremy Pope. 2003. "The 2000 U.S. Presidential Election: Can Retrospective Voting Be Saved?" *British Journal of Political Science* 33: 163–87.

Freedman, Paul, and Ken Goldstein. 1999. "Measuring Media Exposure and the Effects of Negative Campaign Ads." *American Journal of Political Science* 43: 1189–1208.

Funkhouser, Ray. 1973. "The Issues of the Sixties: An Exploratory Study of the Dynamics of Public Opinion." *Public Opinion Quarterly* 37: 62–75.

Gamson, William A. 1992. *Talking Politics*. Cambridge: Cambridge University Press.

Gelman, Andrew, and Gary King. 1993. "Why are American Presidential Election Polls so Variable When Votes are so Predictable?" *British Journal of Political Science* 23: 409–51.

Gerring, John. 1998. *Party Ideologies in America, 1828–1996*. Cambridge: Cambridge University Press.

Graber, Doris A. 1988. *Processing the News: How People Tame the Information Tide*. New York: Longman. Second Edition.

Green, Donald Philip, and Bradley Palmquist. 1990. "Of Artifacts and Partisan Instability." *American Journal of Political Science* 34: 872–902.

Hagen, Michael G., Richard Johnston, and Kathleen Hall Jamieson. 2001. "Partisan Stability in the 2000 Presidential Campaign: Evidence from the Annenberg Survey." Presented at the Conference on Parties & Partisanship, Vanderbilt University, Nashville, Tennessee, October 25–27.

Hagen, Michael G., Richard Johnston, and Kathleen Hall Jamieson. 2002. "Effects of the 2000 Presidential Campaign." Prepared for presentation at the American Political Science Association 2002 Annual Meeting Boston, MA.

Hartz, Louis. 1955. *The Liberal Tradition in America.* New York: Harcourt, Brace.

Hetherington, Marc J. 1996. "The Media's Role in Forming Voters' National Economic Evaluations in 1992." *American Journal of Political Science* 40: 372–95.

Holbrook, Thomas M. 1996. *Do Campaigns Matter?* Thousand Oaks, Calif.: Sage.

———. 2001. "Forecasting with Mixed Economic Signals: A Cautionary Tale." *PS: Political Science and Politics* 34: 39–44.

Hovland, Carl I., and Irving L. Janis, eds. 1959. *Personality and Persuasibility.* New Haven, CT, and London: Yale University Press.

Inglehart, Ronald. 1997. *Modernization and Postmodernization: Cultural, Economic and Political Change in 43 Societies.* Princeton, NJ: Princeton University Press.

Iyengar, Shanto, and Donald R. Kinder. *News That Matters: Television and American Opinion.* Chicago: University of Chicago Press.

Jamieson, Kathleen Hall. 1992. *Dirty Politics.* New York: Oxford University Press.

———. 1996. *Packaging the Presidency: A History and Criticism of Presidential Campaign Advertising.* New York: Oxford University Press.

Jamieson, Kathleen Hall, and Paul Waldman, eds. 2001. *Electing the President, 2000: The Insiders' View.* Philadelphia: University of Pennsylvania Press.

Johnson-Cartee, Karen S., and Gary A. Copeland. 1991. *Negative Political Advertising: Coming of Age.* Hillsdale, NJ: Erlbaum.

Johnston, Richard. 2002. "Prime Ministerial Contenders in Canada." In Anthony King, ed., *Leaders' Personalities and the Outcomes of Democratic Elections.* Oxford: Oxford University Press.

Johnston, Richard, André Blais, Henry E. Brady, and Jean Crête. 1992. *Letting the People Decide: Dynamics of a Canadian Election.* Stanford, CA: Stanford University Press.

Johnston, Richard, and Henry E. Brady. 2001. "The Rolling Cross-Section Design." *Electoral Studies* 21: 283–95.

Johnston, Richard, Michael G. Hagen, and Kathleen Hall Jamieson. 2003. "Priming and Persuasion in the 2000 Presidential Campaign." Paper presented at the Annual Meeting of the Midwest Political Science Association, Chicago, IL, April 3–5, 2003.

Just, Marion R., Ann N. Crigler, Dean E. Alger, Timothy E. Cook, Montague Kern, and Darrell M. West. 1996. *Crosstalk: Citizens, Candidates, and the Media in a Presidential Campaign.* Chicago: University of Chicago Press.

Kahn, Kim Fridkin, and Patrick J. Kenney. 1999. "Do Negative Campaigns Mobilize or Suppress Turnout? Clarifying the Relationship between Negativity and Participation." *American Political Science Review* 93: 877–89.

Katz, Elihu, and Paul F. Lazarsfeld. 1955. *Personal Influence.* New York: Free Press.

Keith, Bruce E., David B. Magleby, Candice J. Nelson, Elizabeth Orr, Mark C. Westlye, and Raymond E. Wolfinger. 1992. *The Myth of the Independent Voter*. Berkeley: University of California Press.

Kern, Montague. 1989. *30-Second Politics: Political Advertising in the Eighties*. New York: Praeger.

Kiewiet, D. Roderick. 1983. *Macroeconomics and Micropolitics: The Electoral Effects of Economic Issues*. Chicago: University of Chicago Press.

Kinder, Donald R. 1986. "Presidential Character Revisited," in Richard R. Lau and David O. Sears, eds. *Political Cognition*. Hillsdale, NJ: Erlbaum. (The 19th Annual Carnegie Symposium on Cognition).

Kinder, Donald R., Robert P. Abelson, and Susan T. Fiske. 1979. *Developmental Research on Candidate Instrumentation*. Ann Arbor: National Election Study Pilot Study Report.

King, Anthony, ed. 2002. *Leaders' Personalities and the Outcomes of Democratic Elections*. Oxford: Oxford University Press.

Kitschelt, Herbert. 1994. *The Transformation of European Social Democracy*. Cambridge: Cambridge University Press.

———. 1996. *The Radical Right in Western Europe: A Comparative Analysis*. Ann Arbor: University of Michigan Press.

Klapper, Joseph T. 1960. *The Effects of Mass Communication*. Glencoe, IL: Free Press.

Kramer, Gerald H. 1971. "Short-term Fluctuations in U.S. Voting Behavior," *American Political Science Review* 65: 131–43.

Kornhauser, William. 1959. *The Politics of Mass Society*. New York: Free Press.

Laakso, Markku, and Rein Taagepera. 1979. "'Effective' Number of Parties: A Measure with Application to West Europe." *Comparative Political Studies* 12: 3–27.

Lau Richard R., Lee Sigelman, Caroline Heldman, and Paul Babbitt. 1999. "The Effects of Negative Political Advertisements: A Meta-Analytic Assessment." *American Political Science Review* 93: 851–75.

Lewis-Beck, Michael S., and Tom W. Rice. 1983. "Localism in Presidential Elections: The Home State Advantage." *American Journal of Political Science* 27: 548–56.

Lewis-Beck, Michael S., and Charles Tien. 2001. "Modeling the Future: Lessons from the Gore Forecast." *PS: Political Science and Politics* 34: 21–3.

Lipset, Seymour M. and Stein Rokkan, 1967. "Cleavage Structures, Party Systems and Voter Alignments. Introduction," in S. M. Lipset and S. Rokkan, eds., *Party Systems and Voter Alignments: Cross-National Perspectives*. New York: Free Press, pp. 1–64.

Lockhart, Julia K. 2002. "Media References to the Gender Gap during September and October 2000." Vancouver, BC: University of British Columbia, unpublished memorandum.

Lodge, Milton, Kathleen M. McGraw, and Patrick Stroh. 1989. "An Impression-Driven Model of Candidate Evaluation." *American Political Science Review* 83: 399–419.

Lodge, Milton, Marco R. Steenbergen, and Shawn Brau. 1995. "The Responsive Voter: Campaign Information and the Dynamics of Candidate Evaluation." *American Political Science Review* 89: 309–26.

McCombs, Maxwell, and Donald Shaw. 1972. "The Agenda-Setting Function of Mass Media." *Public Opinion Quarterly* 36: 176–87.

McGuire, William J. 1968. "Personality and Susceptibility to Social Influence." In Edgar F. Borgatta and William W. Lambert, eds., *The Handbook of Personality Theory and Research*. Chicago: Rand McNally.

———. 1969. "The Nature of Attitudes and Attitude Change." In Gardner Lindzey and Elliot Aronson, eds. *The Handbook of Social Psychology*, 2nd edition, Vol. 3. Reading, MA: Addison Wesley.

McLeod, Jack, Lee Becker, and James Byrnes. 1974. "Another Look at the Agenda-Setting Function of the Press." *Communication Research* 1: 131–66.

Miller, Warren E., and J. Merrill Shanks. 1996. *The New American Voter*. Cambridge, MA: Harvard University Press.

Mutz, Diana C. 1998. *Impersonal Influence: How Perceptions of Mass Collectives Affect Political Attitudes*. Cambridge: Cambridge University Press.

Mutz, Diana C., and Paul S. Martin. 2001. "Facilitating Communication across Lines of Political Difference." *American Political Science Review* 95: 97–114.

Norpoth, Helmut. 2001. "Primary Colors: A Mixed Blessing for Al Gore." *PS: Political Science and Politics* 34: 45–8.

Page, Benjamin I., Robert Y. Shapiro, and Glenn R. Dempsey. 1987. "What Moves Public Opinion?" *American Political Science Review* 81: 23–44.

Palfrey, Thomas R. 1984. "Spatial Equilibrium with Entry." *Review of Economic Studies* 51: 139–56.

Patterson, Thomas, and Robert McClure. 1976. *The Unseeing Eye*. New York: Putnam.

Peffley, Mark A., and John Hurwitz. 1985. "A Hierarchical Model of Attitude Constraint." *American Journal of Political Science.* 29: 871–90.

Price, Vincent, and John Zaller. 1990. "Evaluation of Media Exposure Items in the 1989 NES Pilot Study." Ann Arbor: University of Michigan, National Election Study Board of Overseers, technical report.

Putnam, Robert D. 2000. *Bowling Alone: The Collapse and Revival of American Community*. New York: Simon & Schuster.

Rabinowitz, George, and Stuart E. Macdonald. 1989. "A Directional Theory of Issue Voting." *American Political Science Review* 83: 93–121.

Rahn, Wendy M. 1993. "The Role of Partisan Stereotypes in Information Processing about Political Candidates." *American Journal of Political Science* 37: 472–96.

Rahn, Wendy M., John H. Aldrich, Eugene Borgida, and John L. Sullivan. 1990. "A Social-Cognitive Model of Candidate Appraisal." In James Kuklinski and John Ferejohn, eds., *Information and Democratic Processes*. Urbana: University of Illinois Press.

Romer, Daniel, Kathleen Hall Jamieson, and Joseph Cappella. 2000. "Does Attack Advertising Create a Backlash? Mobilize the Other Side? Depress or Increase Support by Those of the Same Party?" in Kathleen Hall Jamieson, *Everything You Think You Know About Politics . . . And Why You're Wrong*. New York: Basic Books.

Romer, Daniel, Kate Kenski, Paul Waldman, Christopher Adasiewicz, and Kathleen Hall Jamieson. 2004. *Capturing Campaign Dynamics: The National Annenberg Election Survey*. New York: Oxford University Press.

Rosenstone, Steven J. 1983. *Forecasting Presidential Elections*. New Haven, CT: Yale University Press.

Shafer, Byron E., and William J. M. Claggett. 1995. *The Two Majorities: The Issue Context of Modern American Politics*. Baltimore, MD: Johns Hopkins University Press.

Shaw, Daron R. 1999a. "A Study of Presidential Campaign Effects from 1952 to 1992." *Journal of Politics* 61: 387–422.

———. 1999b. "The Effect of TV Ads and Candidate Appearances on Statewide Presidential Votes, 1988–96." *American Political Science Review* 93: 345–61.

———. 1999c. "The Methods behind the Madness: Presidential Electoral College Strategies, 1988–1996." *Journal of Politics* 61: 893–913.

Simon, Adam F. 2002. *The Winning Message: Candidate Behavior, Campaign Discourse, and Democracy*. Cambridge: Cambridge University Press.

Sniderman, Paul M. 1975. *Personality and Democratic Politics*. Berkeley, CA: University of California Press.

Sniderman, Paul M., Richard A. Brody, and Philip E. Tetlock. 1991. *Reasoning and Choice: Explorations in Social Psychology*. Cambridge: Cambridge University Press.

Tuffe, Edward R. 1980. *Political Control of the Economy*. Princeton, NJ: Princeton University Press.

Waldman, Paul, and Kathleen Hall Jamieson. 2003. "Rhetorical Convergence and Issue Knowledge in the 2000 Presidential Election." *Presidential Studies Quarterly* 33: 145–63.

Wattenberg, Martin P., and Craig Leonard Brians. 1999. "Negative Campaign Advertising: Demobilizer or Mobilizer?" *American Political Science Review* 93: 891–99.

Weaver, David. 1981. *Media Agenda-Setting in a Presidential Election*. New York: Praeger.

Weisberg, Herbert, ed. 1995. *Democracy's Feast: Elections in America*. Chatham, NJ: Chatham House.

Weisberg, Herbert, and David C. Kimball. 1995. "Attitudinal Correlates of the 1992 Presidential Vote: Party Identification and Beyond." In Weisberg (1995), pp. 72–111.

West, Darrell M. 1997. *Air Wars: Television Advertising in Election Campaigns 1952–1996*. Washington, DC: Congressional Quarterly, Inc. Second Edition.

Wlezien, Christopher. 2001. "On Forecasting the Presidential Vote." *PS: Political Science and Politics* 34: 25–31.

Wlezien, Christopher, and Robert S. Erikson. 2002. "The Timeline of Presidential Election Campaigns." *Journal of Politics* 64: 969–93.

Zaller, John. 1990. "Bringing Converse Back In: Modeling Information Flow in Political Campaigns." In *Political Analysis.* 1: 181–234.

———. 1991. "Information, Values, and Opinion." *American Political Science Review* 85: 1215–37.

———. 1992. *The Nature and Origins of Mass Opinion.* Cambridge: Cambridge University Press.

———. 1998. "Monica Lewinsky's Contribution to Political Science." *PS: Political Science and Politics* 31: 182–9.

Index